THE AMERICAN
WOMAN IN TRANSITION

Contributions in Women's Studies

The Chains of Protection: The Judicial Response to Women's Labor Legislation
Judith A. Baer

Women's Studies: An Interdisciplinary Collection
Kathleen O'Connor Blumhagen and Walter D. Johnson, editors

Latin American Women: Historical Perspectives
Asunción Lavrin

Beyond Her Sphere: Women and the Professions in American History
Barbara J. Harris

Literary America, 1903-1934: The Mary Austin Letters
T. M. Pearce, editor

Margaret Gibbons Wilson

THE AMERICAN WOMAN IN TRANSITION

The Urban Influence, 1870-1920

Contributions in Women's Studies, Number 6

 GREENWOOD PRESS
Westport, Connecticut • London, England

Library of Congress Cataloging in Publication Data

Wilson, Margaret Gibbons.
    The American woman in transition.

    (Contributions in women's studies ; no. 6 ISSN 0147-104X)
    Bibliography: p.
    Includes index.
    1. Women--United States--History. 2. Social change.
I. Title. II. Series.
HQ1426.W555   301.41'2'0973   78-67911
ISBN 0-313-20638-4

Library of Congress Catalog Card Number: 78-67911
ISBN: 0-313-20638-4
ISSN: 0147-104X

First published in 1979

Greenwood Press, Inc.
51 Riverside Avenue, Westport, Connecticut 06880

Printed in the United States of America

10 9 8 7 6 5 4 3 2 1

To my
husband, **David**

Contents

Illustrations

Tables

Tables:
Appendix A

Tables:
Appendix B

Acknowledgments

Many people have provided assistance as this book passed through its various forms and stages. R. David Weber, Barbara MacEachern, Franklin D. Mitchell, and Peggy Guttenberg offered pertinent criticism and helpful suggestions. As is true with all historians, I owe much to the excellent libraries where I did my research, and to their staffs. These include the Otto G. Richter Library of the University of Miami, the Huntington Library, and the Library of Congress. Special thanks go to the staff of the Otto G. Richter Library for the extensive help given me. I would also like to thank Judy Rabkin for helping me proofread the manuscript. Most of all, I would like to thank my husband, David, who gave me valuable technical and editorial advice, and much needed and appreciated encouragement.

THE AMERICAN
WOMAN IN TRANSITION

Introduction

> The energetic, independent woman of culture is fre-
> quently caricatured as the "New Woman." . . . The
> key-note of her character is self-reliance and the power
> of initiation. She aims at being in direct contact with
> reality and forming her own judgement upon it.[1]

During the latter decades of the nineteenth century and
early years of the twentieth the lives led by middle-class women and the
demarcation of what was considered to be their proper sphere underwent
significant alteration. Increasingly, the active, more independent "New
Woman"[2] of the early twentieth century challenged the ideal of the
home-centered, submissive, pious, and dependent "True Woman" of the
mid-nineteenth.[3]

Between 1860 and 1920 a number of developments intertwined, cre-
ating an atmosphere receptive to a greatly expanded sphere of activity
for women. The Civil War had ripped apart the old order of antebellum
society. Many women who previously had rarely left the protective pale
of the home were thrust, at least temporarily, into the "outside world"
by the exigencies of war. The Fourteenth Amendment, enfranchising
Black men, had left unfulfilled the suffrage demands of women, and the
suffrage movement forcefully agitated for women's rights throughout the
era. Educational opportunities for women spread. But it is to the phenomenal upsurge in urbanization and industrialization occurring between
1870 and 1920 that we must turn to account for the permanent enlarging
of the accepted sphere of activity for women and the change in the image
of feminine propriety.

Between 1870 and 1920, a nation that had been predominantly rural became more than 50 percent urban. Other historians have emphasized the role the city and industrialization played in enlarging women's sphere of activity. They have pointed to expanded employment opportunities, the growing ease of running the urban household, and the cloak of anonymity provided by the concentration of people as important forces in freeing women from their more constricted mid-nineteenth-century roles.[4]

Although many assertions have been made, systematic study of the ways urban living affected women's lives has been lacking. In general, care has not been taken to ascertain whether developments were confined to urban areas or were in fact part of larger trends also present in the rural sector. The failure to distinguish patterns of behavior that were specific to urban areas from those that were more generally present raises serious questions about assertions regarding the role played by "the city" vis-à-vis an expanded sphere of activity for women.[5]

This book investigates those factors that most clearly delineated how women spent their lives for the fifty years between 1870 and 1920. An attempt has been made to determine what differences, if any, existed between the life patterns exhibited in urban and rural areas.[6] Since an extended period of time, rather than a few years or even a single decade, has been studied, it was possible to trace trends that were present during the era. Using the information from the study of urban and rural trends over time, it was also possible to test some of the existing hypotheses regarding the relationship between the degree of urbanization and the extent of difference between the urban and the rural sectors.[7]

Since, traditionally, women's lives have centered upon the home and family, any changes in that orientation would have a significant impact. Were more or fewer women ultimately marrying? At what age did they marry? How many children did they have? What was involved in running a home? Answers to these questions provide key indicators of how women spent their time. In addition to studying changes that happened to women within their traditional sphere of the home, factors that would indicate a movement beyond the confines of tradition were examined. What types of activities involved women—literary societies, reform movements, or other social and activist groups? How widespread was employment?

The literature concerning the lives of urban women has grown in recent years.[8] But for the most part, each study has focused upon a single city. The advantage of the single-city study is obvious: It allows for a penetrating investigation that a broader study does not permit. However, the single-city study has a serious drawback insofar as the general applicability of its findings are concerned. By approaching questions concerning women's lives in an urban setting from a wider perspective, it is possible to determine whether urban life, in general, appeared to encourage particular patterns of behavior among the female residents.

In addition to looking at differences between the urban and rural sectors intercity differences were examined in an attempt to ascertain how factors within an urban environment influenced women's lives.

Economic activity and population size have generally been recognized as key delineators of interurban differences. Numerous studies have been made to see how these two factors have affected particular aspects of women's lives, especially the number of children they have.[9] However, almost all of the studies are for 1920 or later, and many focus upon one census year. Thus many of the assumptions regarding the functioning of certain demographic variables within cities, relied upon by historians and sociologists, have come from relatively modern studies that may or may not reflect the pattern of earlier years.[10] By extending this study to a consideration of how size of city and economic function affect marital status, child/woman ratio (the number of children five years of age or younger per 1,000 women ages twenty to forty-four), and employment back to the late nineteenth century, one can ascertain what patterns existed between 1870 and 1920 and determine whether those patterns correspond to ones found in studies of more recent years.

Census sources provided valuable information regarding the marriage, fertility, and employment patterns of women. However, prior to 1910, information distinguishing between urban and rural areas was not given. In addition, for a number of the years, information for some of the variables was not presented in ready-to-use form by the census.[11] Thus much of the tabular material regarding differences between the urban and rural sectors as well as intercity differences is presented for the first time in this study.

Important as it is to avoid overstating the strides women made toward equality during the early decades of the twentieth century,[12] it is equally vital not to minimize the profound changes that occurred in women's lives during that era. Although the economic, political, and social gains made by women during the period by no means heralded an age of full equality between the sexes, an enlarged sphere of activity for women eclipsed the narrow dimensions of woman's "proper place" that had dominated during the Victorian era.

Between 1870 and 1920 significant changes were occurring in patterns of marriage and fertility. Despite a slightly greater proportion of married women in 1920 than in 1890, and a general trend toward more youthful marriages, the child/woman ratio declined (Table 1). The number of divorces, though still involving a tiny percentage of women, doubled between 1890 and 1920, rising from 0.4 percent of all females fifteen or older to 0.8 percent.[13]

TABLE 1. Percentage of Women Married, Fourteen and Older and Fifteen to Twenty-four, and Child/Woman Ratio, Aggregate Population, 1890 and 1920

	1890	1920
Percent married, 14+	59.4	60.4
Percent married, 15-24	27.5	32.5
Child/woman ratio	685	604

SOURCES: U.S., Department of Commerce, Bureau of the Census, *Statistical Abstract: Supplements, Historical Statistics of the United States from Colonial Times to 1957* (1960); U.S., Department of Commerce, Bureau of the Census, *Seventeenth Census of the United States, 1950*, vol. 2, *Characteristics of the Population*, pt. 1, U.S. Summary, pp. 1-180.

NOTE: Child/woman ratio = the number of children five years of age or younger per 1,000 women ages twenty to forty-four.

More important, for at least a portion of their lives, a growing number of women left the insulating shelter of the home and entered into some type of outside activity. Women's clubs, ranging from literary to social action groups, had over a million participants by 1914. The number of women in the work force rose by 63.3 percent, from 14.7 percent of women sixteen or older in 1870 to 24 percent in 1920.[14]

Some of the changes in life-style first began to appear among younger women. Single, middle-class women, in increasing numbers, found their way into the array of jobs that opened up to women during the late nineteenth and early twentieth centuries. Young, middle-class women did not generally view work as oppressive drudgery, but rather as an avenue toward independence and increased social contact.[15] Moreover, even for those who were not working, the idea of a career loomed as an exciting, desirable opportunity.[16] Thus young women, who in earlier, more sheltered generations would have almost without question accepted the confines of marriage, were coming of age during an era when the idea of a career was increasingly desirable. However, since it was still generally unacceptable for women to combine marriage with a career, most women had to decide between the two. Although the ultimate choice of most women might be a home and family, many expressed a feeling of discontent with the limitations that that decision implied.[17]

The books and articles on the "woman question" that poured forth during the 1890s and early 1900s were an indication of the discontent felt and expressed by women. In response to the unrest, many people made a concerted effort to glorify woman's role in the home and make it appear as desirable and exciting as any other career. Prominent educators such as Charles W. Eliot of Harvard assured women that no task was more important than the cultivation of fine children.[18] Numerous books and articles extolled the wonders and satisfactions of a woman's life in the home. Women were urged to accept the fact that their personality and intellect had made them especially suited for work in the home. Each sex had a natural role to fulfill, and for women that role was to bear and rear children.[19] Clergymen warned women to perform their wondrous duty and not encroach upon the domain of men lest they lose the reverence that men now accorded them.[20] Despite the importuning and the attempt to glorify the home, the number of women who were involved with some form of activity outside the home grew throughout the era.

The transformations that were occurring in women's lives during the late nineteenth and early twentieth centuries were reflected in the changing image of what were believed to be commendable characteristics for a woman to possess, and appropriate activities for her to engage in. Although subscribing to the idea that a certain amount of culture was good for women, an 1850 article in *Putnam's,* entitled "The American Ideal Woman," stressed that "domesticity is [her] honor and glory."[21] By 1880, writers of the day described "The Transitional American Woman." This "transitional woman" was not content to have her life focus upon the home, but instead sought out a variety of activities and causes and ways to improve herself. "Formerly to be a good housekeeper, an anxious mother, an obedient wife, was the *ne plus ultra* of female endeavor—to be all this *for others' sake*. Now it is to be more than one is for one's own sake."[22]

By the early 1890s, the first articles explicitly speaking of the New Woman began to appear. In 1894, *North American Review* and *Cornhill Magazine* discussed "The New Woman." In 1895, *Arena* contained an article about "The New Woman of the South," *Outlook* discussed "The New Woman," and *Review of Reviews* offered "Advice to the New Woman." By 1897 *Westminster Review* described "The 'New Woman' in Her Relation to the 'New Man,' " and in 1902 *Arena* contained an article about "The New Woman."[23]

The New Woman was alternately praised or damned by commentators of the era. To her supporters she was, in contrast to women of the past, "more independent, better educated, a companion to husband and children."[24] She was "not ashamed to know something of the administration of city, state, or Nation. . . . She sees herself as part of a group working to make the world more beautiful for all."[25] But to her critics she was younger than she looked, dark ("for fairness usually goes with an interest in children, and other gentle weaknesses"), very intelligent, not pretty, with "an aggressive air of independence." Moreover, she was unhappy. She failed in her attempt "to prove that woman's mission is something higher than the bearing of children and bringing them up."[26]

The growing acceptance of a woman more independent and active than her mid-century predecessor was perhaps best epitomized by the arrival of the Gibson Girl as the feminine ideal of the 1890s. Though her skirts were long and blouses prim, the Gibson Girl displayed a healthy vitality whether she golfed, played tennis, swam, or just walked along the seashore.

> Her free stride, her direct glance, the arrogant swing of her
> wide shoulders and the haughty tilt of her head. . . . Hers
> was the first generation of American women who had experi-
> enced co-education . . . who had dared to think of "going to
> work" . . . or . . . remaining "bachelor girls" . . . who had used
> slang, played basketball, ridden a bicycle-built-for-two.[27]

By the early 1900s, Boyd Winchester, an American lawyer, congress-man from Kentucky, and U.S. consul to Switzerland, spoke quite positively about the "recognition of the right of woman to her own development—the right of individuals to know, to learn, to perfect themselves to the utmost of their ability, irrespective of sex." He contended that "the improved mental and physical development of the girl [led] to a different ideal for the woman." Independence did not exclude marriage, which Winchester viewed as "the crown of womanhood." But the modern wife was to be "an intelligent companion, a moral helpmate, and equal . . . not a plaything or a slave."[28] By 1910, Margaret Deland, New England-born novelist and frequent contributor to *Atlantic* and *Harper's,* spoke confidently about "The Change in the Feminine Ideal." She described how, during her mother's generation, a woman's life had revolved around the home; involvement in reform movements, except giving money for "the heathens," was considered improper. Her own generation and her daughter's placed much more emphasis upon individualism and "social responsibility."[29]

For the most part, this investigation has been limited to middle-class white women. Although different classes of women undoubtedly shared certain experiences, they also differed in many significant ways. Working-class women, by dint of economic necessity, had never been able to experience the protected lives that had typified mid-nineteenth-century, middle-class women. The two groups likely had different perceptions of the significance of employment. Their access to labor-saving devices, the employment of domestic help, and participation in associations, literary or reform, also probably differed. In short, to attempt to write about women, in general, without taking into account the potential significance of class differences would likely obscure important developments and trends.

Social class is determined by a number of factors, including occupation, income, family background, and level of education.[30] Since much of the data for this study has been drawn from census sources, the attempt to distinguish middle-class women has been shaped by categories used in the census. One of the most important factors delineating social class is occupation, and the relationship between occupation and nativity, an important census classification, can be determined from census data.

Between 1870 and 1920, the middle class in the United States underwent significant change and expansion. To the "old middle class" of independent businessmen and professionals was added a rapidly growing number of new entries: salaried upper-level businessmen and professionals, public service employees, clerical workers, and salespeople.[31] In 1870, 20 percent of the nation's labor force was estimated to be middle class. Members of the "old middle class" dominated, holding approximately two-thirds of all middle-class occupations. By 1920, the middle class had grown, comprising 30 percent of the nation's labor force. In contrast to 1870, more than 70 percent of all middle-class persons in 1920 worked in the "new middle class" occupations.[32]

In both 1890 and 1920, a higher proportion of native whites of native-born parents (NWNP) than members of other nativity groups belonged to those occupational categories that tended to indicate middle-class status: professional, clerical, and much of trade. In 1890, 42.1 percent of all employed persons (excluding those in agriculture and mining) were NWNP. However, NWNP were present in greater proportion in the middle-class occupational categories, making up 68 percent of all professionals, 55 percent of all clerical workers, and 52.9 percent of those in trade. In addition, 30.9 percent of all employed NWNP (excluding those in agriculture and mining) were in middle-class occupations as compared with only 23.2 percent of native whites of foreign-born parents (NWFP) and 14.0 percent of foreign-born whites (FW). The situation was similar in 1920. Forty-six percent of all employed persons (excluding those in agriculture and mining) were NWNP, and 62.5 percent of all professionals, 55.7 percent of all in clerical work, and 51.8 percent of those in trade were NWNP. By 1920, 39 percent of all employed NWNP (excluding those in agriculture or mining) were in middle-class occupations. For NWFP and FW the corresponding percentages were 37.9 and 21.0.[33]

In cities and towns where the majority of the inhabitants were NWNP, the need to distinguish between the aggregate population and NWNP obviously was not of crucial importance. However, many of the cities of the Northeast and Midwest had large immigrant populations, and in such cities distinguishing NWNP from the aggregate population provided significant information regarding middle-class behavior patterns. For example, in Boston in 1890, 44.5 percent of all employed persons were FW and only 13.4 percent of them were employed in middle-class occupations. Since FW comprised such a large proportion of the labor force, the aggregate population had a total of only 24.1 percent employed in middle-class occupations as compared with 42 percent among NWNP. Similarly, in Chicago, FW comprised 54 percent of all employed. There the aggregate population had only 22.5 percent in middle-class occupations, whereas for NWNP the percentage was 40.7. In 1920 the proportion of FW in both cities had declined, but the difference between the aggregate population and NWNP with respect to representation in middle-class occupations was still significant. In Chicago, 39.7 percent of the aggregate population and

55.6 percent of NWNP were in middle-class occupations, whereas in Boston the corresponding percentages were 31.6 and 49.0.[34]

In this study the category NWNP has been used as a rough indicator of the middle class. Although obviously not all NWNP were middle class, at least in many of the urban areas they were more likely than any other nativity group to indicate the behavior patterns of the middle class and for that reason have been distinguished from the aggregate population.

What occurred in the middle class had ramifications beyond class boundaries. Many of the books, magazines, and newspapers of the era reflected the tastes and values of the middle class. Many government officials, especially on the local level, had risen from the ranks of the middle class. Much of the business community was middle class in origin. In terms of the extent of influence if not yet in actual numbers, the middle class was coming to dominate the American scene.[35] Therefore, a study of middle-class behavior patterns and values yields information that extends beyond class confines and presumably reflects the dominant mores of the nation.

Notes

1. Boyd Winchester, "The New Woman," *Arena,* April 1902, p. 367.

2. The phrase "New Woman" began to appear in the mid-1890s in both *Poole's Index to Periodical Literature* and the *Reader's Guide to Periodical Literature.*

3. See Barbara Welter, "The Cult of True Womanhood: 1820-1860," *American Quarterly* 28 (Summer 1966): 151-74.

4. See Arthur M. Schlesinger, Sr., *Rise of the City, 1878-1898* (New York: Macmillan Co., 1933); Howard Furer, "The City as a Catalyst for the Women's Rights Movement," *Wisconsin Magazine of History* 52 (Summer 1969): 285-305; Andrew Sinclair, *The Better Half: The Emancipation of the American Woman* (London: Jonathan Cape, 1966); Carl Degler, "Revolution Without Ideology: The Changing Place of Women in America," *Daedalus* 93 (Spring 1964): 653-70; "The American Woman's Pre-World War I Freedom in Manners and Morals," *Journal of American History* 55 (Spring 1968): 315-33.

5. This criticism holds for the previously mentioned studies.

6. See Appendix A for a detailed description of how data for the variables were collected and how urban/rural differences were calculated.

7. See Appendix B. See also Jack P. Gibbs, ed., *Urban Research Methods* (Princeton, N.J.: Van Nostrand Co., 1967), pp. 461-561 regarding this point.

8. See, for example, Susan Kleinberg, "Technology's Stepdaughters" (Ph.D. dissertation, University of Pittsburgh, 1973); Virginia Yans Mc-Laughlin, "Patterns of Work and Family Organization: Buffalo's Italians," in *The Family in History,* eds. Theodore K. Rabb and Robert I. Rotberg (New York: Harper & Row, 1973), pp. 111-26; Barbara Klaczynska, "Why Women Work: A Comparison of Various Groups—Philadelphia, 1910-1930," *Journal of Labor History* 17 (Winter 1976): 74-87; Susan Kleinberg, "Technology and Women's Work: The Lives of Working Class Women in Pittsburgh, 1870-1900," *Journal of Labor History* 17 (Winter 1976): 58-72; Barbara Berg, *The Remembered Gate: Origins of American Feminism, the Woman and the City, 1800-1860* (New York: Oxford University Press, 1978).

9. See, for example, U.S., Department of Commerce, Bureau of the Census, *The Ratio of Children to Women,* by Warren Thompson, Census Monograph No. 11 (Washington, D.C.: Government Printing Office, 1931); Warren Thompson and Pascal K. Whelpton, *Population Trends in the United States* (New York: McGraw-Hill Book Co., 1933; reprint ed., New York: Kraus Reprint Co., 1969); James Tarver, "Gradients of Urban Influences on the Educational, Employment, and Fertility Patterns of Women," *Rural Sociology* 34 (September 1969): 356-67; Bernard Okun, *Trends in Birth Rates in the United States Since 1870* (Baltimore: Johns Hopkins Press, 1958); William Ogburn and Clark Tibbits, "The Family and Its Functions," in *Recent Social Trends in the United States: Report of the President's Research Committee on Social Trends,* 2 vols. (New York: McGraw-Hill Book Co., 1933), 1: 661-708; Thomas Lynn Smith, *Sociology of Rural Life,* 3rd ed. (New York: Harper & Bros., 1953).

10. In part the limitation of earlier studies has probably stemmed from working within the confines of data that were already presented in reduced form within the censuses.

11. See Appendix A for a detailed discussion of the material available through census sources and the data reduction techniques used.

12. Estelle Davis, in "The New Woman: Changing Views of Women in the 1920s," *Journal of American History* 61 (September 1974): 372-93, has correctly criticized the tendency of historians to view the 1920s as an age of full equality for women. See also Ruth Schwartz Cowan, "Two Washes in the Morning and a Bridge Party at Night: The American Housewife Between the Wars," *Women's Studies* 3 (1976): 147-72, who traces the development of the "feminine mystique" to the years between World War I and World War II.

13. U.S., Department of Commerce, Bureau of the Census, *Fourteenth Census of the United States, 1920: Abstract,* p. 217.

14. U.S., Department of Commerce, Bureau of the Census, *Women in*

Gainful Occupations: 1870-1920, by Joseph A. Hill, Census Monograph No. 9 (Washington, D.C.: Government Printing Office, 1929).

15. Ruth Davidson, interview, April 14, 1970, Pasadena, California. Davidson was born *circa* 1898 in Bradford, Pennsylvania, and worked as a telephone operator before her marriage. Mary Humphreys, "Women Bachelors in New York," *Scribner's,* November 1896, pp. 626-35; Mara Millar, *Hail to Yesterday* (New York: Farrar & Rinehart, 1941); Bethenia Owens-Adair, *Some of Her Life Experiences* (Portland, Ore.: Mann & Beach, 1906); Marie Thérèse (de Solms) Blanc, *The Condition of Women in the United States,* trans. Abby Langdon Alger (Boston: Roberts Bros., 1895; reprint ed., New York: Arno Press, 1972); Grace H. Dodge et al., *What Women Can Earn: Occupations of Women and Their Compensation* (Boston: Frederick A. Stokes Co., 1898). See sections about clerical and telephone work. Martha L. Rayne, *What Can a Woman Do: Or, Her Position in the Business and Literary World* (Petersburg, N.Y.: Eagle Publishing Co., 1893); Helen M. Doyle, *A Child Went Forth* (New York: Gotham House, 1934); Marion Harland, "The Passing of the Home Daughter," *Independent,* July 13, 1911, pp. 88-90; Suzanne Wilcox, "The Unrest of Modern Woman," *Independent,* June 8, 1909, pp. 62-66.

16. Lorine Pruette, *Women and Leisure: A Study of Social Waste* (New York: E. P. Dutton & Co., 1924); Wilcox, "Unrest of Modern Woman," pp. 62-66.

17. Wilcox, "Unrest of Modern Woman," pp. 62-66. See also Carolyn Forrey, "The New Woman Revisited," *Women's Studies* 2 (1974): 37-56, for a discussion of the conflicts experienced by "new women" as portrayed in novels of the era.

18. Charles W. Eliot, "The Normal American Woman," *Ladies' Home Journal,* January 1908, p. 15.

19. T. Cave-North, "Woman's Place and Power," *Westminster Review,* September 1908, p. 265.

20. Cardinal Gibbons, "Pure Womanhood," *Cosmopolitan,* September 1905, pp. 559-61.

21. "The American Ideal Woman," *Putnam's,* November 1853, p. 531.

22. Kate Gannett Wells, "The Transitional American Woman," *Atlantic,* December 1880, p. 824.

23. See Ouida, "The New Woman," *North American Review,* May 1894, pp. 610-19; Josephine K. Henry, "The New Woman of the South," *Arena,* February 1895, pp. 353-62; "The New Woman," *Cornhill Magazine,* October 1894, pp. 365-68; "Advice to the New Woman," *Review of Reviews,* June 1895, pp. 84-85; Lillian Betts, "The New Woman," *Outlook,* October 12, 1895, p. 587; Emma C. Hewitt, "The 'New Woman' in Her Relation to the 'New Man,' " *Westminster Review,* March 1897,

pp. 335-37; Winchester, "The New Woman," p. 367. *Cornhill Magazine* and *Westminster Review* were British.

24. Hewitt, "The New Woman," pp. 335-37.

25. Betts, "The New Woman," p. 587.

26. "The New Woman," *Cornhill Magazine,* October 1894, pp. 365-68.

27. Elsie Robinson, *I Wanted Out* (New York: Farrar & Rinehart, 1934), p. 130. Coeducation had been introduced at Oberlin in 1837. Between 1840 and the Civil War, a small number of colleges and universities had followed the example set by Oberlin. It was between 1870 and 1900 that the number of co-ed institutions exhibited a marked increase. In 1870 women were admitted to 30.7 percent of all colleges (excluding technical schools and schools strictly for women). By 1880 the percentage of colleges admitting women stood at 51.3, in 1890 it was 65.5 percent, and in 1900, 71.6 percent. See Woody, *History of Women's Education,* 2: 231-52.

28. Winchester, "The New Woman," pp. 367, 371-72.

29. Margaret Deland, "The Change in the Feminine Ideal," *Atlantic Monthly,* March 1910, pp. 291-302.

30. See Seymour Lipset and Reinhard Bendix, *Social Mobility in Industrial Society* (Berkeley: University of California Press, 1963); Joseph A. Kahl, *The American Class Structure* (New York: Rinehart & Co., 1957); William Lloyd Warner, Marchia Meeker, Kenneth Eells, eds., *Social Class in America* (Chicago: Science Research Associates, 1949).

31. For discussions regarding the composition and growth of the middle class in late nineteenth- and early twentieth-century America see Richard Hofstadter, *The Age of Reform* (New York: Vintage Books, 1955); Robert H. Wiebe, *The Search for Order, 1877-1920* (New York: Hill & Wang, 1967); Lewis Corey, "Problems of the Peace: IV. The Middle Class,' *Antioch Review* 5 (Spring 1945): 68-87.

32. Corey, "The Middle Class," pp. 69-70. Percentages were calculated from the data presented in Corey's article.

33. U.S., Department of the Interior, Office of the Census, *Eleventh Census of the United States, 1890: Population,* pt. 2, Ages and Occupations, p. cxviii; U.S., Department of Commerce, Bureau of the Census, *Fourteenth Census, 1920,* vol. 4, *Population: Occupations,* pp. 34, 341.

34. U.S., Department of the Interior, *Eleventh Census, 1890: Population,* pt. 2, pp. 638, 650-51; U.S., Department of Commerce, *Fourteenth Census, 1920,* vol. 4, *Population: Occupations,* pp. 1062-65, 1076-80.

35. Wiebe, *Search for Order,* especially pp. 111-32, discusses the importance of the middle class in late nineteenth- and early twentieth-century America.

1 Nineteenth-Century Changes in Family Dynamics

By marriage the husband and wife are one person in law . . . the very being or legal existence of the woman is suspended during marriage or at least incorporated and consolidated into that of her husband.[1]

In the rural areas of the United States, especially prior to the Industrial Revolution, the family had typically been a unit of production as well as consumption. Within this unit, each member performed a particular function necessary to the well-being and ultimate survival of the family. For the most part, the father and grown sons worked in the fields, tended the animals, and hunted while the mother, daughters, and younger sons prepared food and made clothing, fed the animals, hauled the water, and in general tended to the running of the house. Each household was relatively self-sufficient.

Despite the fact that all members of the family, with the exception of the very youngest, contributed to the economic maintenance of the family, the rural family exhibited a rigid hierarchy. Within the hierarchy, each person had a clearly defined place, with the father holding the highest, most powerful position. Wife, sons, daughters—all were subordinate to the father. Women would almost always be subordinate to the male members of the family. As daughters they were expected to submit to the authority of their fathers; as wives they were under the control of their husbands. Only as widows or as adult, single women could they possibly escape from their subordinate position. However, in a rural society it was not easy for women or men to survive alone; so most women remained within a family, as daughters or wives or sisters, subordinate to fathers or husbands or brothers.[2]

The functions of the rural, American family were obviously not confined to the economic sphere. Education of the young, the imparting of religious beliefs, protection against hostile outsiders, and even recreation— all tended to be centered in the home and around the family.[3] Both parents were involved with all aspects of family life, especially with the socializing process of education and religious training.

Though not as self-sufficient as rural households, families in colonial cities led relatively integrated lives with often only an ill-defined line separating the private and public spheres. Home and work most often were in identical locations. Given the chronic labor shortage of colonial America, it was not uncommon for the wife and even the children to work alongside the husband in the family business. However, since the business was literally a part of the home, the wife who worked did so as part of a family enterprise, under the watchful eye of her husband.

As the urbanization and industrialization of the nineteenth century progressed, many functions that formerly had belonged almost exclusively to the family began to move outside the home. Education, which in the colonial family had often been centered in the home, began to be taken over by schools. Until well into the nineteenth century, most elementary schools were private. Although a few states in the Northeast and Midwest began to lay the foundation for public education systems during the 1830s, generally individual cities established free schools prior to the states as a whole. By 1850 the 80,000 elementary schools in the nation, mostly in the Northeast and Midwest, enrolled about 3.5 million pupils. At about that time Massachusetts introduced the first compulsory education law, but not until 1918 did all states finally follow the Massachusetts example. At first only a few years of school were made mandatory, but the number of years required expanded as the century progressed.[4]

Prior to the Civil War, high schools were rare and most of them were private, but after the war a system of public high schools began to grow. In 1870 public high schools numbered about 500, in 1890 nearly 2,500, and by 1915 almost 12,000. Thus during the course of the late nineteenth and early twentieth centuries, education, which often had been solely within the domain of the family, was increasingly transferred to outside agencies—the schools.[5]

For some groups, in some areas, recreation also began to lose its family focus. The nineteenth-century American city offered an ever-expanding array of entertainment that drew people out of the home and away from family-centered activities. Theaters, lectures, and concerts served to make recreation a matter of individual interest and involvement rather than familial interaction.

The transfer of activities that previously had been centered in the home in effect narrowed considerably the role played by the family, and significant changes began to develop in the relationships among family members. Perhaps the most important changes came about as a result of the separation of a major facet of the production function from the home.

In the thriving commercial cities of the late eighteenth and early nineteenth centuries a growing number of families began to lead increasingly segmented lives. For some adult males, work became something divorced from the home. Each day the home and its activities were left behind as the men went out to work in a wide variety of occupations. Left at home, for the most part, were adult females and children. Prior to the 1890s many of the same duties that occupied rural women also filled the days of urban women—cooking, child care, sewing, cleaning. In the rural areas those tasks performed by women were valued because they were intimately related to the survival of the family unit. But in the city those same tasks were deemed tangential to the major economic variable that influenced the survival of the family—the success or failure of those employed in the working world. Woman's status, which even in the colonial era had not been as high as man's slipped a few notches in the early nineteenth-century commercial city.[6]

The growing separation between work and home directly affected the role played by the father within the family. In the colonial era he had often been involved with the daily activities of the household and closely associated with education and training, especially of the sons. In the antebellum urban setting he was increasingly absent. More and more the home was becoming woman's domain, and the work associated with it valued less highly than the moneymaking work outside the home. As the character of economic interdependence of the family unit shifted, the economic basis of the marriage began to diminish in importance while the companionable aspects grew.[7] Especially among the rising urban middle class, wives were no longer chosen mainly because they were hard and adept workers. Other considerations such as personality and attractiveness grew in importance. However, economic considerations still remained quite important in the selection of a husband, since the family's economic success largely depended upon him.

The rising affluence and growth of the urban middle class during the first half of the nineteenth century brought important changes to the American middle-class family and the role of women within it. Increased wealth allowed a growing number of Americans to copy a life-style that previously had been reserved for the upper class, where the "idle" wife loomed as the ultimate symbol of her husband's success. Class divisions began to sharpen between working-class and middle-class women, and the fact that a woman did not have to be employed because the husband, alone, could support the family became an important status symbol.[8]

The confinement of women to the home, however, coming at the very time when work outside the home carried the highest status, posed a serious dilemma for the middle-class family. Would women be content to remain in the home when it was from work outside the home that one derived respect and status? If women did not remain in the home, but instead decided to enter the working world, a serious challenge to the male's status within the family hierarchy could develop. Unlike working within the context of the family unit in a rural area, working outside the home for money gave a woman the potential to be financially independent of her husband and thus could diminish his authority over her.[9] This dilemma was not necessarily conceived of at a conscious level, but the changes brought about by the growing affluence of the urban middle class made adjustments regarding male and female family roles essential.

In urban, middle-class families not only did the wife's economic value decrease relative to that of the husband's, but so did the children's. Whereas in rural areas the older children had participated in helping the family economically, in the urban setting they were increasingly considered to be an economic burden. The concept of childhood as a distinct period in an individual's development had begun to develop among the upper class during the seventeenth century. By the nineteenth century this concept of childhood had spread to other classes, and took especially firm root in the urban middle class.[10] The years allotted to "childhood" grew, and greater emphasis was placed upon the need for parents to nurture and protect their offspring over a longer period of time.

As sharing economic responsibility in the family unit declined in importance, the child-rearing role gained. Despite the fact that some of the educating and socializing functions of the family were being taken over by the school and the church, the duties of the mother increasingly revolved around child rearing. This development was due in large part to stretching the number of years designated as "childhood" and the fact that with the father's increased absence from the home, child rearing, which formerly both parents had shared, increasingly became the exclusive task of the mother.

The idea, which developed during the early 1800s, of woman as the protector and teacher of the young and as the guardian of society's morals was exceedingly significant. In the first place, the whole emphasis upon the importance of child rearing meant that whoever was rearing the children was performing a valuable function. Women, whose value as partners in an economic unit had declined, now had a different source for gaining a sense of worth and purpose. It was therefore not surprising to find a growing literature during the pre-Civil War era that glorified woman's role in the home, especially as the inculcator of proper values in children.[11]

However, the idea of woman as the protector of society's morals was a two-sided argument used both by those who believed that woman should confine her activities to the home, and also by those who believed that she should enlarge her sphere of activity. The former insisted that to raise one's own children was the most important task, and the one for which women were especially suited. The latter argued that woman's higher morality made it essential that she not restrict herself to the home, but rather that she bring her moral superiority to bear upon finding solutions for society's woes.[12]

Between the early 1800s and 1860 a way developed to deal with changes that had occurred within the middle-class family as it adjusted to the antebellum urban setting. Although not as pronounced as toward the close of the nineteenth century, the pre-Civil War city still was a place of upheaval. The antebellum urban home came to be viewed as a place to which a man could escape from the turmoil of the world.[13] As a retreat it should in no way resemble the competitive, rough and tumble ways of the working world, and those who stayed in it—women and children—would remain pure and unsullied. Conversely, constant contact with the outside world would ultimately corrupt. Women, actually middle- and upper-class white women, were idealized and idolized and elevated to a pedestal that demanded from them "piety, purity, domesticity, and submissiveness," and

made them almost totally dependent on men for their survival. To be a lady
was the ideal, but to be a lady meant that one had to marry and be supported by a man, and that opportunity simply was not available to all
women. Moreover, for some women total dependence and immersion of
oneself in the home were not desired.

Although the majority of women, happily or unhappily, followed the
dictates of a code that insisted that they stay in the home, a significant
minority did not. Stimulated in part by the religious fervor of the Second
Great Awakening during the early nineteenth century, and in part by the
very conditions that had constricted their role in the commercial cities,
thousands of middle- and upper-class urban women threw themselves into
organizing a myriad of benevolent associations. Urban women who had
been bored, trapped in their homes, cut off from contacts, found a sense
of purpose in their many associations. Between 1800 and 1860 thousands
of middle- and upper-class women stepped beyond the confines of their
constricted domestic role and reached out to assist less fortunate members
of their communities. They organized foreign and domestic missions, assisted
workingwomen, widows, and orphans, and even worked with prostitutes.
In the benevolent associations women began to sense both their own individuality and self-worth as well as their shared oppression. For many women
these associations served as the wellspring of feminist awareness.[14]

Another source of feminist consciousness and activism for women
sprang from involvement in the abolition movement. Women such as
Lucretia Mott, Angelina and Sarah Grimké, Lydia Child, Lucy Stone, and
Susan B. Anthony were active participants in the antislavery movement
that grew in strength from the 1830s on, constantly prodding at the con-
science of the nation.[15] Many of those women also expressed their belief
in equality by involvement in the women's rights movement, which came
into official existence at the Seneca Falls Convention of 1848.

One who struggled to break out of the confines of the early nineteenth
century's role for women was Lucy Stone. Born in Massachusetts in 1818,
Stone rebelled against the position of inferiority assigned to her by a
domineering father. From an early age, she was aware of the numerous
burdens that weighed so heavily on her mother. At age sixteen Stone began
to teach at the district school. The low wages, relative to men, received
by women teachers, reinforced her indignation toward the inequities visited
upon women. In 1843 Stone entered Oberlin. She wanted to practice

public speaking but found such activities closed to women. Invited to write a commencement address in 1847, Stone refused because she would not have been allowed to present the speech. Following graduation, Stone received an appointment as lecturer in William Lloyd Garrison's American Anti-Slavery Society. She also began in earnest her campaign for women's rights. Stone's sensitivity to the oppression suffered by women had disposed her against marriage. In 1855, she finally capitulated to the adamant pursuit of reformer Henry Blackwell, who promised her "perfect equality" in marriage. Marriage did not end Stone's activism, and she remained a prominent member of the feminist movement until her death in 1893.

Although the benevolent societies, the antislavery struggle, and the women's rights movement did propel some middle- and upper-class women out of the drawing room and into "outside" activities, neither the pre-Civil War commercial cities nor the nascent manufacturing centers provided much opportunity for middle-class women to enter the working world. A small proportion of middle-class women without higher education found employment. Some worked in the factories of Lowell, Lawrence, or other New England towns during the early days of the 1830s.[16] Others taught school, took in boarders, worked as milliners, or in the few other occupations initially deemed genteel for those middle-class women who had to or chose to work. In the few coeducational colleges of the West, Oberlin, Antioch, and the State University of Iowa, a small number of women pursued the goal of a higher education and in some cases a professional career. However, for most antebellum, middle-class women, life was relatively circumscribed, with few viable options outside of home and marriage.

Not until the Civil War did larger numbers of women begin, at least temporarily, to emerge from the confines of the home. The upheaval engendered by the war, the removal of hundreds of thousands of men from their civilian jobs, and the death of fathers and husbands forced many women, who in normal times would have relied upon men for economic support, to fend for themselves.[17] For many women, this entrance into the working world was temporary. For others, employment remained a necessity of life. Especially in the South, the war shredded the social fabric of the old order, and in both the North and the South the circumscribed, antebellum role defined as "proper" for middle- and upper-class women was modified by the realities of the times.

The Civil War served an important function as a disrupter of the existing order, but it alone did not bring about lasting changes to the lives of American women. In order to explain the massive and enduring changes that were taking place in women's lives during the late nineteenth and early twentieth centuries, the role played by the post-Civil War city must be examined.

Notes

1. Justice Blackstone, quoted in Willystine Goodsell, *A History of Marriage and the Family* (New York: Macmillan Co., 1939), pp. 360-61. The quote dates from the late eighteenth century.
2. For a discussion of the structure and function of the rural family see: Charles P. Loomis and J. Allan Beegle, *Rural Social Systems* (New York: Prentice-Hall, 1950); Muzaffer Sherif and Carolyn Sherif, *An Outline of Social Psychology* (New York: Harper & Row, 1948); Noel P. Gist and Sylvia F. Fava, *Urban Society,* 5th ed. (New York: Thomas Y. Crowell Co., 1964); Edmund S. Morgan, *The Puritan Family* (New York: Harper & Row, 1944); Paul Pierce, *Social Survey of Three Rural Townships in Iowa,* University of Iowa Monograph Series, vol. 5, no. 2 (Iowa City: The University of Iowa Press, 1917); William Forrest Sprague, *Women and the West* (Boston: Christopher Publishing House, 1940).
3. Adolph S. Tomars, "Ethical Frontiers," quoted in Thomas Earl Sullenger, *Sociology of Urbanization: A Study in Rurban Society* (Ann Arbor, Mich.: Braun-Brumfield, 1956), pp. 24-26.
4. Henry Bamford Parkes, *The United States of America* (New York: Alfred A. Knopf, 1968), pp. 269-70, 479; Harry S. Good and James D. Teller, *A History of American Education* (New York: Macmillan Co., 1973), pp. 127-30.
5. Ephraim Gordon Ericksen, *Urban Behavior* (New York: Macmillan Co., 1973), pp. 328-29; Tomars, "Ethical Frontiers," in Sullenger, *Sociology of Urbanization,* pp. 24-26, points out that religion, too, is removed from the family as specialized organizations develop to take over this function.
6. Gideon Sjoberg, "Familial Organization in the Pre-industrial City," *Marriage and Family Living* 18 (February 1956): 30-36. Sjoberg contends that family structure in the pre-industrial and industrial city is very different. In the former, women are clearly subordinate to men and do not work outside the home. With the industrialized city there is more possibility of independence for women. See also Gideon Sjoberg, "The Rural-Urban

Dimension in Pre-industrial, Transitional and Industrialized Societies,"
in *Handbook of Modern Sociology*, ed., Robert E. Faris (Chicago: Rand
McNally Co., 1964); Gerda Lerner, "Woman's Rights and American Feminism," *American Scholar* 40 (Spring 1971): 235-48; Ethel Peal, "The Atrophied Rib: Urban Middle-Class Women in Jacksonian America" (Ph.D.
dissertation, University of Pittsburgh, 1970); Barbara J. Berg, *The Remembered Gate: Origins of American Feminism: The Woman and the
City, 1800-1860*. Peal and Berg both specifically discuss the decline in
women's status in American cities between about 1800 and 1840.

7. William Ogburn and M. F. Nimkoff, *Technology and the Changing
Family* (Boston: Houghton Mifflin Co., 1955), pp. 46-47, 53-54; Loomis
and Beegle, *Rural Social Systems*, p. 67.

8. Gerda Lerner, "The Lady and the Mill Girl: Changes in the Status
of Women in the Age of Jackson," *American Studies* 10 (Spring 1969):
5-15; Barbara Welter, "The Cult of True Womanhood: 1820-1860,"
American Quarterly 28 (Summer 1966): 151-74; Berg, *The Remembered
Gate*.

9. Sherif and Sherif, *Social Psychology*, pp. 704-5; Gist and Fava,
Urban Society, p. 365; David M. Heer, "Dominance and the Working
Wife," *Social Forces* 36 (May 1958): 341-47. Work outside the home did
not always threaten the family hierarchy. See Virginia Yans McLaughlin,
"Patterns of Work and Family Organization: Buffalo's Italians," in *The
Family in History*, eds. Theodore K. Rabb and Robert I. Rotberg (New
York: Harper & Row, 1973), pp. 111-36, regarding this point.

10. Phillipe Ariès, *Centuries of Childhood* (New York: Alfred A. Knopf,
1962); Christopher Lasch, "Divorce American Style," *New York Review
of Books*, February 17, 1966, pp. 3-4.

11. Welter, "True Womanhood," pp. 151-74; William Bridges, "Family
Patterns and Social Values in America, 1827-1875," *American Quarterly*
27 (September 1965): 3-11.

12. Glenda Gates Riley, "From Chattel to Challenger: The Changing
Image of the American Woman, 1828-1848" (Ph.D. dissertation, Ohio
State University, 1967); Welter, "True Womanhood," especially pages
163, 172-74; Ann D. Gordon, Mari Jo Buhle, and Nancy Schrom, "Woman in American Society," *Radical America* 5 (July-August 1971): 3-
66.

13. Berg, *Origins of American Feminism*. Richard Sennett, *Families
Against the City* (Cambridge, Mass.: Harvard University Press, 1970).
Sennett describes such a development for the 1870s in Chicago.

14. Berg, *Origins of American Feminism*. Keith Melder, *Beginnings of
Sisterhood: The American Woman's Rights Movement, 1800-1850* (New

York: Schocken Books, 1977). Melder also sees nascent feminism in benevolent association activity.

15. Melder, *Beginnings of Sisterhood,* emphasizes the importance of the abolitionist movement. See also Lerner, "Woman's Rights and American Feminism," pp. 235-48.

16. Hannah G. Josephson, *The Golden Threads* (New York: Duell, Sloan & Pearce, 1949). At first native white, single women flocked to the new factory towns which attempted to attract them by offering a protected environment and a variety of cultural activities. However, by 1850 conditions had deteriorated considerably and the "golden days" had passed. The factories soon were filled with newly arrived immigrants and the short era of factory work being considered respectable was over.

17. Anne Firor Scott, *The Southern Lady: From Pedestal to Politics, 1830-1930* (Chicago: University of Chicago Press, 1970), especially pages 80-133; Blanc, *Condition of Women,* p. 25; David McRae, *America Revisited* (Glasgow: John Smith & Son, 1908), p. 25; Eližabeth F. Baker, *Technology and Women's Work* (New York: Columbia University Press, 1964), pp. 63-65.

2   The City in the Industrial Age

Woman is not only drifting to the cities but setting
them in order and making a new environment therein
for herself and her arriving sisters.[1]

In the late nineteenth-century city a variety of factors
coalesced, ultimately forming an environment conducive to the growth
of a less restricted life-style for middle-class women. The development
of cities after the Civil War was closely intertwined with the Industrial
Revolution. Not all late nineteenth-century cities were predominantly
industrial, but the technological developments that occurred as a result
of the Industrial Revolution had a profound influence upon urban life in
the United States.

Prior to the Civil War, the vast majority of cities in the United States
were commercial in origin and orientation and most were comparatively
small. In 1850 only eight cities had populations of more than 100,000,
but by 1920 sixty-eight cities fell into this category. Between 1800 and
1870, the urban population of the United States, though increasing almost thirtyfold, grew by only 9.5 million people to a total of almost 10
million. From 1870 to 1920, although the increase was only eightfold,
44 million people were added to the urban roster.[2] Between 1870 and
1920 a nation that had been predominantly rural had become more than
50 percent urban.

The post-Civil War city was a place of almost frenetic activity and
seemingly endless and sometimes wondrous change. During the thirty-
year period from 1870 to 1900, the American city was transformed.

From what had been a city whose boundaries were within walking distance of its inhabitants, a city largely darkened and silenced by nightfall, offering a small number of diversions such as theater, lectures, and concerts, emerged the city of the industrial age. The new city was an astounding fairyland of lights, offering a wide assortment of amusements and covered with a web of public transportation that allowed the city to prosper and expand. At the center of this activity were machines—machines to move people, machines to light the streets, machines to make clothes, steel and food, machines to send messages, machines to print words. Change was the order of the day, or so it must have seemed as invention followed invention.

In 1870, public transportation relied almost exclusively on horse-drawn vehicles, but by 1900 cable cars, electric trolleys, and elevated and subway trains whisked city inhabitants from place to place. Horse-drawn transit cars had begun to appear in the 1850s and remained the most efficient and widespread form of public transportation for more than thirty years. By 1880 over 3,000 miles of track were in operation and most cities of more than 50,000 inhabitants had a horse-drawn rail system. But from the 1860s on, the search was underway for improved forms of urban transportation. In the 1870s a steam-powered, elevated rail system was constructed in New York City. Similar systems were built in Brooklyn and Chicago during the 1880s and 1890s. That, however, was a dirty, noisy, and expensive form of transportation whose popularity waned by the 1890s. Another form of public transit, the cable car, appeared during that period, and by the mid-1890s more than six hundred miles of track were in service, mainly in the larger cities of the nation. The cable car system, however, had the disadvantage of being expensive to install and did not permit the cars to run at different speeds.

In the 1870s, the development of the dynamo, a steam-powered machine that transformed the mechanical energy used to operate it into electrical energy, revolutionized urban transportation. For the first time a clean, rapid, flexible transit system was possible. In the late 1880s, Frank Julian Sprague built the first electric railroad in Richmond, Virginia, and by 1895 more than 850 electric railway systems operated 10,000 miles of track. During the 1890s and early 1900s, the technology used in the electric street railway was applied to both elevated and subway systems.[3] In the space of thirty years, urban transit had grown so rapidly that more than 23,000 miles of track, ranging from 10,000 in the

North Atlantic states to 1,300 in the South Central, assisted travel in American cities (Table 2).

TABLE 2. Increase in Miles of Track, 1890-1902

	1890	*1902*	*Percent Increase*
United States	8,123	22,589	178.1
North Atlantic	2,952	10,175	244.7
South Atlantic	612	1,670	172.9
North Central	2,754	7,818	183.9
South Central	969	1,322	36.5
West	837	1,604	91.7

SOURCE: U.S., Department of Commerce and Labor, Bureau of the Census, Special Reports, *Street and Electric Railways* (1903), p. 34.

The development of the dynamo, so important to the modernization of urban transportation, was also critical to other sectors of city life. In 1870 the streets of most cities were dimly lit by gaslights. The 1876 invention of the arc lamp was followed in 1879 by the introduction into Cleveland of a small arc lamp system. That same year, Thomas Edison perfected the incandescent lamp. The dynamo permitted the rapid spread of electric light systems. Also important was the transmission of electricity by alternating rather than direct current. Alternating current removed the distance limitations inherent in a direct-current system. George Westinghouse, the major proponent of alternating current, saw the principle triumph in 1894-95, when an alternating-current system was installed at Niagara Falls.[4] There were 38 central power stations in 1882, 600 in 1888, and over 3,000 by 1898.[5] Electric lights peppered the urban landscape, seemingly turning night into day. The significance of adequate streetlighting to women was commented upon by one author. She noted that the lights gave women much greater freedom to do things at night, be it going to a theater or restaurant, or working.

> When Mr. Edison was experimenting with the subdivision
> of the electric light, it seemed to have no special bearings

on the evolution of the woman bachelor. The brilliance of the
streets at night has been so conspicuous a factor that the
latest goddess, Electra, may well be adopted as the patron and
guardian of the sex. The duties of legions of women take them
out at night. . . . Accompanied by the chivalrous umbrella,
many a women has braved the powers of night and not infre-
quently done battle. . . . The increase in the number of women
abroad at night, with no other protector than the benign
beams of the electric light, affords a new and interesting man-
ifestation of the streets. They are found in the streetcars at
hours that once would have been called unseemly; they are
substantial patrons of the theater.[6]

The field of communication also changed radically during the latter
years of the nineteenth century. The telephone, invented by Alexander
Graham Bell in the early 1870s, was first put into commercial use in
1878 when a switchboard was installed in New Haven. In 1879 an intercity line between Boston and Lowell was established. By 1880, telephones
serviced eighty-five towns, with a total of about 50,000 subscribers, or
about 1.1 telephones for every 1,000 inhabitants. By 1900 there were
approximately 17.6 telephones per 1,000 people, in 1910, 82.0, and in
1920, 123.0.[7]
    Residents were finding major aspects of their lives altered by changes
occurring in the cities. Whereas in a rural setting it had been difficult and
unusual for men or women to remain single, such was not the case in an
urban environment. There had long been a place in the American city for
the single individual—boardinghouses had provided an easy answer to the
problem of where to live and take meals. But in the late nineteenth- and
early twentieth-century city, the options open to single individuals multiplied, reflecting the need to accommodate those people who either did
not want to or were unable to marry. J. Bixby, writing for the *Nation*
in 1868, noted that large cities were most likely to have a number of
single individuals. He contended that the city of 1868 was more conducive
to single life than the city of 1818 had been because it offered so much
more for single people to do.[8]
    Many of the northern cities contained considerably more women than
men, whereas in the West the opposite was often the case. In 1890, the
sex ratio (the number of men per 100 women) in Albany was 89.9, in

Lowell 78.3, in Lawrence 82.3, and in Utica 83.1; but in San Francisco it was 139.5, in Los Angeles 112.9, and in Denver 145.3.[9] Obviously, not all of the individuals in these and other cities would or could marry, and alternatives to marriage were essential. For men, the idea of an "alternative to marriage" was not especially critical, since men generally worked and supported themselves. However, where the ideal for a woman dictated that she be supported by a father or a husband—that her only profession was marriage—the growing acceptance of the idea that options other than marriage were needed was a radical development.

With an increasing number of women living apart from their families for at least a certain period of their lives, alternatives to the family home were indispensable. Single women lived not only in boardinghouses, but increasingly in individual apartments and sometimes took over entire apartment buildings.[10] According to one author, "In 1886 a determined effort was made to secure an apartment-house for women, modestly copying the numerous apartment-houses for men." The author saw the rise in apartment living for women in New York as a reaction against the dismal "hall bedroom," a narrow, cramped room with little more than a bed and a dresser.[11] For the single woman, the shared apartments provided a feeling of home and an "air of confidence that once was the enviable property of only married women."[12] Also available were "homes" for workingwomen. They were inexpensive, protected, but oftentimes quite regimented.[13]

During the era, certain types of living quarters became more common, not only to meet the needs of single individuals, but also to satisfy those who were married and could not or did not want to establish a traditional home. Boardinghouses, popular from at least as early as the 1830s, numbered among their inhabitants married couples with children as well as single men and women. Apartments and apartment-hotels gained in popularity around the turn of the century. Oftentimes, children were not permitted in the apartment hotels, whose average suite consisted of two rooms and a bath.[14]

For those who either could not or did not wish to bother with preparing meals, an assortment of options was available. Boardinghouses, "hall bedrooms," and workingwomen's homes generally provided food as well as lodging. Hotels had their own dining rooms, which made meal-taking especially convenient for their own residents. In addition, the growing number of restaurants ranged from the simplest of lunchrooms to the most sumptuous and elegant of places to dine. There were restaurants to suit almost any budget, and people from all walks of life frequented them. In *Condition of Women in America,* Mme de Blanc, a French novelist and journalist, commented upon the ease with which single women frequented restaurants: "I saw the girls known as bachelor girls call for the bill of fare as naturally as if they were bachelors indeed."[15] And for those who desired a more exclusive atmosphere, there was always the private club— even for women! Mme de Blanc described a club to which a Philadelphia woman took her, a club where the woman frequently had breakfast when her husband was out of town. The club also offered temporary lodging.[16]

Even those who lived in more traditional homes found that life was changing. Preparation of food and clothing, which had consumed a large portion of women's time, was increasingly removed from the home as "ready-mades" in both food and clothing began to proliferate. Advertisements for ready-made clothing appeared in a variety of different newspapers, with the number and size of the ads increasing as the years progressed.[17] Now a woman could go to grocery stores and bakeries for prepared food, and department stores or smaller specialty stores for clothing. A variety of appliances, all designed to ease the burden of house care, began to appear from the 1880s onward, while more and more middle-class city homes had indoor plumbing, eliminating the traditional female task of hauling water.[18]

In addition to changes that were occurring in the day-to-day running of the household, an increasing number of activities offered in the city tended to draw people out of the home away from family-centered activities. Although the antebellum city had by no means been devoid of recreational activities, what was offered was limited in scope and often accessible only to the more affluent residents. In the larger metropolitan centers of the East, New York, Philadelphia, and Boston, an array of theaters, concerts, operas, museums, and libraries enriched the lives of at least some of the inhabitants. Even in the hinterlands some cultural activities were available. Tyrone Power, the Irish actor, toured a number of American cities in the 1840s, including Charleston, New Orleans, St. Louis, and Cincinnati. Jenny Lind, the Swedish singer, captivated American audiences during the 1840s. Some cities other than the eastern metropolitan centers had small natural history museums, most often filled with a hodgepodge of curios. For most cities, not until after the Civil War did a recreation explosion occur, an explosion that vastly multiplied the activities available and the audience reached.

After 1870, in cities large and small, theaters, concerts, operas, vaude-ville, lending libraries, and museums of all sorts proliferated. Art museums flourished. The Corcoran Gallery in Washington, D.C. opened in 1869; the Museum of Art in Philadelphia in 1876; the Art Institute of Chicago in 1879; the Indianapolis Museum of Art in 1883; the Milwaukee Art Center in 1888; San Francisco's Fine Arts Museum in 1895; and the Los Angeles County Art Museum in 1910. More cities opened natural history museums. There was the California Museum of Science and Industry in Los Angeles (1880); the Milwaukee Public Museum (1882); the Louis-ville Natural History Museum (1884); the Arizona State Museum in Tucson (1893); and the Field Museum in Chicago (1893). Between 1890 and 1910 cities organized musical societies, orchestras, and in some cases professional symphonies: Cincinnati (1895); Philadelphia (1900); Minne-apolis (1903); San Francisco (1911).

From the 1880s onward, a wide assortment of recreational sports grew in popularity, including roller and ice skating, bicycling, tennis, golf, and swimming. During the same era, amusement parks began to make their appearance on the American scene. Coney Island was begun during the 1870s. Other parks soon followed: Ohio Grove near Cincinnati (1883); Elitch Gardens in Denver (1892); Riverview Park in Chicago (1904); Glen Echo in Washington, D.C. (1911). These permanent carnivals drew thou-sands and thousands of Americans into their make-believe worlds. After the turn of the century, movie houses attracted a steady clientele. And there was more. According to a 1916 survey, American cities had a total of 82 zoos, 61 indoor pools, and 149 beaches, all publicly run.[19]

For the more adventuresome, there was always a chance to peek at the bawdier side of the city. One author described an "escorted slum tour" in which she was taken to "Jack's," where "college boys and prostitutes met," and also to places where "girlish young men danced and sang for us and asked us to slip money into their stockings."[20]

The urban working world itself was revolutionized during the latter decades of the nineteenth century, and a growing array of jobs opened up. In particular, work opportunities for women expanded. Factory work, especially in textiles, had been available since the 1830s, and after the late 1870s, food-processing plants demanded a growing number of workers. The expanding assortment of personal services available in the city offered another set of work possibilities: restaurants, department stores, grocery stores, bakeries, laundries, beauty shops—all multiplied during that period. Yet another important source of employment appeared in the rapidly expanding field of office work. With the introduction of the typewriter in 1873, office work, which had previously been dominated by men, was flooded with women. The majority of typists, or "typewriters" as they were known for a brief while, and stenographers were women.[21] From the mid-1870s on, another steady supply of jobs was provided by the telephone company. Professional careers for women were also on the rise. The number of teaching positions climbed steadily, and the domination of this field by women was pronounced.[22] The post-Civil War years also saw the development of two new, important professions for women—nursing and librarianship.[23]

A symposium begun by *Harper's Bazaar* in 1908 attested to the significance of the city with respect to employment opportunities for women. "How many girls, the land over," the magazine queried, "come to the city to find work or begin a career. . . . Everyone knows the number is great and yearly increasing."[24] *Harper's Bazaar* invited its readers to share their personal experiences in an ongoing column, "The Girl Who Came to the City."

One woman, a native of the South, launched a successful career as a stenographer in New York. She attached great importance to both the training facilities and employment opportunities available in New York.[25] Another woman took up a career as a teacher in Baltimore. In addition to her job, she took courses at Johns Hopkins, joined a literary club, went to the theater, and to concerts.[26] The experiences of the women who wrote varied, but the general tenor of their letters emphasized the opportunities that living in a city had brought to them.

The theme of the city as a place of opportunity for women was reiterated in a 1911 *Ladies' Home Journal* article, "Her Sister in the Country Who Wants to Come to the City to Make Her Way." The author of the article described the ample career options open to women in cities. The varied possibilities offered by a city stood in sharp contrast to life in "Centerville, where there seems to be nothing . . . to do."[27]

Radical alterations also occurred in the social composition of the city. Between 1870 and 1920, millions of immigrants crowded into American cities, especially those of the North. Although large-scale immigration was not a new phenomenon, the massive influx from 1880 on dwarfed anything that had occurred earlier. Between 1840 and 1880 an average of 2.5 million immigrants arrived during each decade. During the 1880s, more than 5.2 million immigrants came to the United States; but between 1900 and 1910 the number rose to almost 9 million! The first wave of immigrants, those arriving between 1840 and 1880, had been mainly Irish and German Catholics, and German, English, and Scandinavian Protestants. During the second flood of immigration, new groups outnumbered the old ones as massive numbers of Jews from Russia and Eastern Europe, and Catholics from Italy poured into America. More of the "new" immigrants settled in urban areas than had been true for the older immigrant groups.[28]

As Italians, Slavs, Russians, Greeks settled in the older sections of the cities, a patchwork of ethnic neighborhoods emerged, each with its own set of churches, stores, restaurants, and clubs. To the native white residents, the arrival of a seemingly ever-increasing stream of immigrants presented a series of problems. Many of the immigrants were poor peasants unaccustomed to urban living. The inability to speak English, overcrowded living quarters, problems associated with waste disposal, the spread of disease, and the lack of jobs and money—all were difficulties that plagued the immigrant and frightened the more affluent urban residents. Jacob Riis in *How the Other Half Lives* vividly captured the flavor and the strangeness of the immigrant community as seen by an outsider.

> Between the tabernacles of Jewry and the shrines of the Bend
> ... [is Chinatown]. ... Stealth and secretiveness are as much
> part of the Chinaman in New York as the catlike tread of his felt
> shoes. ... The very doorways of his offices and shops are fenced
> off by queer forbidding partitions. ... The tenements grow taller
> as we cross the Bowery, and ... invade the Hebrew quarter. ...
> No need of asking here where we are. The jargon of the street,
> the signs of the sidewalk, the manner and dress of the people
> ... betray their race. ... It is said that nowhere in the world
> are so many people crowded together on a square mile as here.[29]

One can almost sense the fear mixed with some compassion that native whites felt as they listened to the hodgepodge of languages, saw the swarm of children, the poverty, the disease, the rough-looking gangs of the immigrant communities. Here, in their midst, in their city were these hordes of aliens—and what could be done?

Although many industrialists may have welcomed the supply of cheap labor that the immigrants provided, many native white urban residents greeted the newcomers with fear and hatred. Friction between native whites and immigrant groups was of course not unique to the late nineteenth century. Nativism had erupted during the 1830s, 1840s, and 1850s as American Protestants lashed out against what they viewed as the "Popish menace" of Catholic immigrant groups. The post-Civil War years saw a continued hostility, and native whites devised varied solutions to what they viewed as the problems created by the massive influx of immigrants. For some native whites the answer seemed to lie in stopping the flow of newcomers, and throughout the era the demand for limits on immigration grew stronger until in 1924 Congress passed the restrictive Immigration Act. To others, the major menace was the very high birth rate of the foreign born, which came at a time when the birth rate of native whites was declining. The eugenics movement of the late nineteenth century was in part a reaction to such concerns.

To many middle- and upper-class native whites, as ominous a development as the massive immigration of the era was the growth of "Boss Politics." Bossism had arisen in a number of American cities from mid-century on, filling the vacuum created by the lack of adequate city services and the needs of the populace. Much of the support for urban political machines came from immigrant groups whose interests and concerns had rarely been considered by the old, native white leadership. By the last quarter of the nineteenth century, men such as Richard Croker in New York, Abe Ruef in San Francisco, Jim Pendergast in Kansas City, and ward bosses "Bathhouse John" Coughlin and Michael "Hinky Dink" Kenna in Chicago controlled powerful political machines. Between the political bosses and the new industrial tycoons of the era, lucrative links were often established.[30]

In such a climate the reform movements that would ultimately blossom into Progressivism got under way. It started first at the local level. Men and women, some of whom had been former leaders of their communities, displaced by the new industrial plutocracy, others of whom were members of the new middle class of salaried professionals, began to question, analyze, and, ultimately, push to reorder the communities to which they belonged.

The reformers were not always a unified group. For some the answer seemed to lie in "cleaning up" government by initiating a number of electoral reforms designed to make government more responsive to the people and more efficiently and honestly run. The referendum, the recall, and the establishment of the city manager form of government were among the changes pushed for. It was hoped that the latter reform would remove favoritism from government and allow cities to be run efficiently, in a businesslike manner. Other reformers emphasized the need to better the physical environment of the city, to solve some of the physical problems confronting urban residents. From this group arose the movements for tenement reform, city planning, and park beautification. Yet other reformers concentrated their efforts on dealing with the social and economic problems of the cities: unemployment, inadequate pay, poor education, health problems. It was this group that continued and expanded the focus of philanthropy and made the settlement house a popular and effective agent of social reform.[31]

Jane Addams in *Twenty Years at Hull House* captured the ideals and feelings of those who became involved in the social reform movements of the era.

> These young men and women, longing to socialize their democracy, are animated by certain hopes which may be thus loosely formulated; that if in a democratic country nothing can be permanently achieved save through the masses of the people, it will be impossible to establish a higher political life than the people themselves crave . . . that the blessings which we associate with a life of refinement and cultivation can be made universal and must be made universal if they are to be permanent; that the good we secure for ourselves is precarious and uncertain, is floating in mid-air, until it is secured for all of us and incorporated into our common life.[32]

As will be seen in Chapter 5, the city, its problems, and its reform movements played a significant role in drawing hundreds of thousands of women out of the home and plunging them into the turmoil of urban life.

Numerous technological and social changes altered the late nineteenth-century city. In addition, urban characteristics, not unique to the late nineteenth-century city, combined with other developments occurring at the time to play a significant role in bringing changes into women's lives. In contrast to rural areas or villages, cities and towns contained sufficient populations to provide a certain degree of anonymity to the inhabitants. The larger the city, at least up to a certain point, the greater the anonymity.[33] The anonymity meant that people could more easily deviate from a prescribed standard of conduct and escape detection. Numbers alone precluded the possibility of close scrutiny of everyone's actions.

Moreover, the city tended to contain such a conglomeration of people with widely diverse backgrounds that a single standard of conduct was difficult to maintain. Each ethnic group brought with it a particular way of behaving. The various social classes tended to have somewhat different expectations regarding conduct. Within a particular group there indeed were often very specific rules governing behavior. However, the fact that a number of different groups were present meant that one group's code of conduct could not completely dominate. Rural areas and smaller towns and villages lacked that kind of diversity and made individual divergence from the norm more difficult.

The rapid communication of information was another significant aspect of urban life. Newspapers and magazines abounded, serving as a forum for a variety of topics. Perhaps as important was the proximity of the inhabitants and the ease with which ideas could be shared. Both of those factors meant that information could be quickly passed along to a relatively large number of people. As women began to emerge from the isolation of the home into various activities, they were more easily able to share ideas about a wide variety of topics. This ease of communication was probably quite important to women in the dissemination of information, for example, about methods of birth control.[34]

The city of late nineteenth- and early twentieth-century America was a dynamic place. It offered a growing selection of opportunities that drew women out of the home. Not all cities offered the same number or types of options. But despite the differences, the cities and towns of this period exhibited a great similarity with respect to how they affected women's lives.

Notes

1. James Collins, "She Drifted to the City," *Saturday Evening Post,* January 1, 1921, p. 11.

2. U.S., Department of Commerce, Bureau of the Census, Statistical Abstract: Supplements, *Historical Statistics of the United States from Colonial Times to 1957* (1960). Urban is defined as 2,500 or larger.

3. For discussions of the development of urban public transportation see Arthur M. Schlesinger, Sr., *Rise of the City, 1878-1898* (New York:

Macmillan Co., 1933), pp. 87-93; Charles N. Glaab and A. Theodore Brown, *A History of Urban America* (New York: Macmillan Co., 1967), pp. 147-53.

4. Edward C. Kirkland, *A History of Economic Life* (New York: F. S. Crofts & Co., 1947), p. 426.

5. Schlesinger, *Rise of the City,* p. 101; Glaab and Brown, *Urban America,* pp. 163-64.

6. Mary Humphreys, "Women Bachelors in New York," *Scribner's* (November 1896): 635.

7. Schlesinger, *Rise of the City,* p. 96; U.S., Department of Commerce, *Historical Statistics,* p. 480.

8. J. Bixby, "Why Is Single Life Becoming More General," *Nation,* March 5, 1868, pp. 190-91.

9. U.S., Department of the Interior, *Eleventh Census, 1890: Population.* See also Katherine G. Busbey, *Home Life in America* (New York: Macmillan Co., 1910), pp. 85-86.

10. Brenda Ueland, *Me* (New York: G. P. Putnam's Sons, 1939), p. 101; Humphreys, "Women Bachelors," p. 634; Busbey, *Home Life in America,* pp. 85-86.

11. Humphreys, "Women Bachelors," pp. 630-34.

12. Ibid., p. 634.

13. Dorothy Richardson, "The Long Day," in *Women at Work,* ed. William O'Neill (New York: Quadrangle, 1972), pp. 157-73.

14. Pownall Papers, Senger letter, July 15, 1877 (PW 862), and Senger letter, December 16, 1877 (PW 887), Huntington Library, San Marino, California; Schlesinger, *Rise of the City,* pp. 97-103; John Modell and Tamara K. Hareven, "Urbanization and the Malleable Household: An Examination of Boarding and Lodging in American Families," *Journal of Marriage and the Family* 35 (August 1973): 467-79; Arthur Calhoun, *A Social History of the American Family from Colonial Times to the Present,* 3 vols. in one (Cleveland: A. H. Clark, 1917-19; reprint ed., New York: Arno Press, 1973), pp. 182-84.

15. Marie Thérèse Blanc (de Solms) *The Condition of Women in the United States,* trans. Abby Langdon Alger (Boston: Roberts Bros., 1895; reprint ed., New York: Arno Press, 1972), p. 266.

16. Ibid.

17. See, for example: *Daily Oklahoman* (Oklahoma City), May 5, 1894, and July 11, 1914; *Chicago Daily Journal,* November 2, 1905; *Kansas City* (Missouri) *Star,* January 9, 1901, and May 24, 1919; *Morning Oregonian* (Portland), May 1, 1900; *Detroit Free Press,* November 22, 1885; *Los Angeles Times,* February 2, 1913.

18. See the following for information regarding labor-saving devices: Valerie Kincade Oppenheimer, "The Female Labor Force in the United States: Factors Governing Its Growth and Changing Composition" (Ph.D. dissertation, University of California, Berkeley, 1966); Schlesinger, *Rise of the City*, pp. 140-41. The *Daily Oklahoman*, November 2, 1914, contained an ad for a "new invention," a self-heating iron, indicating that at least in Oklahoma City the use of electric irons was not that widespread. The rural areas lagged behind the city with respect to indoor plumbing. Paul Pierce, *Social Survey of Three Rural Townships in Iowa*, University of Iowa Monograph Series, vol. 5, no. 2 (Iowa City: University of Iowa Press, 1917), found that few had indoor plumbing.

19. For an idea of the types of amusements available in urban areas see the following: Humphreys, "Women Bachelors," p. 635; Marian Bowlan, *City Types* (Chicago: T. S. Denison & Co., 1916); David McRae, *America Revisited* (Glasgow: John Smith & Son, 1908), p. 23; Millar, *Hail to Yesterday* (New York: Farrar & Rinehart, 1941), pp. 121, 142-43; Eugenie Longerman Spearman, *Memories* (Los Angeles: Private Printing by Modern Printers, 1942), pp. 13-21; Robert E. Riegel, *American Women: A Story of Social Change* (Rutherford, N.J.: Fairleigh Dickinson University Press, 1970), pp. 53-54; Pownall Papers, diary of Lucy Pownall Senger, 1876-77; *Daily Oklahoman*, May 12, 1894; *Boston Weekly Transcript*, April 4, 1890, April 25, 1902, and March 6, 1903; *Chicago Times*, August 7, 1893; *Morning Oregonian*, February 20, 1872; *Detroit Free Press*, October 12, 1884; Blake McKelvey, *The Urbanization of American [1860-1915]* (New Brunswick, N.J.: Rutgers University Press, 1963); Glaab and Brown, *History of Urban America*, p. 98; American Association of Museums, *The Official Museum Directory, 1977* (Washington, D.C.: National Register Publishing Co., 1976); William F. Mangels, *The Outdoor Amusement Industry: From Earliest Times to the Present* (New York: Vantage Press, Inc., 1952); Foster-Rhea Dulles, *A History of Recreation: America Learns to Play*, 2nd ed. (New York: Appleton-Century-Crofts, 1965).

20. Millar, *Hail to Yesterday*, pp. 113-15.

21. The following studies discuss the typewriter as an emancipator of women: Bruce Bliven, Jr., *The Wonderful Writing Machine* (New York: Random House, 1954); Richard N. Current, *The Typewriter and the Men Who Made It* (Champaign: University of Illinois Press, 1951); Herkimer County Historical Society, *The Story of the Typewriter, 1873-1923* (Herkimer, N.Y.: Herkimer County Historical Society, 1923). For another perspective, see Margery Davies, "Woman's Place Is at the Typewriter: The Feminization of the Clerical Labor Force," *Radical America* 8 (July-

August 1974): 1-28. Women's entrance into clerical occupations is discussed more fully in Chapter 6.

22. Elizabeth F. Baker, *Technology and Women's Work* (New York: Columbia University Press, 1964), p. 60. In 1870, two-thirds of all teachers were women, and by 1900 the percentage had risen to 76 percent.

23. Women and their occupations are discussed more fully in Chapter 6. See Baker, *Technology and Women's Work,* for an excellent summary of occupations open to women.

24. "The Girl Who Comes to the City," *Harper's Bazaar,* January 1908, pp. 54-55. The symposium ran from January 1908 to January 1909.

25. "The Girl Who Comes to the City," *Harper's Bazaar,* January 1909, pp. 54-55.

26. "The Girl Who Comes to the City," *Harper's Bazaar,* November 1908, p. 1142.

27. Clara E. Laughlin, "Her Sister in the Country Who Wants to Come to the City and Make Her Way," *Ladies' Home Journal,* August 1911, p. 16.

28. Howard P. Chudacoff, *The Evolution of American Urban Society* (Englewood Cliffs, N.J.: Prentice-Hall, Inc., 1975), p. 94.

29. Jacob Riis, *How the Other Half Lives: Studies Among the Tenements of New York* (New York: Charles Scribner's Sons, 1890; reprint ed., New York: Hill & Wang, 1957), pp. 67-70, 76-78.

30. For studies of the urban political machine see, for example, Lyle W. Dorset, *The Pendergast Machine* (New York: Oxford University Press, 1968); Lloyd Wendt and Herman Kogan, *Lords of the Levee: The Story of Bathhouse John and Hinky Dink* (Indianapolis, Ind.: Bobbs-Merrill, 1943); Harold Zink, *City Bosses in the United States: A Study of Twenty Municipal Bosses* (Durham, N.C.: Duke University Press, 1930); William L. Riordon, *Plunkitt of Tammany Hall* (New York: E. P. Dutton & Co., Inc., 1963). Also see sections on boss politics in: Chudacoff, *Evolution or American Urban Society;* Glaab and Brown, *History of Urban America;* McKelvey, *Urbanization of America.*

31. Chudacoff, *Evolution of American Urban Society,* provides an insightful analysis of different types of reformers. For studies of urban reform and the Progressive movement see: David P. Thelen, *The New Citizenship: Origins of Progressivism in Wisconsin, 1885-1900* (Columbia: University of Missouri Press, 1972); Roy Lubove, *The Progressives and the Slums: Tenement House Reform in New York City, 1890-1917* (Pittsburgh: University of Pittsburgh Press, 1962); Arthur Mann, *Yankee Reformers in the Urban Age* (Cambridge, Mass.: Harvard University Press, 1954); Robert H. Wiebe, *Search for Order, 1877-1920* (New York: Hill

& Wang, 1967); Richard Hofstadter, *The Age of Reform: From Bryan to F.D.R.* (New York: Vintage Books, 1955); Allen F. Davis, *Spearheads for Reform: The Social Settlements and the Progressive Movement, 1890-1914* (New York: Oxford University Press, 1967); David P. Thelen, "Social Tensions and the Origins of Progressivism," *Journal of American History* 56 (September 1969): 323-41; J. Joseph Huthmacher, "Urban Liberalism and the Age of Reform," *Mississippi Valley Historical Review* 49 (September 1962): 231-41.

32. Jane Addams, *Twenty Years at Hull-House* (n.p.: Phillips Publishing Co., 1910; reprint ed., New York: Macmillan Co., 1960), p. 92.

33. Samuel P. Hays, "The Changing Political Structure of the City in Industrial America," *Journal of Urban History* 1 (November 1974): 6-38. Hays contrasts the preindustrial city, which had been small, compact, and where one lived under the scrutiny of others, with the larger, industrial city.

34. See Chapter 3 for a detailed discussion of fertility trends in late nineteenth-century America. Also, *Los Angeles Times,* February 2, 1913, contained an illustrated ad for a douche; *Daily Oklahoman,* October 14, 1904, had an ad for a vaginal syringe.

3 Marriage and Fertility: 1890-1920

Acquaintance, "So you have determined to marry?"
Girl of the Period (sadly), "Yes, I see nothing else
before me."[1]

The decisions of women whether or not to marry, when
to marry, how many children to have, how much time to devote to child
rearing and household tasks—all were crucial in determining how women
spent their lives. If a woman married at a young age, had a large number
of children, oversaw the running of an entire household without assistance
from servants or labor-saving devices, she would have had little time or
energy to spend on other pursuits. Conversely, if she married later or even
if she married early and was able to limit the number of children she bore,
and had the burden of maintaining a household lightened either by servants
or labor-saving aids, she would have had the time and energy for other
forms of activity. The conditions of the era as well as the mores of the
particular society would be involved in determining what form the activities took.

For the majority of urban women, the trend between 1890 and 1920
was for more to marry, for marriages to take place at an earlier age, but
for fewer children to be born. Prior to 1890, data distinguishing between
the number of married women in cities and rural areas were not available.
Between 1890 and 1920, in rural and urban areas, it is possible to determine that proportionately more women were marrying and the number
of children they were having was decreasing (Table 3). During that time
period, the percentage increase of women who married in urban areas was

almost double that in rural areas, and the decrease in the child/woman ratio was slightly higher in the cities (Table 3). Although the general urban trend was toward earlier marriages, an important minority of women tended to postpone marriage or not to marry at all.

TABLE 3. Percentage of Females Fifteen or Older Who Were Married, and Child/Woman Ratio, 1890 and 1920, and Percent Change, 1890-1920, Aggregate Population

| | PERCENT MARRIED | | CHILD/WOMAN RATIO | |
	Urban	Rural	Urban	Rural
1890	52.0	59.3	489	753
1920	57.0	63.2	429	674
Percent change 1890-1920	11.4	6.6	−12.2	−10.5

SOURCES: U.S., *Censuses, 1890-1920.*

In America of the late nineteenth and early twentieth centuries, most women had married by the time they reached their mid-twenties. That was true in the cities as well as in the rural areas, although the proportion of married women always tended to be greater in the countryside. The biggest increase in the percentage of married women came between ages nineteen and twenty-four, with the next largest addition occurring among those twenty-four to twenty-nine (Appendix A, Table 1). After that point, the percentage of those married continued to rise until women reached their mid-forties, but at a slower rate. After the age of forty-five, the proportion of married women declined as the number of widows grew. Despite a gradual increase in the overall percentage of married women between 1890 and 1920, the greatest growth really occurred in the fifteen- to twenty-four-year-old age group. The proportion of those married in the older age categories changed very little during the period (Appendix A, Table 1).

The proportion of married women in the urban sector was lower than that in rural areas for both the aggregate population and NWNP (Appendix A, Table 2). However, the difference between the urban and rural sectors diminished over time (Appendix A, Table 2).

Although the overall proportion of married women was increasing, the rate of increase was greater in urban areas than in rural. For the aggregate population the percent of urban married women rose by 5 percent between 1900 and 1920; in the rural areas the increase was only 3.4 percent. Between 1910 and 1920, the urban rate rose slightly to 5.9 percent, but the rural rate stood at 3.1 percent. The pattern for NWNP women was similar to that found for the aggregate population: The urban increase from 1910 to 1920 was 5.4 percent, whereas that in the rural areas was only 2.1 percent.[2] In brief, the percentages of women who married in urban and rural areas were converging, not because the rural percentage was declining and thus approaching the urban, but rather because the urban increase was considerably higher, thus allowing the urban rate to approach the rural one.

Between 1910 and 1920 the most marked increase in percent married occurred among the fifteen to twenty-four year olds in the urban sector. In contrast, the rural areas saw a decline in that age group (Appendix A, Table 3).

Although a breakdown between the urban and rural sectors for the fifteen- to twenty-four-year-old age group was not available prior to 1910, information given for the entire United States indicated that an increase in the total percentage married had begun at least as early as the 1890-1900 decade (Appendix A, Table 1). Furthermore, the greatest decrease in the rural/urban difference in percentage of women married occurred in the fifteen- to twenty-four-year-old age group. Despite a higher percentage of young, married women in the countryside, the city women were rapidly closing the gap (Appendix A, Table 4).

Between 1890 and 1920, at a time when more women, especially young ones, married, the child/woman ratio tended to decline[3] (Table 4). The trend, especially pronounced in urban areas, toward a higher percentage of married women and younger marriages, coupled with a decrease in fertility, appeared linked to the greater availability and use of birth control measures.[4] In this book, the term "birth control" will be used to apply to all methods used to limit the birth of children, including abortion and abstinence as well as contraception. Although not limited to urban areas, birth control practices appeared to have been initially more widespread in the urban sector.

Within urban areas, the greater use of birth control measures among middle- and upper-class women was suggested by the consistently lower native white[5] child/woman ratio (Table 4). As will be seen shortly, the

TABLE 4. Child/Woman Ratio for Urban and Rural Areas and Percentage Change by Decades, Aggregate and Native White Population, 1890-1920

	AGGREGATE POPULATION			NATIVE WHITE POPULATION		
	Urban	Rural	Percent Greater Urban Is than Rural	Urban	Rural	Percent Greater Urban Is than Rural
1890	489	753	54.0	364	651	78.8
1900	452	728	61.1	333	628	88.6
1910	429	702	63.6	a	a	—
1920	429	674	57.1	388	643	65.7
Percent change 1890-1900	−8.2	−3.4	—	−9.3	−3.7	—
Percent change 1900-1910	−5.1	−3.6	—	a	a	—
Percent change 1910-1920	0	−4.2	—	16.5	2.4	—

SOURCES: U.S., *Censuses, 1890-1920.*
NOTE: See Table A.2 for method used to calculate urban and rural totals. Prior to 1920, the Tables of Ages were used to calculate the urban and rural child/woman ratios. Child/woman ratio = the number of children five years old or younger per 1,000 women twenty to forty-four years of age.
aData not available for 1910.

mode of birth control used appeared to divide along class lines. Effective methods of contraception became increasingly common among middle- and upper-class women between 1890 and 1920, whereas for poorer women, abortion probably remained the major method of birth control.

Prior to the development and dissemination of information about effective methods of contraception, a limited number of options were open to those who wished to marry and yet curtail the size of their families. One way, of course, was to postpone the age of marriage. Francis Place, early English population theorist, commented that such a practice was found among the middle class in England.[6] As long as premarital abstinence was practiced, the number of offspring would be reduced. Another method was to employ one of the not very effective modes of contraception known at the time. Through the ages, different contraceptive procedures had been tried. Some of them were outright dangerous, such as douching with mercuric chloride as suggested by an anonymous author in 1831;[7] and others, simply ridiculous such as one advised by a tenth-century physician:

> The woman should rise up when coitus is finished and then take seven jumps backward, sneezing at the same time and endeavouring to jump higher each time. Great care must be taken in remembering to jump backwards, to dislodge the sperm, for jumping forward will cause the sperm to remain where it is.[8]

The development and spread of contraceptive devices during the nineteenth and early twentieth centuries will be explored in greater detail shortly, but, first, other modes of limiting family size used during the past century will be examined.

In nineteenth-century America an unwanted pregnancy did not necessarily mean an unwanted child. From at least as early as the 1820s, attempts to limit family size became more common in the United States.[9] Numerous sources indicate that abortions were common in the United States from at least as early as the 1830s. Auguste Carlier, a Frenchman, traveled in the United States during the late 1850s. He was an astute observer of the mores of the era. In his book, *Marriage in the United States,* Carlier referred to an 1839 speech made to a medical school class that decried the rising abortion rate in towns and cities. The speaker observed that many of the women who sought abortions were married and did not want the trouble and expense of having more children.[10] As for the late 1850s, Carlier found that abortions for married women persisted, often at the instigation of the husband: "That such practice should be deliberately brought into marriage, with the consent and under the direction of the husband [is deplorable]."[11] In 1870, physicians writing for the *Boston Medical and Surgical Journal* commented upon the use of abortion by married couples who wished to limit the number of children they had. At least in some cases, the use of abortions to limit family size appeared linked to a desire for a higher standard of living. "The families who resort to this [abortion] . . . are not . . . the vile and degraded, but far oftener prudent and thoughtful young people."[12]

In the mid-1880s, abortion continued to be used by married women, some of whom at least believed that additional children would interfere with their personal pleasures. Dr. Alice Stockham, author of several marriage manuals, described one case in which the wife of a well-to-do lawyer wanted an abortion because her pregnancy was interfering with a planned trip to Europe. Stockham reiterated Carlier's observation that many abortions were instigated by the husband.[13] That abortion continued to be used in the early twentieth century as a means of limiting family size could be seen from the warning given by Edith Belle Lowery in her 1911 medical advice book for women. Lowery urged women not to submit to abortions, since permanent damage could result. She was especially concerned that young women would decide to terminate their pregnancies and then because of botched abortions be unable ever to have children.[14]

Throughout the nineteenth and into the beginning of the twentieth century, information regarding the availability of abortions—at least in urban areas—was readily obtainable, if not always straightforward. All one had to do was know the correct code. According to Carlier, "Advertisements [were] published in the newspapers . . . saying that one must be careful not to take certain medicines in the situation denoted, which signifies that they are recommended in the special case."[15] An 1862 advertisement for "Dr. Harvey's Chromo-Thermal Pills" was a case in point.

> Dr. Harvey's Chromo-Thermal Pills have never yet failed when the directions have been strictly followed, in removing difficulties arising from an obstruction or stoppage of nature . . . [they are safe but] they should never be taken during the first

three or four months of pregnancy, though safe at any other time, as miscarriage would be the result.[16]

Physicians who specialized in performing abortions often took care to disguise their lucrative trade. For example, Carlier observed that certain New York doctors who performed abortions let the fact be known by a "particular mark" attached to their names.[17] At times the abortion advertisements were more straightforward. Two found in New York promised "A cure for ladies immediately. Madame _____'s female antidote . . . certain to have the desired effect in twenty-four hours, without any injurious results. [Or the ad would read:] Sure cure for ladies in Trouble. No injurious medicines or instruments used."[18]

Some indication regarding the prevalence of abortions came from comments made by physicians in their medical journals. Writing in 1870, one doctor observed that he thought there were "one hundred times more abortions today than there were thirty years ago," while during the same year another physician commented, "I venture the assertion that there is not a gentlemen present who has not, more or less frequently, been importuned to interfere in cases of this kind." An 1881 study by the Michigan Board of Health reported that one-third of all pregnancies were voluntarily terminated by abortions. In 1885 another physician stated that "according to recent estimates, the proportion of abortions and miscarriages to deliveries at term is not less than one to three." Since that number included miscarriages, it is impossible to determine what portion was deliberately induced abortions. An 1887 article in the *Journal of the American Medical Association* also suggested that abortions were probably quite prevalent. In the article, one American physician questioned the applicability of Parisian abortion statistics (one abortion per every child carried to term) to the United States, stating that he had seen only one-tenth the number of abortions as full-term pregnancies. Writing in 1922, Margaret Sanger asserted that certain American authors estimated that between one and two million abortions occurred annually. Sanger contended that, especially for working-class women, abortion continued to be the primary way to limit family size. Until the development and dissemination of effective means of contraception, abortion undoubtedly remained a major method of limiting family size.[19]

Another method of limiting family size used in nineteenth-century America was child abandonment. Statisticians of the era were quite interested in the extent of the "dependent" sectors of the population, and the 1880 and 1890 censuses contain information regarding the number of "homeless" children in various sorts of benevolent institutions. In both years, the numbers were small: 2.6 "homeless" children per 1,000 children sixteen or less in 1880, and 3.0 per 1,000 children under sixteen in 1890. For infants under one year of age the rate in 1890 was 1.0 per 1,000. Of the 68,011 "homeless" children in institutions in 1890, 50.6 percent had one parent living and 17.9 percent had both parents living. The practice of child abandonment may have been more common among certain groups of women. Evidence from the 1890 census indicates that native white children of foreign-born parents were the most likely to be found in the various benevolent institutions: Of all children age sixteen or less, 4.0 per 1,000 native white children of foreign-born parents, 2.0 per 1,000 "colored" children, and 1.0 per 1,000 native white children of native-born parents and foreign-born white children were in such institutions.[20] Future research will have to determine the accuracy and significance of such differences.

In addition to the children just discussed were most probably other children who remained uncounted and untended as they wandered the city's streets. Still others were placed with foster or adoptive parents. The New York Children's Aid Society estimated that it found homes, mainly in the Midwest, for 100,000 New York City waifs between 1850 and 1899.[21] Although additional research is needed to determine the extent of child abandonment, the evidence suggests that the practice was probably not a major method used to limit family size.

Although apparently not common, nineteenth-century women sometimes resorted to more drastic means of eliminating unwanted children. Magazine and newspaper articles documented instances of infanticide. Such cases seemed to occur most frequently among unwed, poor, often very young women. A typical case was that of twenty-year-old Lizzie Miller, a domestic servant in a Quincy, Massachusetts, home who, in 1875, was accused of drowning her newborn child. In the same year, Elizabeth Arbuckle, a "maid-servant of the Brooklyn Club House," was accused of murdering her newborn infant. Another case was that of a "poor, unwed, young Irish girl" brought to trial and sentenced to death in 1876. Yet another instance involved a thirty-year-old New Bedford domestic servant who was suspected of killing her fourth illegitimate child.[22] That unwed women were far more likely to resort to infanticide than their married sisters was attested to by one author who claimed that he had never been able to find a case in which a married woman premeditated the murder of her infant.[23]

How common was infanticide? Writing in 1877, one author said that during the previous thirty years, only sixty-four women had been convicted of murdering their children.[24] An 1885 article by the coroner of Richmond City, Virginia, claimed that in thirteen years 139 women (44 white and 96 Black) had been brought to trial for infanticide and none had been convicted.[25] Yet lack of convictions or a small number of convictions did not necessarily mean the absence of infanticide. One author claimed that coroners' inquests were held every month over the bodies of 5,000 children under twelve months of age, and that there was no way to know how many were killed at birth. He suspected that most cases of infanticide went unpunished.[26]

Information from U.S. censuses strongly suggests that infanticide was relatively rare and certainly not a widespread method of limiting family size. In 1890 and 1900 a separate category for infanticide was included under causes of death. Infanticides accounted for 0.03 deaths per 1,000 births in 1890 and 0.01 per 1,000 in 1900. Between 1860 and 1900, additional information regarding the possible occurrence of infanticide was obtained by comparing the frequency of certain types of accidental deaths for infants to the total number of births for a particular year. Accidental deaths judged possibly suspicious were "burns and scalds," "exposure and neglect," and "suffocation." Of these, suffocation consistently comprised the largest number. In the census years between 1860 and 1900 less than 2.0 such "suspicious" deaths occurred per 1,000 births.[27] Of course, it must be remembered that many of the deaths due to the previously mentioned causes were likely to have been true accidents.

Throughout the nineteenth century and into the twentieth, abortion undoubtedly remained the most important postconception method of limiting family size. However, during the nineteenth century, a serious and ultimately profitable search for safe and effective contraceptives began to gather momentum. The significance of effective, safe contraceptives to women cannot be overemphasized. Without such devices, women were caught in an endless round of pregnancy and child rearing. Abortions could be used to break the cycle, but they, as was true with pregnancy itself, carried their own dangers.[28] Nineteenth-century medical literature is filled with references to various sorts of uterine disorders—prolapses, retroversions, inflammations—which seemed to affect a large proportion of the adult, female population. A fair proportion of such ailments was quite possibly due to venereal disease or some of the barbaric treatments, such as the use of caustic substances to treat uterine disorders, that gynecologists inflicted upon their patents.[29] However, it seems quite likely that complications of pregnancy or a series of abortions were probably also important causes of such disorders.[30] Not until the advent of effective contraceptives were women able to break out of the pregnancy, child-rearing cycle with its concomitant drain on health and time. The ability to limit conception safely brought to women both increased control over their lives within the traditional sphere of the home as well as the potential for becoming more active participants in the "outside" world.[31]

Despite major disagreement in both the medical profession and the articulate lay public regarding the propriety of contraception in general, and certain forms of contraception in particular, effective contraceptives, knowledge about them, and use of them grew dramatically in America between 1860 and 1920.[32] Nineteenth-century reticence about sexual matters makes it difficult to determine what contraceptive measures people employed, how extensive the use was, and how contraceptive advice was obtained. However, information from a series of popular marriage manuals that appeared from the 1830s on, knowledge of particular technological developments in contraceptive devices, comments from physicians in their journals and textbooks, observations from social commentators, and evidence about marriage and fertility rates combine to outline the growth of contraceptive use during the past century.

The marriage manuals, which began to appear in the United States during the 1830s, offered some advice to those seeking contraceptive information. *Fruits of Philosophy,* by Charles Knowlton, an American physician, was one of the century's earliest and perhaps one of the most influential books on the subject. Knowlton's book, published in 1832, was reputed to be the first to emphasize douching as a contraceptive method, stressing the desirability of placing birth control under the control of women.[33] By 1839, 10,000 copies of Knowlton's book had been sold in the United States. Between 1840 and 1870, several popular books containing contraceptive information appeared. The first was the *Married Woman's Private Medical Companion* (1847), by A. M. Mauriceau, a popularizer of medical information who totally lacked medical credentials. In 1856, Harry Knox Root, a physician who popularized medical information, produced *The People's Lighthouse of Medicine*, which recommended the condom and powders for douching. The *Science of Reproduction and Reproductive Control*, by J. Soule, a mid-century physician, was published that same year. He advocated coitus interruptus, the condom, douching, and safe periods. Although other marriage manuals appeared during the era, the ones mentioned were representative of the popular advice books available during the mid-nineteenth century.[34]

Between 1840 and 1870, two especially important technological advances in contraception occurred. First, the vulcanization of rubber in the 1840s allowed the condom, which had been in use since at least the 1750s, to become more generally obtainable.[35] Second, from the mid-1860s on, cervical caps became available to American women. In 1864 Edward Bliss Foote, newspaperman, physician, and birth control advocate, claimed to have invented the cervical cap.[36] Called the "womb-veil" by Foote, it was described thus in his 1864 edition of *Medical Common Sense:*

> [It is] an India-rubber contrivance which the female easily adjusts in the vagina before copulation, and which spreads a thin tissue of the rubber before the mouth of the womb so as to prevent the seminal aura from entering. Its application is easy and accomplished in a moment, without the aid of a light. . . . Since its invention I have introduced it quite extensively, and to all it appears to give the highest satisfaction.[37]

Foote estimated that over 250,000 copies of *Medical Common Sense* were sold between 1858 and 1869.[38]

By 1870 an assortment of contraceptive devices ranging greatly in terms of their effectiveness was potentially available to the interested public. In addition to condoms, cervical caps, and douches of varying sorts were different types of tampons and possibly even some intracervical and intrauterine devices. The gynecological literature of the mid- and late 1800s is filled with descriptions of a multitude of solid pessaries, purportedly used for various uterine disorders. One 1865 article published in the *Transactions of the American Medical Association* had illustrations of 123 different pessaries.[39] Some of the pessaries could have been used to prevent conception. That such devices were sometimes used as contraceptives was at least suggested by medical journal articles such as that written by George Granville Bantock in 1878 in which he discussed the "use and abuse of pessaries." One abuse pointed to by Bantock was the "misuse of a properly fitting instrument."[40]

The proliferation and dissemination of contraceptive information was attested to by the harsh reaction against it. In 1873 Congress passed the Comstock law ostensibly to halt the trafficking in pornographic material. However, the law specifically forbade mailing anything related to contraception:

> Every article or thing designed, adapted, or intended for preventing conception or producing abortion, or for any indecent or immoral use; and every article, instrument, substance, drug, medicine, or thing which is advertised or described in a manner calculated to lead another to use or apply it for preventing conception or producing abortion, or for any indecent or immoral purpose; and every written or printed card, letter, circular, book, pamphlet, advertisement, or notice of any kind giving information . . . where, or how, or of whom, or by what means any of the hereinbeforementioned matters, articles or things may be obtained or made, or where or by whom any act or operation of any kind for the procuring or producing of abortion will be done or performed or how or by what means conception may be prevented or abortion may be produced.[41]

The federal law was followed by a series of state statutes that, though similar to the original, specified prohibitions against other ways of giving out contraceptive information. Twenty-four states forbade the publishing, advertising, or giving out of information, fourteen made it illegal to tell anyone about birth control measures, and Connecticut even made it illegal to use contraceptives. However, the state bans regarding contraceptive information were not complete. Some states such as Colorado, Indiana, and Pennsylvania exempted medical colleges and medical books from the prohibition. Other states such as Arkansas, Delaware, Florida, Georgia, and Illinois had laws that dealt more generally with obscenity, but did not specifically mention contraception.[42] Though the bans against the dissemination of contraceptives and information about them was not complete, the general impact of the federal and state Comstock laws was to create a climate of repression that few were willing or able to oppose. Despite the prohibitions and the repressive climate, the search for more effective contraceptives and the debate as to which of the existing methods were best continued.

Popular manuals containing contraceptive information continued to appear even after the passage of the Comstock law. Dr. Alice B. Stockham published a trilogy of books, *Tokology, Karezza,* and *Parenthood,* during the 1880s and 1890s in which she popularized the contraceptive idea of prolonged coitus without ejaculation proposed by John Humphrey Noyes in his 1872 tract, *Male Continence.* For those who could not practice continence, Stockham recommended the rhythm method. Unfortunately, at that time the fertile period was generally believed to occur immediately after menstruation, with the "safe period" coming about fifteen days later. It was not until the 1930s that the relationship between ovulation and menstruation was fully understood and ovulation recognized as occurring approximately nine days after the menstrual flow ceased.[43] Women who followed Stockham's advice regarding a safe time for intercourse were likely to end up with a fair share of unplanned pregnancies.

Stockham's book *Tokology* contained information about other contraceptive methods, most of which did not meet with her approval. She condemned withdrawal as leading to impotence in males, sterility in females, and "nervous symptoms" in both sexes. Her objection to unmedicated douches was a practical one. If the sperm had already passed into the uterus, the water would not reach it. As for medicated douches, "drugs," Stockham feared that "they are usually injurious and cannot accomplish the purpose beyond the vagina." In the 1886 edition of *Tokology,* Stockham registered a mild complaint against "mechanical interference." "If the material is pliable, the only positive injury is from preventing a complete interchange of magnetism."[44]

Another set of important late nineteenth-century authors of marriage manuals were Edward Bliss Foote, whom as I have already noted claimed to be the American inventor of the cervical cap, and his son Edward Bond Foote. In addition to *Medical Common Sense,* Edward Bliss Foote also published a small tract in the 1870s, *Words in Pearl,* for which he was jailed under the Comstock law, and *Plain Home Talk,* which first appeared in 1870. In the latter work, "mechanical devices" to prevent conception were discussed. However, the 1876 edition was forced to eliminate all reference to such devices in order to comply with the Comstock law, a development greatly lamented by Foote, who, in 1904, entered a "solemn protest, as a physician, to this piece of meddlesome impertinence on the part of the hasty law-makers."[45] Foote contended that he was besieged for information regarding birth control devices but could not give out such information until the Comstock law was repealed.[46] Foote favored placing the control of conception in the hands of woman, tempered by advice from her physician. "With contraceptics [sic] in the hands of the mother of the race, the family physician could intelligently and effectively advise woman when she might safely parent a child."[47]

Foote's outspoken advocacy of contraception and his early run-in with the Comstock law probably made it difficult for him to give out information regarding birth control devices. But what of the attitudes and actions of other members of the medical profession? Since it was to physicians that many people probably turned for contraceptive information, the attitude of medical professionals was of significance.[48] In the late nineteenth century, the attitude of medical doctors toward contraception can at best be described as mixed. There were undoubtedly many like William Goodell, author of an 1879 gynecology text, who opposed virtually all contraceptive practices. Interestingly, one of his objections to withdrawal, a major method of birth control at the time, was his belief that it deprived the wife of orgasm, a deprivation which he believed led to various uterine disorders. "By forfeiting her conjugal rights, she does not reach that timely conjuncture which loosens the tension of the . . . muscles of her erectile tissues . . . thus arises engorgements, erosions and displacements of the uterus."[49] In contrast to Goodell's anticontraceptive stance, an article in the *Medical and Surgical Reporter* commented on the "diversity of opinion among specialists" regarding contraception and contested Goodell's conclusions that contraception led to uterine disorders. The same article contained a quote from a Dr. O. E. Herrick, characterized by the journal as a "gynecologist of repute," who asserted that "there are means of preventing conception that are absolutely harmless to the woman . . . all this mawkish sentiment about its being wrong, or . . . doing damage to the health is simply bosh."[50] In 1882, an article published in the *Michigan Medical News* advocated that women decide how many children to have and recommended douching as a contraceptive measure.[51]

In 1888, the *Medical and Surgical Reporter* presented what was possibly the first published symposium regarding the propriety of contraception.

An editorial that appeared in the September issue called for readers to write in and express their attitudes toward birth control. During the next three months, twelve letters appeared. Most of those who responded favored some form of contraception. Dr. David E. Matteson, author of one of the letters, indicated that at least a portion of the medical community was favorably disposed toward contraception. Matteson claimed to have had a letter favoring contraception published in a medical journal. In response to his letter, Matteson asserted he received letters from "Texas to Maine," mostly from physicians who supported his stand.[52]

Further indication of the acceptance of contraception by at least a segment of the medical profession was suggested by another letter in the *Medical and Surgical Reporter*. The letter referred to remarks made by a Dr. J. Ford Thompson to the 1888 meeting of the Gynecological Society of Washington, D.C. At the meeting, Thompson stated that much of the anticontraceptive literature was "nonsense."[53] Thompson's remarks also contained an evaluation of various birth control methods and offered a detailed description of contraceptive practices of the era. Thompson contended that withdrawal, which he believed was the most common form of birth control, had no ill effects. Both condoms for males or "hoods" (cervical caps) for women were harmless since neither "interfered with the act of coition." While he thought that cold water douches might be harmful, he contended that tepid water or "water impregnated with carbolic acid or astringent" were probably safe.[54]

In another letter, David Matteson offered additional information regarding birth control practices. He contended that douching was the most prevalent form of contraception. According to Matteson, withdrawal "has grown in popularity of late," but although effective he rejected it along with the condom as "aesthetically unpleasing." He thought that the various "veils" (cervical caps) required too much skill for most women and instead recommended placing a moistened sponge in the vagina that "at the needed time will be carried onward, covering and shielding the os uteri, while its meshes will catch and hold the seminal fluid." He suggested attaching a string to the sponge so that the device could be easily removed following intercourse.[55] In 1890 another symposium appeared, this time in Cincinnati's *Medical News*. Eight participants favored contraception, one abstinence, and three opposed any form of birth control.[56] An article in *The Maryland Medical Journal* of 1895 advocated the cervical cap and douching, but condemned the condom as harmful.[57]

While some physicians were willing to express openly a procontraception stance, others presented one viewpoint in public and another in communicating with their medical colleagues. Dr. W. R. D. Blackwood criticized such medical hypocrites and in doing so revealed one of the ways fearful physicians transmitted birth control information to one another and to their students.

> I never saw a more ludicrous display of double cunning than
> appeared in a medical journal, where in a professor warned his
> class against the wickedness and baneful effect of simple aqueous
> or medicated vaginal douches when employed as a preventive means
> after coition, when in the same journal further on this man
> begged his pupils not to forget his repeated injunction as to the
> value of just such injections in large quantity under all conditions
> of uterine excitement, engorgement, or inflammation. One talk
> was for the religious public, the other a genuine piece of advice
> to his students, and a good one as we all know.[58]

The medical profession was clearly deeply divided as to the general propriety of contraception, its use in particular instances, and which procedures or devices were the most effective. Furthermore, few physicians appeared willing to take a public stand favoring contraception. However, at least some of them, in the privacy of their offices, and probably especially with their middle- and upper-class patients, shared what knowledge they had.[59]

During the latter decades of the nineteenth century and early years of the twentieth, the effectiveness and availability of different methods of contraception continued to increase. For many couples, coitus interruptus and abstinence probably remained the most commonly used forms of birth control.[60] Douching as a contraceptive measure appeared to grow in popularity during the early 1900s, and a wide variety of components ranging from the dangerous mercuric chloride to quinine to simple cold water were used.[61] Advertisements for douches appeared in urban newspapers, though in keeping with the prohibitions of the era, the hygenic rather than contraceptive value of douching was emphasized. One paper advertised a "vaginal syringe . . . with a marvelous whirling spray . . . the best . . . more convenient."[62] There is some evidence that various types of "mechanical devices," probably condoms and cervical caps, grew in popularity following the turn of the century. Writing in 1907, Henry Lyman, in his *Practical*

Home Doctor, asserted that "the most popular and generally used means [of contraception] . . . are the various mechanical devices, 'barriers' which are extensively advertised and even vended around the street."[63]

A survey by Hornell Hart of articles indexed in the *Reader's Guide to Periodical Literature* indicated a public receptiveness toward easier access to birth control information. Looking at both the mass circulation and more intellectual magazines of the era, Hart found that a highly favorable attitude toward birth control prevailed during the 1905-14 period—more so than during most of the 1920s (Appendix A, Table 5).

It is clear that effective contraceptive measures grew in number in the United States during the late nineteenth and early twentieth centuries and that knowledge of them was eagerly if furtively sought after by much of the American public. The possibility of limiting family size by safe methods of contraception was becoming a reality. That the process was a gradual one with women of the upper and middle class reaping the first benefits was indicated both by observations from commentators of the era and by fertility statistics. Although not until Margaret Sanger courageously and forcefully undertook her birth control campaign did information about contraception begin to permeate all layers of society,[64] significant numbers of the middle and upper class appeared to have been practicing birth control for at least the few preceding decades.

An 1887 article in *Medical Age* complained that "the devices of the brothel [contraceptives] have been so freely introduced into classes of society which stand most in need of multiplication . . . to have practically nullified the divine decree to multiply."[65] In 1888, Dr. Thomas A. Pope stated that "very frequent conception is now mostly confined to the poorer class. The rich, in town and country, already limit their offspring." Pope advocated making contraceptive information available to poorer women, commenting that "I have no doubt that most of the criminal abortions occasionally seen in the country and so often occurring in the city are due to a mother feeling she cannot adequately care for another child rather than simply not wanting another."[66] The knowledge and the use of contraceptives, though much more prevalent among middle- and upper-class women, were not limited to them. According to Dr. James E. Free, "We know that many in all classes are experimenting for the purpose of limiting the number of offspring, and that many women who marry nowadays either have a preventive . . . or hope to find one."[67]

Writers in the early 1900s reiterated the comments of earlier observers.

Ethel Wadsworth Cartland was a thirty-one-year-old, college-educated
native white woman of native-born parents. She was married to a clergy-
man and lived in New England. Cartland contended that, from what she
had observed, the norm among native whites of native-born parents was
to have no more than two children.[68] According to a 1915 article in the
New Republic, "A large minority of husbands and wives already know
how not to have too many children and it is only a question of a decade
or two when the rest will know."[69]

Writing in 1916, Dr. Rachelle S. Yarros pointed out that not only had
"birth control . . . been practiced more and more for the past several
decades by the intelligent, comfortable, and professional classes of this
country and abroad," but that such classes apparently had "little difficulty in obtaining the information from competent physicians."[70] The
disparity in birth control information available to rich and poor was also
commented upon by Dr. Mary Hunt, who criticized "Fifth Avenue Doctors"
for giving information and services to the rich that were denied to the
poor.[71] Some of the strongest statements regarding the class differences
in terms of knowledge of contraceptives and practices used to limit family
size were made by Margaret Sanger in 1922. She asserted that

> . . . most of the women of the middle and upper classes in all
> countries seem secure in their knowledge of contraceptives as a
> means of birth control. . . . Contraceptive measures among the
> upper class and the practice of abortion among the lower class
> are the real means employed to regulate the number of offspring.[72]

Although the general trend between 1890 and 1920 was toward more
youthful marriages and fewer children, by 1920, the higher percentage of
younger married women in the urban areas had combined with other
factors to halt the decline in the number of children born (Table 4). First,
none of the birth control devices was 100 percent effective. In addition,
a much more positive and open attitude toward women's sexuality
emerged during the early twentieth century.[73] Those more liberal views
first emerged in the city and had their initial impact upon women of the
upper and middle classes.[74] Perhaps an increase in illegitimate births accompanied the new morality. In addition, despite the development and proliferation of more effective contraceptives, the combination of a higher
marriage rate plus a greater acceptance of female sexuality within marriage

were probably influential in accounting for part of the rise in the child/ woman ratio. Another factor whose effect would have been especially pronounced in the urban areas would have been the inclusion in the native white category of a large number of daughters of foreign-born parents who may have tended toward the higher reproduction rates of the foreign born rather than the lower rates of the earlier groups of native-born whites.[75] Finally, the generally higher child/woman ratio figures for 1920 possibly reflected a post-World War I baby boom.

Although the majority of urban women tended toward earlier marriages with fewer children, a visible minority of women moved toward a later marriage or no marriage at all. That minority trend evoked a great deal of concern among certain members of the more affluent and highly educated portions of society, because it was precisely in that group where the trend was most evident. A survey published in the 1931 *American Journal of Sociology* revealed that for women who had gotten married between 1900 and 1905, the higher the social class (defined on the basis of the husband's occupation), the later the marriage age[76] (Appendix A, Table 6).

A 1900 study made by Mary Roberts Smith supports the contention that educated women of higher social classes tended to marry relatively late. In her study, Smith looked at college-educated and non-college-educated women who came from the same social class and compared the ages at which they married (Appendix A, Table 7). Compared with the findings of the 1931 study, both groups of women married relatively late. However, college-educated women in the Smith study tended to marry later than their non-college-educated sisters. The disparity in marriage age between the two groups was probably linked to their different premarital employment experiences. The college-educated women tended to be more career oriented than their non-college-educated counterparts. Of the college-educated women, three-fourths had some form of occupation prior to marriage, whereas only one-third of the non-college-educated women had worked.[77] For both groups, the younger the women, the higher the average marriage age. The increase in the average marriage age was probably linked to the increase in employment opportunities that would have drawn more women in both groups into the labor force. Since the turn of the century, middle- or upper-class women who wished to pursue a higher education and/or a career were in most instances forced by the dictates of society to postpone or forsake marriage. A pattern of delayed marriage or no marriage at all began to emerge.

As has been seen, a pattern of relatively early marriage coupled with low fertility was present in American cities around the turn of the century. What similarities or differences were present among cities with respect to female marriage and fertility patterns? Did cities tend to be much alike in the way they affected women's propensity to marry and bear children, or did factors such as size of city, economic function, sex ratio, and the percentage of Catholic or foreign-born women cause significant differences?

A major distinguishing feature among cities is the size of the population. How did city size affect the percentage of women who married and the child/woman ratio? Was a gradual change evident as one moved from the largest of urban units to the rural areas, or was there a more abrupt jump from rural to urban without much variation within the urban category?[78] Little concrete evidence has been presented regarding marriage and fertility patterns in the late nineteenth- and early twentieth-century city. Often the pattern of one census year has been assumed to have existed in previous and subsequent decades.

Between 1890 and 1920, size of city appeared to bear almost no relationship to the percentage of married women (Appendix A, Table 8). Only in 1910 was a slight inverse relationship between the two variables evident, and even for that year the correlation was weak and not highly significant.[79]

Similarly, female fertility did not appear to be strongly associated with city size during the 1890-1920 period.[80] A small negative relationship between the two variables was present. The relationship, although statistically significant for 1890 and 1920, was not strong for any of the three census years (Appendix A, Table 9).

The evidence suggests that once a certain population size was reached, a distinct urban pattern of marriage and fertility emerged. In this study, a population of 25,000 was generally used as the cutoff point between urban and rural. It is possible, however, that during the 1870-1920 time period, towns having between 2,500 and 25,000 people exhibited marriage and fertility patterns that were more urban than rural. In the 1920 census, information was presented for urban areas in the 2,500-25,000 population range. Towns of that size comprised 30.4 percent of the total urban population.[81] For the percentage of women married or single and for the child/woman ratio, the differences between the urban and the rural sectors were slightly greater when the 2,500-25,000 group was included in the urban category, suggesting that towns of that size exhibited a more urban than rural pattern of behavior (Appendix A, Table 10).

Whether an abrupt shift between urban and rural marriage and fertility patterns occurred at a population of about 2,500 or whether a gradual transition took place between rural areas and towns of 2,500 people was not determined. What was clear was that once a population of 25,000, and possibly as low as 2,500 had been reached, little additional variation was evident.

The lack of a strong association between community size and female marital status and fertility, at least once a population of 25,000 or possibly 2,500 had been reached, was probably due to a number of factors. Some of the attitudes motivating urban women to have fewer children would not likely have been related to community size. Town and city dwellers tended to regard children as not contributing to the economic well-being of the family. Among urban middle-class families, perhaps the increased emphasis upon the complexities of child rearing was related to a decrease in the number of offspring. A growing desire for a higher standard of living most likely also played a role in reducing fertility. Such attitudes probably cut across city-size boundaries. At the same time, more effective means of contraception meant that urban women, with their easier access to birth control information and products, would tend to find it increasingly easy to marry at an earlier age and still limit family size.

The impact of a higher percentage of Catholic women or foreign-born women upon the child/woman ratio of a city was also studied. In 1900, the year investigated, the higher the percentage of Catholic women or foreign-born women, the greater the aggregate child/woman ratio (Appendix A, Table 11). Such a relationship was anticipated because foreign-born women were less likely than native whites to have knowledge of or access to birth control devices, and because many of the foreign-born women came from rural areas and would have followed the rural pattern of having more children. Catholic women, even if aware of birth control measures, would probably not have used them because of religious prohibitions.[82]

In contrast to the aggregate population, the relationship between the percentage of Catholic women and the native white child/woman ratio was negative; as the percentage of Catholic women in a city rose, the native white child/woman ratio declined (Appendix A, Table 12). The negative relationship between the two variables was probably due to the tendency for Catholic women to be found in cities with a high manufacturing and mechanical component (Appendix A, Table 12). In 1900, such cities were positively associated with the percentage of employed NWNP women and negatively correlated with the native white child/woman ratio

(Appendix A, Table 12). In short, the percentage of Catholic women in
a city did not itself appear to influence the native white child/woman ratio.

One factor that was an important indicator of marriage and fertility
patterns was the relative proportion of men and women in a city. Although
not always considered an important differentiator among urban areas,
sex ratio[83] (the number of men per one hundred women) was quite significant insofar as the marriage patterns of women were concerned. A strong
positive association existed between sex ratio and the percentage of married
women (Table 5). The association was considerably stronger for the aggregate population than for NWNP. Moreover, between 1890 and 1920, the
strength of the correlation increased for the aggregate population, but
it appeared to decrease for NWNP (Table 5). By 1920, among the aggregate population, sex ratio accounted for almost half of the variation
among cities with respect to the percentage of married women (Table 5).

It was not surprising to find the availability of men closely associated
with the percentage of married women. But how was the different impact
that sex ratio had upon the marital patterns of the aggregate population
and NWNP to be explained? The evidence suggests that although for the
aggregate population the availability of men was of paramount importance
in determining whether or not women married, for NWNP women other
factors tended to play a more pronounced role. In particular, employment
opportunities seemed to be important. As will be discussed more fully
in Chapter 6, the percentage of married women and the percentage of
employed women tended to be correlated negatively. The better-paying,
more desirable white-collar jobs were dominated by NWNP women. Among
such women employment was more likely to be a conscious, positive
choice and marriage less likely to be looked upon as something entered
into as an escape from the drudgery of a job. Indeed, one author, writing
in 1905, spoke of married women, mainly middle class, who looked back
with some longing on their premarriage days, "when as self-supporting
women they were comfortably assured of a definite weekly or monthly
salary, and there is in them an undertone of dissatisfaction."[84] In contrast,
the oppressive nature of much factory or sweatshop work would have
made it less likely for women in such occupations to want to stay with
their jobs.

A city's economic orientation[85] also seemed to be closely related to the
marriage and fertility patterns of urban women. In general, the greater the
proportion of all workers employed in manufacturing and mechanical occu-

TABLE 5. Correlation Between Sex Ratio and Marital Status, Aggregate Population and Native Whites of Native-Born Parents, 1890-1920

	Aggregate Population		Native Whites of Native-Born Parents	
	AGGREGATE SEX RATIO VS.:		*AGGREGATE SEX RATIO VS.:*	
	Percent Married	*Percent Single*	*Percent Married*	*Percent Single*
1890[a]	$r = 0.57^{e}$	$r = -0.31^{d}$	$r = 0.67^{e}$	$r = -0.47^{d}$
	$N = 58$	$N = 58$	$N = 27$	$N = 27$
1900[b]	$r = 0.56$	$r = -0.41^{e}$	$r = 0.37^{c}$	$r = -0.29$
	$N = 158$	$N = 158$	$N = 30$	$N = 30$
1910	—	—	$r = 0.45^{e}$	$r = -0.26^{e}$
			$N = 231$	$N = 231$
1920	$r = 0.73^{e}$	$r = -0.55^{e}$	$r = 0.39^{e}$	$r = -0.33^{e}$
	$N = 285$	$N = 285$	$N = 285$	$N = 285$

SOURCES: U.S., *Censuses, 1890-1920.*

NOTE: The aggregate sex ratio was calculated on the basis of males and females fifteen or older. The percentage of women fifteen or older who were married was calculated for each city. Then the strength of the correlation between sex ratio and marital status was tested. r = the correlation coefficient; N = the number of observations.

[a] For 1890, marital status for the aggregate population was calculated for cities 50,000+, whereas for native white women of native-born parents it was calculated for cities of 100,000+, excluding Massachusetts.

[b] For 1900, marital status of native whites of native-born parents was calculated for cities of 100,000+, excluding Massachusetts, Rhode Island, and New Jersey.

[c] Significant at the 0.05 level.

[d] Significant at the 0.01 level.

[e] Significant at the 0.001 level.

TABLE 6. Correlation Between Economic Function, Marital Status, and Fertility for the Aggregate Population, Native Whites, and Native Whites of Native-Born Parents, 1890-1920

	AGGREGATE POPULATION			*NATIVE WHITES OF NATIVE-BORN PARENTS*		
	1890	*1900*	*1920*	*1890[a]*	*1900[b]*	*1920*
Manufacturing and mechanical vs.:						
Percent single	r = 0.35[g] N = 124	r = 0.33[g] N = 158	r < 0.1 N = 285	r < 0.1 N = 27	r = 0.40[g] N = 30	r = 0.18[c,g] N = 285
Percent married	r < 0.1 N = 124	r < 0.1 N = 158	r = 0.31[g] N = 285	r = −0.17 N = 27	r = −0.28 N = 30	r < 0.1[c] N = 285
Native white child/woman ratio	—	—	—	r = −0.42[g] N = 58	r = −0.28[g] N = 158	r = −0.16[c,g] N = 285
Trade and transportation vs.:						Trade[d] / Transportation[d]
Percent single	r = −0.18[e] N = 124	r = −0.14[e] N = 158	r = −0.34[g] N = 285	r = −0.39[e] N = 27	r = −0.44[f] N = 30	r = 0.24[g], N = 285 / r = −0.22[g], N = 285

Table 6 continued

Percent married	$r = 0.24^f$ $N = 124$	$r < 0.1$ $N = 158$	$r < 0.1$ $N = 285$	$r = 0.44^f$ $N = 27$	$r = 0.39^e$ $N = 30$	$r < 0.1$ $N = 285$	$r = 0.22^g$ $N = 285$
Native white child/woman ratio	—	—	—	$r = 0.28^e$ $N = 58$	$r < 0.1$ $N = 158$	$r = 0.29^g$ $N = 285$	$r < 0.1$ $N = 285$

SOURCES: U.S., *Censuses, 1890-1920.*

NOTE: The percentage of the work force in each city engaged in occupations classified as (1) trade and transportation and (2) manufacturing and mechanical was calculated for each year. For 1920, trade and transportation were also calculated separately. Then the strength of the correlation between economic activity and marital status or child/woman ratio was tested. Unless otherwise stated, calculations were based on cities of 25,000+. N = the number of observations. r = the correlation coefficient. p = the level of significance.

[a]For 1890, information regarding the marital status of native whites of native-born parents was available only for cities of 100,000+, excluding Massachusetts. For the native white child/woman ratio, information was given for cities of 50,000+.

[b]For 1900, information regarding the marital status of native whites of native-born parents was available only for cities of 100,000+, excluding Massachusetts, New Jersey, and Rhode Island.

[c]For 1920, information regarding the marital status of native whites of native whites of native-born parents was available for all cities of 25,000+. In order to ascertain whether the inclusion of cities of the 25,000-100,000 category had skewed the correlations, correlations were calculated using only those cities looked at in 1890. For marital status, cities of 100,000+ (in 1890) were included. For the percentage of single women, $r = 0.11, N = 25, 0.4 > p > 0.3$. For the percentage of married women, $r = -0.28, N = 25, 0.1 > p > 0.05$. For the native white child/woman ratio, cities of 50,000+ (in 1890) were looked at: $r = 0.27, N = 58, p \sim 0.025$.

[d]As was done with mechanical and manufacturing occupations, the correlations between trade and transportation and the variables were tested for cities that had been looked at in 1890. For marital status, cities of 100,000+ were examined. For the percentage of single women, $r = -0.32, N = 25, p \sim 0.05$. For the percentage of married women, $r = 0.20, N = 25, 0.2 > p > 0.1$. For the native white child/woman ratio, cities of 50,000+ were used: $r = 0.09, N = 58$.

[e]Significant at the 0.05 level.

[f]Significant at the 0.01 level.

[g]Significant at the 0.001 level.

pations in a city, the higher the percentage of single women, the lower the percentage of married women, and the lower the child/woman ratio (Table 6). Conversely, as the proportion of the work force engaged in trade and transportation occupations grew, the percentage of married women rose and the percentage of single women decreased (Table 6).

The temporal trends in women's marriage and fertility patterns support the contention that 1890 to 1920 was a time of transition for the American urban woman. For example, although the percentage of married NWNP women continued to be associated positively with the proportion of the work force in trade and transportation jobs, the strength of the relationship decreased between 1890 and 1920 (Table 6). A positive correlation that had existed between trade and transportation jobs and the native white child/woman ratio in 1890 had vanished by 1900 (Table 6). Similarly, the slight negative relationship between manufacturing and mechanical occupations and the percentage of married NWNP women disappeared between 1900 and 1920. At the same time, the relationship between manufacturing and mechanical occupations and the native white child/woman ratio, which had been negative in 1890, became slightly positive by 1920 (Table 6).[86]

As will be explored more fully in Chapter 6, economic function also tended to be correlated closely with the percentage of employed women. Cities that leaned more heavily toward manufacturing and mechanical occupations appeared to draw women into the work force at an earlier date than did those cities that had a greater percentage of their total work force in trade and transportation occupations. However, as white-collar occupations burgeoned, the initial advantage with respect to female employment held by manufacturing and mechanical cities appeared to undergo a comparative decline. Since marriage and employment tended to be associated negatively for women, the changing employment opportunities offered by cities with different economic functions probably were reflected in the marriage and fertility patterns. Thus the positive association between trade and transportation occupations and the percentage of married NWNP women declined during the same time period that white-collar occupations expanded. Not surprisingly, as the positive association between cities inclining toward trade and transportation jobs and the percentage of married women declined, so did the positive correlation between cities with a higher proportion of trade and transportation occupations and the native white child/woman ratio.

During the late nineteenth and early twentieth centuries, significant changes were occurring in the marriage and fertility patterns of American, urban women. In general, the trend was toward earlier marriages but fewer children, a development made possible by the increasing effectiveness and availability of birth control measures. Although distinct urban and rural patterns of female fertility and tendency to marry were evident, variations also existed among cities. Important differentiators among urban areas included economic function and sex ratio. In general, both a high sex ratio and a high percentage of the work force in trade and transportation occupations tended to be related positively to the percentage of married women and the child/woman ratio and negatively associated with the percentage of single women. The opposite tended to be true for cities with a high percentage of their work force in manufacturing and mechanical occupations. In contrast to economic function, city size, at least once a population of 25,000 or possibly as low as 2,500 had been reached, appeared to bear little relationship to the percentage of married women or the child/woman ratio. Although intercity variations in female fertility and marital patterns were evident, a movement toward earlier marriages coupled with a decrease in fertility appeared generally to be associated with urban areas during the late 1800s and early 1900s.

Notes

1. *Boston Weekly Transcript,* March 4, 1890.

2. Data regarding the conjugal status for native white women of native-born parents in 1900 were given only for cities of 100,000 or larger rather than for 25,000 or larger as in 1910 and 1920. Therefore, it was impossible to separate accurately the percent married in urban and rural areas prior to 1910.

3. The child/woman ratio is the number of children under five per 1,000 women twenty to forty-four years of age. In the absence of more precise fertility statistics, the child/woman ratio gives an estimation of a population's fertility. The child/woman ratio in the United States began to decline around 1810. Wilson H. Grabill, Clyde V. Kiser, and Pascal K. Whelpton, "A Long View," in *The American Family in Social-Historical Perspective,* ed. Michael Gordon (New York: St. Martin's Press, 1973), pp. 374-96, present statistics for the 1800-40 period and 1910-50. Between 1800 and 1840 they point out that there was a decrease of approximately the same number of children per 1,000 women in both urban and

rural areas. However, the percentage decline was more precipitous in the urban sector due to the already smaller child/woman ratio. For the 1840-90 period little is known about general fertility patterns in the urban and rural sectors of the United States.

4. The relationship between the trend toward earlier marriages in urban areas and the use of contraceptives had been suggested, but not documented, by other authors. See Warren Thompson and Pascal K. Whelpton, *Population Trends in the United States* (New York: McGraw-Hill Book Co., 1933; reprint ed., New York: Kraus Reprint Co., 1969), p. 226; Regine K. Stix and Frank W. Notestein, *Controlled Fertility: An Evaluation of Clinic Service* (Baltimore: Williams & Wilkins, 1940); William Ogburn and M. F. Nimkoff, *Technology and the Changing Family* (Boston: Houghton Mifflin Co., 1955).

5. Data were not available regarding the fertility rates for native whites of native-born parents. Therefore, the rates for native whites have been calculated.

6. Francis Place, *Illustrations and Proof of the Principles of Population* (n.p.: Longman, Rees, Hurst & Orme, 1820; reprint ed., Augustus, Me.: Kelley, 1967), p. 162.

7. Bernard Ephraim Finch and Hugh Green, *Contraception Through the Ages* (Springfield, Ill.: Charles C Thomas, 1963), pp. 34, 36. The authors point out that this method of douching was responsible for many deaths and much damage to health.

8. Ibid., p. 62.

9. See Linda Gordon, *Woman's Body, Woman's Right: A Social History of Birth Control in America* (New York: Grossman Publishers, 1976); Norman Himes, *Medical History of Contraception* (Baltimore: Williams & Wilkins Co.; reprint ed., New York: Schocken, 1970); Daniel Scott Smith, "Family Limitation, Sexual Control, and Domestic Feminism in Victorian America," *Feminist Studies* 1 (Winter-Spring 1973): 40-57; R. Sauer, "Attitudes to Abortion in America, 1800-1973," *Population Studies* 28 (March 1974): 53-67; James C. Mohr, *Abortion in America: The Origins and Evolution of National Policy, 1800-1900* (New York: Oxford University Press, 1978). Mohr describes a great upsurge of abortions between 1840 and 1880 (see pp. 46-85).

10. Auguste Carlier, *Marriage in the United States,* trans. by B. Joy Jeffries (Boston: De Vries, Ibarra & Co., 1867; reprint ed., New York: Arno Press, 1972), p. 158.

11. Ibid., p. 154. Carlier was much more sympathetic toward a parent's use of abortion to protect a daughter's reputation.

12. "Reports of Medical Societies," *Boston Medical and Surgical Journal*

6 (December 1, 1870): 359-60; O. C. Turner, "Criminal Abortion," *Boston Medical and Surgical Journal* 5 (April 21, 1870): 299-300. Mohr, *Abortion in America,* pp. 86-118, contends that between 1840 and 1880 abortions became increasingly common among married, native white, Protestant women who wished either to delay having children or limit the total number of children they had.

13. Alice Stockham, *Tokology* (Boston: George Smith & Co.), pp. 247-49. Stockham (p. 250) was sympathetic toward unmarried women who wanted abortions but still felt that it was morally wrong.

14. Edith Belle Lowry, *Herself* (Chicago: Forbes & Co., 1911), p. 95.

15. Carlier, *Marriage in the United States,* p. 153.

16. *Cincinnati Daily Gazette,* March 18, 1862.

17. Carlier, *Marriage in the United States,* p. 153. Carlier did not specify what the mark was.

18. George Ellington, *Women of New York: Underworld of the Great City* (New York: New York Book Co., 1869), p. 396.

19. Turner, "Criminal Abortion," p. 300; "Reports of Medical Societies," p. 359; J. L. Sullivan, "Treatment of Abortion with Cases," *Boston Medical and Surgical Journal* 123 (September 3, 1885): 223; Medico-Legal Society of Chicago, "Medico-Legal Aspects of Criminal Abortion," *Journal of the American Medical Association* 9 (December 10, 1887): 764; Margaret Sanger, *The New Motherhood* (London: Jonathan Cape, 1922; reprint ed., Elmsford, New York: Maxwell Reprint Co., 1970), pp. 142-43; Walter Franklin Robie, *Rational Sex Ethics: Further Investigations* (Boston: Gorham Press, 1919), p. 194. For discussions regarding changing attitudes toward abortion in the United States see Gordon, *Woman's Body, Woman's Right,* and Sauer, "Attitudes to Abortion."

20. U.S., Department of the Interior, Office of the Census, *Tenth Census of the United States, 1880,* vol. 21, *Report on the Defective, Dependent and Delinquent Classes,* p. 443; U.S., Department of the Interior, Office of the Census, *Eleventh Census of the United States, 1890: Crime, Pauperism and Benevolence,* pt. 2, pp. 954, 1011-20; *Population,* pt. 2, p. 2.

21. "Finding Homes for the Homeless," *Review of Reviews,* August 1899, pp. 124-25.

22. *New York Times,* February 19, 1875, and August 25, 1875; C. A. Fyffee, "The Punishment of Infanticide," *Nineteenth Century,* June 1887, pp. 583-95; W. H. Taylor, "A Case of Infanticide," *Boston Medical and Surgical Journal* 123 (November 12, 1885): 459-60. See Gordon, *Woman's Body, Woman's Right,* p. 50, where infanticide is described as primarily a crime of the very poor.

23. Fyffee, "Punishment of Infanticide," pp. 583-95.

24. Ibid.

25. "Infanticide," *Journal of the American Medical Association* 5 (October 17, 1885): 440.

26. Fyffee, "Punishment of Infanticide," pp. 583-95.

27. U.S., Department of the Interior, Office of the Census, *Eighth Census of the United States, 1860: Mortality and Miscellaneous Statistics,* pp. 44-45, 52-53; U.S., Department of the Interior, Office of the Census, *Ninth Census of the United States, 1870,* vol. 2, *Vital Statistics,* pp. 18-21; vol. 1, *Population and Social Statistics,* p. 552; U.S., Department of the Interior, Office of the Census, *Tenth Census of the United States, 1880,* vol. 2, *Mortality and Vital Statistics,* pt. 1, pp. 44-53; vol. 1, *Population,* p. 548; U.S., Department of the Interior, Office of the Census, *Eleventh Census, 1890: Vital and Social Statistics,* pt. 3, Statistics of Death, pp. 16-22; *Population,* pt. 2, p. 2; U.S., Department of the Interior, Office of the Census, *Twelfth Census, 1900,* vol. 4, *Vital Statistics,* pt. 2, Statistics of Death, pp. 228-50. Births for a given year were calculated on the basis of the total under one year of age plus the total deaths for those under one year of age.

28. Gordon, *Woman's Body, Woman's Right,* pp. 52-54, suggests that the mortality rate from abortions has tended to be overestimated, and that abortions were probably much safer than is generally believed. However, she presents little evidence to support her contention at least insofar as the nineteenth century was concerned. Even if the mortality from abortions during that era has been overstated, the health problems resulting from the abortion procedure itself or complications that followed may have been quite debilitating.

29. See Stockman, *Tokology,* p. 270, who criticized the use of nitrate of silver, sulphate of zinc, corrosive sublimate, tannic acid, and nitric acid in treating uterine inflammation. According to Stockham, such practice had been in vogue for the preceding twenty-five years, but was beginning to be looked upon with disfavor by physicians.

30. Ann Douglas Wood, " 'The Fashionable Diseases': Women's Complaints and Their Treatment in Nineteenth Century America," in *Clio's Consciousness Raised: New Perspectives on the History of Women,* eds., Mary S. Hartman and Lois Banner (New York: Harper & Row, 1974), pp. 1-22, suggests that many of the uterine disorders reported in the nineteenth century may have been in large a result of male physicians' antagonism toward women, which resulted in an "unscientific even obsessive focus upon woman's womb" (p. 28). Wood's analysis may have some validity. However, given the rather primitive state of medicine and the types of physical problems that could result from too frequent conception or complications of pregnancy, abortions, or venereal disease, a high incidence

of uterine disorders does not seem implausible. As for criticism of the specific treatments, Regina Morantz, "The Lady and Her Physician," in *Clio's Consciousness Raised,* pp. 38-53, offers an excellent assessment of the general backwardness of medicine during the nineteenth century and cautions against condemnation of medical practices of that era from a mid-twentieth-century perspective.

31. For discussions regarding the significance of birth control to women see: Gordon, *Woman's Body, Woman's Right;* Carroll Smith-Rosenberg and Charles Rosenberg, "The Female Animal: Medical and Biological Views of Woman and Her Role in Nineteenth Century America," *Journal of American History* 60 (September 1973): 332-56; Smith, "Family Limitation and Domestic Feminism."

32. For discussions regarding the divergent attitudes toward contraception in nineteenth-century America, see Gordon, *Woman's Body, Woman's Right;* David Kennedy, *Birth Control in America* (New Haven: Yale University Press, 1970); James Reed, *From Private Vice to Public Virtue: The Birth Control Movement and American Society Since 1830* (New York: Basic Books, Inc., 1978).

33. Himes, *History of Contraception,* pp. 227, 229. The value of douching as a contraceptive measure had been recognized for centuries. Finch and Green, *Contraception Through the Ages,* p. 30, assert that douches of wine and garlic were suggested in Egyptian papyrus as early as 1850 B.C.

34. See Himes, *History of Contraception,* for an excellent discussion of contraceptive literature in the United States.

35. Gordon, *Woman's Body, Woman's Right,* p. 64, contends that it took World War I and the United States Army to make the use of condoms widespread. However, as with other birth control devices, it seems quite possible that use of condoms was already common among the middle and upper classes prior to World War I.

36. A cervical cap probably had been invented in 1838 by Friedrich Adolphe Wilde, a German gynecologist. Himes, *History of Contraception,* p. 321; Vincent J. Cirillo, "Edward Foote's *Medical Common Sense:* An Early American Comment on Birth Control," *Journal of the History of Medicine* 25 (July 1970): 341-45.

37. Edward Bliss Foote, quoted in Cirillo, "Edward Foote's *Medical Common Sense,"* p. 344. The first edition of *Medical Common Sense* appeared in 1858.

38. Edward Bliss Foote, *New Plain Home Talk* (New York: Murray Hill Publishing Co., 1904), p. iii.

39. Augustus K. Gardner, "On the Use of Pessaries," *Transactions of the American Medical Association* 15 (1865): 108-22. The article contains illustrations of all 123 pessaries.

40. George Granville Bantock, "On the Use and Abuse of Pessaries," *Lancet* 1 (February 2, 1878): 162. A contemporary article by Norman Glazer, M.D., "A History of Mechanical Contraception," *Medical Times* 93 (August 1965): 865-69, corroborates the view that some nineteenth-century pessaries indeed were used as intrauterine and intracervical contraceptive devices. Gordon, *Woman's Body, Woman's Right*, also discusses the use of such devices as contraceptives.

41. Mary Ware Dennett, *Birth Control Laws* (New York: Frederick H. Hitchcock, 1926), p. 9.

42. Millard S. Everett, *The Hygiene of Marriage* (New York: Vanguard Press, 1932), pp. 182-86.

43. Stockham, *Tokology*, pp. 324-26. Reed, *From Private Vice to Public Virtue*, p. 13 points out that although there was much confusion during the nineteenth century as to when the safe period was, at least some physicians offered relatively accurate advice. See also L. L. Langley, ed., *Contraception*, Benchmark Papers in Human Physiology (Stroudsburg, Pa.: Dowden, Hutchinson & Ross, Inc., 1973), especially pages 96-131, for a brief history of knowledge regarding the relationship between menstruation and ovulation.

44. Stockham, *Tokology*, p. 326. The reference to mechanical devices is not present in the 1891 edition. See Gordon, *Woman's Body, Woman's Right*, for a discussion of theories of sexual energy, "magnetism," in vogue during Stockman's time.

45. Foote, *New Plain Home Talk*, pp. 1136-37.

46. Ibid., p. 1138.

47. Ibid., p. 1148.

48. See, for example, XYZ (pseud.), "The Prevention of Conception," *Medical and Surgical Reporter* 59 (November 10, 1888): 600, and L. Huber, "The Prevention of Conception," *Medical and Surgical Reporter* 59 (November 10, 1888): 580-81. Both authors refer to the frequent requests physicians received regarding information about contraceptives.

49. William Goodell, *Lessons in Gynecology* (Philadelphia: D. G. Brinton, 1879), p. 372. Writing in favor of contraception in 1888, Dr. W. R. D. Blackwood, "The Prevention of Conception," *Medical and Surgical Reporter* 59 (September 29, 1888): 394, contended that many physicians publicly opposed contraception. Blackwood asserted that the physicians feared public opinion if they took a procontraception stand.

50. "The Limitation of Births," *Medical and Surgical Reporter* 44 (April 2, 1881): 382-84.

51. Himes, *History of Contraception*, p. 287.

52. David E. Matteson, "Professional Cowardice," *Medical and Surgical Reporter* 59 (November 3, 1888): 568.

53. J. Ford Thompson, quoted in Thomas A. Pope, "Prevention of Conception," *Medical and Surgical Reporter* 59 (October 27, 1888): 522-25.

54. Ibid., p. 525.

55. David E. Matteson, "Prevention of Conception," *Medical and Surgical Reporter* 59 (December 15, 1888): 759-60.

56. Himes, *History of Contraception*, p. 300.

57. Ibid., pp. 301-2.

58. Blackwood, "Prevention of Conception," p. 395.

59. See Rachelle S. Yarros, "Some Practical Aspects of Birth Control," *Surgery, Gynecology and Obstetrics* 23 (August 1916): 188-90, and "Trials of Birth Control Advocates," *Survey*, February 10, 1917, p. 555, regarding this point.

60. Himes, *History of Contraception;* Edward Shorter, "Female Emancipation, Birth Control and Fertility in European History," *American Historical Review* 78 (June 1973): 605-40; Thompson, quoted in Pope, "Prevention of Conception," p. 525.

61. Finch and Green, *Contraception Through the Ages*, p. 33. They contend that douching did not reach its peak as a contraceptive device until the 1930s. See also Himes, *History of Contraception*, pp. 248-49; Matteson, "Prevention of Conception," pp. 759-60.

62. *Daily Oklahoman*, September 4, 1904. The *Los Angeles Times*, February 2, 1913, also had illustrated ads for douches.

63. Henry M. Lyman et al., *The Practical Home Doctor: Twentieth Century Household Medical Guide*, revised ed. (Chicago: American Publishing Co., 1907), p. 991. Lyman opposed such devices.

64. For discussions of the role of Margaret Sanger and the spread of birth control knowledge see, Kennedy, *Birth Control in America;* Gordon, *Woman's Body, Woman's Right;* Sanger, *The New Motherhood;* Margaret Sanger, *My Fight for Birth Control* (New York: Farrar & Rinehart, 1931).

65. Article in *Medical Age*, quoted in "Obstacles to Fecundation," *Medical and Surgical Reporter* 56 (January 1, 1887): 48-49.

66. Pope, "Prevention of Conception," p. 523.

67. James E. Free, "Prevention of Conception," *Medical and Surgical Reporter* 59 (December 8, 1888): 726.

68. Ethel Wadsworth Cartland, "Childless Americans," *Outlook*, November 15, 1913, pp. 585-88. Cartland deplored the low birth rate of native whites of native-born parents.

69. "The Age of Birth Control," *New Republic*, September 25, 1915, p. 196.

70. Yarros, "Practical Aspects of Birth Control," pp. 188-90.

71. "Trials of Birth Control Advocates," p. 555.

72. Sanger, *The New Motherhood*, pp. 144, 146.

73. For discussions concerning pre-World War I attitudes toward female sexuality see: James McGovern, "The American Woman's Pre-World War I Freedom in Manners and Morals," *Journal of American History* 55 (Spring 1968): 315-33; Daniel Scott Smith, "Family Limitation, Sexual Control and Domestic Feminism in Victorian America, *Feminist Studies* 1 (Winter-Spring 1973): 40-57; Carl Degler, "What Ought to Be and What Was: Woman's Sexuality in the Nineteenth Century," *American Historical Review* 79 (December 1974): 1467-90.

74. McGovern, "Freedom in Manners and Morals," pp. 315-33.

75. Himes, *History of Contraception,* p. 372, suggests this possibility. See also Tamara Hareven and Maris A. Vinovskis, "Marital Fertility, Ethnicity, and Occupation in Urban Females: An Analysis of South Boston and the South End in 1880," *Journal of Social History* 8 (Spring 1975): 69-93. Hareven and Vinovskis conclude that the fertility rates of native whites of foreign-born parents resembled those of foreign-born whites rather than those of native whites of native-born parents.

76. Frank Notestein, "Differential Age at Marriage According to Social Class," *American Journal of Sociology* 37 (June 1931): 22-48. Notestein sampled almost 60,000 women from thirty-three cities plus 243,000 from rural areas. For a sample of arguments presented by eugenicists of the era see: Charles Davenport, *Heredity in Relation to Eugenics* (New York: Henry Holt & Co., 1911); William J. Robinson, *Eugenics, Marriage and Birth Control* (New York: The Critic & Guide Co., 1917).

77. Mary Roberts Smith, "Statistics of College and Non-College Women," *American Statistical Association* 8 (March 1900): 1-26.

78. In particular, Thompson and Whelpton, *Population Trends in the United States,* found an inverse relationship between size of community and the percent of women who were married for 1910, and between size of community and the native white child/woman ratio for 1920. In contrast, Ogburn and Tibbits, "The Family and Its Functions," pp. 661-708, pointed to communities of over 2,500 as acting as a deterrent to marriage. For other discussions regarding the impact of community size, see the following: Thomas Lynn Smith, *The Sociology of Rural Life,* 3rd ed. (New York: Harper & Bros., 1953); Bernard Okun, *Trends in Birth Rates in the United States Since 1870* (Baltimore: Johns Hopkins Press, 1958); James Tarver, "Gradients of Urban Influence on the Educational, Employment and Fertility Patterns of Women," *Rural Sociology* 34 (September 1969): 356-67.

79. In 1910, $r = -0.15$, $p < 0.01$. r, the correlation coefficient, gives one an estimate of the *strength* of a linear relationship between two sets of observations. The closer to 1 or -1 that r is, the more highly correlated, either positively or negatively, the two sets of observations are. p expresses

the significance of the correlation. The closer to 1, the weaker the significance and the more likely the correlation is due to chance. For example, $p = 0.01$ means that there is only one chance in one hundred that the results have occurred due to chance. Thompson and Whelpton, *Population Trends in the United States,* pointed to an inverse relationship between size of city and the number of married women for 1910.

80. See Okun, *Trends in the Birth Rate,* and Thompson and Whelpton, *Population Trends in the United States.* Their emphasis on an inverse relationship between fertility and city size was based in large upon data from the 1920 census.

81. U.S., Department of Commerce, *Fourteenth Census, 1920,* vol. 1, *Population: Number and Distribution,* p. 56.

82. A 1955 study by Clyde V. Kiser found that a high percentage of Catholic wives were opposed to the use of contraceptives, and Catholic wives were less likely than any other group to use contraceptives. It seems likely that similar, if not stronger attitudes, prevailed earlier in the century. See Clyde V. Kiser, ed., *Research in Family Planning* (Princeton, N.J.: Princeton University Press, 1962), pp. 178-79.

83. For 1890 through 1920, sex ratio was measured for the population fifteen years or older rather than for the entire population. See Appendix A for an explanation.

84. Margaret E. Sangster, "Shall Wives Earn Money?" *Woman's Home Companion,* April 1905, p. 32.

85. See Appendix A for a detailed description of how economic function was determined.

86. Trade and transportation were differentiated in the 1920 census. U.S., Department of Commerce, *The Ratio of Children to Women,* pp. 49-56, pointed to a lower child/woman ratio when trade was dominant and a higher one when manufacturing was dominant.

4   The Home

> With AMERICAN Radiators and IDEAL Boilers. . . .
> There is not daily struggle with flying embers, ghostly
> ashdust, soot and coal gases, as in the use of old-time
> heating devices. IDEAL heating halves woman's house-
> hold cleaning work.[1]

       Within the cities of late nineteenth- and early twentieth-
century America significant changes were occurring in what remained the
major focus of most women's lives, the day-to-day running of the household. During the latter decades of the nineteenth century and continuing
to the present day, a bountiful array of time-saving inventions has appeared
to ease the burden of caring for the American home. The appearance of
labor-saving devices for the home was gradual, and at first confined to
urban areas. In addition, the tendency to move out of the larger, more
time-consuming single-family home accelerated. Those developments
brought to women an incalcuable savings of time and energy, time and
energy that could be redirected in other channels.
    During the nineteenth century, a growing number of urban families
entered the middle class and amassed the money to allow for a higher
consumption level of goods and services. The middle class attempted to
mimic, at least as much as they could afford, the elegant life-style formerly reserved for a small minority of wealthy families. But the more elegant
and elaborate the house, the more necessary it became to have some form
of assistance for the woman of the family in the day-to-day running of the
household. Moreover, in attempting to copy the life-style of the wealthy,

it was considered desirable for the wife to be a "lady" who did not have
to be involved with the physical labor of household tasks. For some of the
wealthier middle-class families, the answer lay in securing servants. Many
families, however, could not afford the number of servants they wanted,
or could not find them at any price. For such families, living in large,
single-family homes became impracticable. The solution, for at least some
urban families, was to move into boardinghouses, a trend commented
upon by native and foreign observers from the 1830s on.

From at least as early as the 1830s, foreign visitors noted the shortage
and unreliability of servants in American cities. In *Society in America,*
published in 1837, Harriet Martineau commented upon the "difficulty
of obtaining domestic service." Auguste Carlier, a visiting Frenchman,
made similar observations about the 1850s, and during the 1880s, the
Detroit Free Press noted that domestics were becoming scarcer.[2] One
author writing in 1909 commented upon the sharp decline in the number
of families having domestic servants. He contended that thirty or forty
years earlier, one out of every eight or nine families had had servants. By
1909 the number had dropped to one out of every fifteen or sixteen
families.[3] The number of those employed in a variety of domestic occupations (servant, waiter, housekeeper, and steward) declined more than 49
percent between 1870 and 1920, whereas overall population grew from
40 million to over 106 million, an increase of 165 percent. In only twenty
years, between 1900 and 1920, the number of those employed as servants
dropped 46.7 percent (Appendix A, Table 13).

Why did the number of domestic workers decrease so dramatically
following the Civil War? Traditionally, most domestic workers were women
and for many years that occupational category had provided the bulk of
jobs to women who worked. With the advent of the Industrial Revolution,
women who might have earlier become servants opted for the greater independence and oftentimes better pay of factory work. In 1884 the *Detroit
Free Press* commented upon the relationship between the decline in the
number of domestic servants and the increase in the number of factory
positions.[4] It was difficult to determine precisely what wages the "average"
domestic worker earned, since the earlier censuses did not report the earnings of domestics as they did with factory workers. Helen Campbell, author
of *Women Wage Earners,* contended that domestic work was more highly
paid than work in the needle trades, but information from other sources
indicated that factory work generally paid higher wages than domestic

work. According to the 1890 census, the annual average earnings for female factory workers ranged from $255 for piece workers, $276 for skilled or unskilled operatives, and $462 for "officers, firm members and clerks." In contrast, nine years later, historian Lucy Salmon, in her classic survey of wages for domestic workers, found that the pay ranged from $153 a year for general servants to $198 a year for cooks.[5] However, it must be remembered that most domestics lived with their employers, who provided shelter, food, and sometimes clothing, certainly an additional financial benefit.

There was little doubt that to most women domestic service was exceedingly distasteful employment. Not only did it mean a loss of independence and a lack of personal privacy, it meant submitting, often on a twenty-four-hour basis, to employer demand. As one woman summed it up, "To go into houseservice . . . is to lose caste in our world."[6] Lucy Salmon reiterated that point, asserting that entering into domestic service meant a blow to one's pride and a feeling of a loss of dignity.[7] With other employment options opening up to them, women turned away from domestic work. The percentage of women employed in "domestic and personal" work, and more specifically as servants, dropped precipitously between 1890 and 1920; moreover, between 1900 and 1920 the actual number of women employed as servants declined (Appendix A, Table 13).

But a lack of servants was not the only factor propelling the nineteenth-century urban dweller out of the single-family home. Congestion was endemic to the nineteenth-century city. Housing rarely seemed able to keep pace with the pressures of a growing population. The inability to find a single-family dwelling, and the high cost of the single-family home constantly plagued nineteenth-century urban Americans. Although the single-family home may have been the American dream, the realities of the situation were often quite different.

Some nineteenth-century moderately well-off urban residents found that the combined forces of a housing shortage, high rents, and the lack of servants pushed them first into boardinghouses and hotels and later in the century into apartments and apartment-hotels. Boardinghouses had been observed in New York as early as 1800, and according to reports made in the 1830s by Harriet Martineau and James Silk Buckingham, an English traveler, such residences were quite common, especially in New York City.[8] In addition, from the late 1820s, hotels grew in popularity with urban residents. The first hotel in the United States, the Tremont, was

built in Boston in 1828-29. It was very well received, and the idea soon
spread to other cities. Hotels numbered among their guests permanent
residents as well as transient visitors. Boardinghouses and hotels, though
varying from the fashionable to the impoverished, tended at best to offer
a relatively small suite of rooms to residents, and thus much of the
lodgers' time was spent in the shared public rooms.[9]

Neither the housing shortage nor high rents abated following the Civil
War, and new solutions to the chronic problem were sought. Some relief
came as developments in urban transportation allowed the city to expand
beyond its previously circumscribed boundaries, and rapid suburbaniza-
tion became a common phenomenon. Indeed, escape to the suburbs often
appeared to be the only alternative for many middle-income families, at
least in New York, prior to the construction of apartment buildings.[10]
But for those residents who did not choose to leave the city, other solutions were needed.

Mid-century technological developments such as the use of iron rather
than masonry for building supports, and the invention of the elevator increasingly allowed cities to expand vertically as well as horizontally. Multiple-family buildings of various designs, which were first built for the poor
during the 1850s, spread rapidly as cities attempted to absorb the massive
influxes of new arrivals. However, it was not until the 1880s that multiple-
family buildings began to be accepted by the middle class, who apparently
had continued to associate such buildings with the poor and therefore
with a loss in status.[11]

The first definitive example of the new, "better class" of apartment
buildings was the Stuyvesant, built in New York in 1869.[12] The apartments in the Stuyvesant, "some of six, others of ten rooms, including
kitchen and servants rooms were designed for strictly independent housekeeping in good but not extravagant style."[13] Also beginning to appear
at that time were apartment-hotels, a cross between the hotel and the
apartment building, where separate suites with limited cooking facilities
were offered, but a common dining room was also present. Apartments
appeared to win acceptance only slowly during the 1870s, but by the
1880s they began to catch on with middle- and upper-income urban
dwellers.

Population pressure and the high cost of real estate quickly pushed
Manhattan toward the large-scale building of apartments. At first most
of the new apartments in New York were luxury ones, designed for the

wealthy. One author, writing in 1874, fretted that without more apartments a whole class of moderately well-to-do New Yorkers faced four housing alternatives: "banishment from the city; the occupation of a part of a home not made for multiple housekeeping; boarding; or keeping boarders."[14] Boarding continued to be a common phenomenon, but from the 1880s on apartments and apartment-hotels grew rapidly in popularity, and by the early 1900s the New York papers "overflowed with ads for flats" of all types and sizes. A fairly decent flat of seven small rooms with steam heat rented for $40 a month. A luxury suite at the newly built apartment-hotel, the Ansonia, complete with "climate control," elevators, telephones, pneumatic tubes, a central laundry, a pool, a Turkish bath, dumbwaiters connected to a downstairs dining room for those who did not want to do their own cooking, and a variety of shops on the ground floor, might rent for $10,000 a year.[15] One author writing in 1903 estimated that over 90 percent of all Manhattan residents lived in multiple-family dwellings of one kind or another.[16]

Although New York may have moved more quickly and more fully toward building multiple-dwelling units, other cities followed similar patterns. In Chicago during the 1880s, observers referred to the rapid spread of apartment living as "flat fever." More than 1,100 apartment buildings were constructed during 1883. The first buildings erected were three to five stories high; by the 1890s they often were eight stories high. Apartments varied greatly in size and luxury from modest ones on the Westside to luxury flats on Lake Shore Drive at $1,000 a month. In 1910 apartment buildings accounted for 34.4 percent of all new construction in Chicago. By 1915 the percentage had risen to 49.0. In contrast, in 1915 single-family homes accounted for only 10.8 percent of all new construction.[17]

The exodus of urban dweller from single-family homes did not go uncriticized. From as early as the 1830s, observers commented upon and often condemned the trend because of the effect they believed it had upon family life. Writing in the 1830s, Harriet Martineau characterized boardinghouses as a threat to domestic happiness:

The uncertainty about domestic service is so great, and the economy of boarding house life so tempting . . . that it is not to be wondered that many young married people use the accommodation. . . . But no sensible husband, who could before-

hand become acquainted with the liabilities incurred, would
willingly expose his domestic peace to the fearful risk.[18]

According to Martineau, boardinghouse life offered too many temptations
to the "young married ladies," provided a bad milieu in which to raise
children, and afforded no peace to the tired husband after a day's work.[19]
During the late 1850s, Auguste Carlier noted the tendency of families
in some northern cities to move into boardinghouses and hotels because
of the shortage of servants. He criticized that trend because of its "ill
effects" upon women:

> Relieved of all domestic occupation, she forgets the domestic
> life, constructs bad habits and thoughtlessness, sometimes
> dangerous liaisons and the husband and children . . . withdraw
> themselves . . . till there is nothing left of the domestic circle
> but the name.[20]

By 1870 a British observer even felt compelled to assure his readers that
"It is not at all true that people prefer hotels and boardinghouses." He
contended that young couples did stay in them but only as a "purgatory
through which they pass to the traditional delights of 'love in the cottage.'" [21]
The trend toward simplified apartment or hotel living continued, and
in 1899 one critic asserted that "the proportion of married people who, in
cities and towns, live in hotels, is continuing to be one of the most curious
and grave phenomena of our modern civilization."[22] One such married
person was economist, feminist, and reformer Charlotte Perkins Gilman.
In 1900, Gilman, her husband, and daughter lived in an apartment on
Seventy-sixth Street in New York and took their meals at a nearby boardinghouse. Their rent was $40 a month and their meals another $20. Gilman
seemed pleased with the convenience and cost of such an arrangement:

> We liked it. We had a "home without a kitchen," all the privacy
> and comfort, none of the work and care—except for beds and a
> little cleaning. We all went out together to breakfast, then
> Houghton [her husband] went to his office and Katherine to
> her school, while I had the morning for my work. I met Katherine
> for lunch there [the boardinghouse], and at night we met
> Houghton at the train and dined together in peace. We had a

table to ourselves, but found much entertainment in the talk of
the other boarders.[23]

By 1910, one American author, commenting upon the tendency of
American women to consider housekeeping such a chore, estimated that
more than 15,000 married people had moved into apartment hotels in
New York, with equal proportions in Chicago and Boston.[24]

The movement out of the larger, more time-consuming single-family
home, first into boardinghouses and hotels and later into apartments and
apartment-hotels was but one important trend affecting the life of the
American woman that originated in the nineteenth-century city. Although
that trend undoubtedly somewhat eased the nineteenth-century American
woman's domestic burden, of even more significance was the post-Civil
War growth in labor-saving wares of all sorts.

Independent of size of home, single or multiple in type, a rapidly growing assortment of appliances and commodities, with the potential to reduce
significantly the burden of household chores, appeared during the late
nineteenth and early twentieth centuries. The creative ingenuity of inventors
may indeed have been directed toward the development of such devices in
response to an increased demand. Between 1869 and 1909, the prepared-
food industry exhibited a truly phenomenal growth (Appendix A, Table
14). The number of establishments and persons involved with the preparation of foodstuffs ranging from canned fruits and vegetables, dairy products,
and meat, increased markedly during the era. Rapid growth also prevailed
in the men's and women's ready-made clothing industry between 1860
and 1910 (Appendix A, Table 15).

The revolution in the economy of the middle-class household further
appeared in the huge growth in retail sales during the 1869-1919 period.
Those retail outlets whose products could either lighten the burden of
household chores, or whose services could provide an escape from food
preparation, multiplied their sales manyfold during the latter years of the
nineteenth and early ones of the twentieth (Appendix A, Table 16).

In addition, the manufacturing of appliances for use in the home began
to grow, especially after 1900. Gas stoves were first introduced in the
1880s. By 1904 more than 33,000 people were employed in the production of gas and oil stoves, and by 1919 the number had risen to more than
43,000. Washing machines, hand-cranked at first, began to replace the
washboard around 1900, and by 1919 almost 6,000 people were involved

in their production. Iceboxes also increased in popularity. In 1899 over 3,000 people worked to produce them, and by 1919 the number had risen to almost 6,000. By that time the refrigerator had made its appearance. Figures for its production were not available prior to 1927 when more than 17,000 workers were employed in producing refrigerators.[25] Other appliances that gained in popularity from 1900 on included the portable vacuum cleaner and the electric iron. At first those appliances tended to be concentrated among the upper and middle classes in urban areas, and only gradually did they spread to other sectors of society.

During the 1870s and 1880s, and even into the 1890s, the household responsibilities of the middle-class, urban woman were somewhat less demanding than those of the farm woman, but few modern conveniences lightened either woman's burden. In the urban areas, though some packaged and processed foods such as bread and dairy products were becoming available, much food preparation, especially canning and baking, was still carried on in the home. A great deal of time was devoted to sewing, since much clothing was still made in the home, though ready-made clothing was available at least in some of the larger cities. The laundry often was done by someone else, usually by a woman hired either to work in her employer's house or to take the laundry to her own home. General house-cleaning tasks rounded out the chores of the urban, middle-class woman.

Writing in 1875, A. M. Diaz, a suffragist, asserted that only a small group of women had the time to do what they wished, while the vast majority had either to do their own housework or oversee that others did it well. "In the present state of things it is impossible for women . . . to enjoy the delights of culture."[26] Even in those homes where servants or household helpers were present, the women of the family still spent their days doing much of the family's sewing and generally overseeing the running of the house. One middle-class Chicago housewife in the mid-1860s had a cook and a washerwoman. Still the mother rose at 5:30 A.M. to oversee the cook's making of the breakfast. In addition, as was typical of many families, because of the father's time-consuming job, the running of the house was left up to the mother.[27] In a small Minnesota town during the 1880s, a hired girl helped in the house because the mother was ill. Despite her illness, the mother still cooked, made clothes, and knit stockings.[28]

The rural woman of the same era confronted a larger array of chores. Food preparation included not only canning and baking, but making butter as well. The rarity of ready-made food, at least in some rural areas, is illustrated by the story of a North Carolina farm woman who related how all of the neighbors came to see a loaf of "store-made" bread brought home by her father.[29] In rural areas, not only were clothing, quilts, and the like sewn at home, but often the fabric itself was made on the farm. Laundry, usually an all-day chore, was done by farm women in their own homes. In addition to those house chores, there was generally gardening, tending to the animals, and sometimes even work in the fields.

Between 1900 and 1920, the time that urban women, especially the more affluent ones, had to devote to household chores was diminished by numerous appliances and the proliferation of ready-made commodities. Gas stoves were replacing the cumbersome wood-burning models. Ready-made clothing and food were becoming increasingly available in the stores of towns and cities. Though the number of women engaged in laundry work decreased, the growth in the number of steam laundries plus the introduction of the electric washer helped make laundering a somewhat less odious chore for many urban women. In 1900, only 21,945 persons worked in steam laundries. By 1910 the number had risen to more than 124,000 and about 83 percent of those were in cities with populations of 10,000 or more. In 1920, a census report noted the decrease in the number of women working as "laundresses" and attributed the decline to an increase in steam laundries and electric washing machines.[30]

In 1907 only 8 percent of all dwellings had electricity. By 1920 the percentage had risen to 34.7 percent. The contrast between urban and rural areas in 1920, with respect to electrification, was sharp: Only 1.6 percent of all farms had electricity, but over 47 percent of the urban and rural nonfarm dwellings were electrified.[31] An increasing number of urban, middle-class households had iceboxes, hot and cold running water, and indoor baths and toilets. Electrical appliances such as the "self-heating" iron, vacuum cleaner, and refrigerator began to find their way into urban homes. All of those developments simplified the maintenance of the urban, middle-class home, greatly enlarging the free time available to women. Writing in 1916, one author asserted:

> Today the woman who would attend to society, club, or suf-
> fragist duties, but who cannot support a maid, find[s] all sorts
> of labor-saving devices to help her. . . . Any woman—at least
> any woman who lives within reach of gas and electricity—can
> banish most of the ordinary cares of housework.[32]

In contrast, the rural household of the early twentieth century still demanded a tremendous amount of women's time. Few farms had iceboxes, gas or oil stoves, indoor baths or toilets. The lack of electricity meant no vacuum cleaners, power washers, or self-heating irons. Most farm women still did their own laundry, using either a tub and washboard or a hand-cranked washer. Many still churned their own butter, canned fruits and vegetables, baked bread, tended the animals, and worked in the garden. The biggest change took place in the area of ready-made clothing, which had become more available to farm families after the turn of the century. However, the myriad of chores, generally unrelieved by modern conveniences, left the farm woman with little spare time or energy.[33]

A reduction in the time actually needed to complete the day-to-day tasks of the urban home did not necessarily mean that women would in fact spend less time on such work.[34] For many women the early twentieth century brought a revitalized emphasis upon the value and virtue of home and motherhood and a glorification of the many wonderful and important tasks that could fill the day of the "home" woman. Perhaps the very reduction of woman's household burdens consciously or unconsciously threatened women and men of the era. For many women, a reduction in the time needed for housework and child rearing could mean many empty hours coupled with a sense of worthlessness. For men, free time for women meant the potential for women to leave the home and enter the outside, "working" world. For many men, such a development would loom as a serious threat to their position in the family's hierarchy. Theories that emphasized the complexities of the home role and demanded all of women's time and energy had potential appeal for both men and women. Thus during the very time period when woman's household role could have been contracting, for many women it expanded.

Women's magazines vividly illustrated the divergent trends that pulled women of the early twentieth century in two conflicting directions. Some of the magazines emphasized the domestic aspect of women's lives and presented a picture of dutiful, beautiful wives and mothers, raising better and healthier children, making elaborate and better meals, and cleaning their homes better than ever before. The February 1906 edition of *Good Housekeeping* was typical. It included articles advising homemakers how to make an inexpensive music room, and instructing brides how to use a stove safely, how to buy beef, how to do laundry, together with numerous recipes, and a drawing of a beautiful young mother tucking in her child for the night.[35] Other women's magazines very clearly illustrated the ambivalent feelings of their readers. For example, the December 1903 issue of *House Beautiful* contained articles about "how to furnish a house," and "Scientific Training as Applied to the Household," but also "The Woman's Forum," a new section of the magazine "which will present the larger interests of the civic life, especially on the lines of woman's work."[36] Similarly, in *Harper's Bazaar,* February 1909, articles ranged from "The Housemother's Problems," "Yesterday's Dishes Made Over," and "Menus for the Month," to a symposium about "The Best Thing Our Club Ever Did," and "What the Suffragists Are Doing."[37]

The late nineteenth and early twentieth centuries clearly were a time of great flux for women, especially those of the urban middle class. Significant changes had occurred in the day-to-day functioning of the urban middle-class home. Although many women continued to confine their activities to the home, the combination of fewer children, an extended period of time during which children were in school, a proliferation of labor-saving commodities and services, and easier-to-maintain homes coalesced to create an environment conducive to the development of an expanded sphere of activity for women. As will be discussed in the next two chapters, for married women various types of associations provided the major focus for outside-the-home activity; for single women, employment became increasingly common.

Notes

1. *Ladies' Home Journal,* March 1913, advertisement, p. 29.

2. Harriet Martineau, *Society in America,* 3 vols. (London: Saunders & Otley, 1837), 3: 131; Auguste Carlier, *Marriage in the United States,* trans. B. Joy Jeffries (Boston: De Vries Ibarra & Co., 1867; reprint ed., New York: Arno Press, 1972), p. 68; *Detroit Free Press,* October 12, 1884.

3. I. M. Rubinow, "Discussion: Women and Economic Dependence," *American Journal of Sociology* 14 (March 1909): 614-19.

4. *Detroit Free Press,* October 12, 1884.

5. Helen Campbell, *Women Wage Earners* (Boston: Roberts Bros., 1893), p. 237; Lucy Salmon, *Domestic Service* (New York: Macmillan Co., 1901), p. 88.

6. Campbell, *Women Wage Earners,* p. 244.

7. Salmon, *Domestic Service,* p. 140.

8. Christopher Tunnard and Henry Hope Reed, *American Skyline* (n.p.: 1953; also in paperback edition, New York: Mentor Books, 1956), p. 82; Martineau, *Society in America,* 3: 131-36.

9. Joseph C. Furnas, *The Americans: A Social History of the United States* (New York: G. P. Putnam's Sons, 1969), pp. 468-69; Barbara J. Berg, *The Remembered Gate: Origins of American Feminism: The Woman and the City, 1800-1860* (New York: Oxford University Press, 1978), pp. 96-97; Martineau, *Society in America,* 3: 131-36.

10. James Richardson, "The New Homes of New York," *Scribner's Monthly,* May 1874, p. 65.

11. Lady Blanche Murphy, "American Boardinghouse Sketches," *Catholic World,* July 1885, p. 455.

12. Tunnard and Reed, *American Skyline,* p. 122.

13. Richardson, "New Homes of New York," p. 68.

14. Ibid.

15. Albert Bigelow Paine, "The Flat Dwellers of a Great City," *The World's Work,* April 1903, pp. 3287-90; Reginald Pelham Bolton, "The Apartment-Hotel in New York," *Cassier's Magazine,* November 1903, pp. 31-32.

16. Paine, "Flat Dwellers of New York," p. 3281.

17. Homer Hoyt, *One Hundred Years of Land Values in Chicago* (Chicago: University of Chicago Press, 1933), pp. 136, 215, 231; Bessie Louise Pierce, *A History of Chicago,* 3 vols., vol. 3, *The Rise of the Modern City, 1871-1893* (New York: Alfred A. Knopf, 1957), p. 57.

18. Martineau, *Society in America,* 3: 131-36.

19. Ibid.

20. Carlier, *Marriage in the United States,* p. 68.

21. George Towle, *American Society* (London: Chapman & Hall, 1870), pp. 259-60.

22. Arthur Calhoun, *A Social History of the American Family from Colonial Times to the Present,* 3 vols. in one (Cleveland: A. H. Clark, 1917-19; reprint ed., New York: Arno Press, 1973), 3: 180.

23. Charlotte Perkins Gilman, *The Living of Charlotte Perkins Gilman: An Autobiography* (New York: D. Appleton-Century Co., 1935), p. 283.

24. Katherine Busbey, *Home Life in America* (New York: Macmillan Co., 1910), pp. 369-72.

25. U.S., Department of Commerce, Bureau of the Census, *Fifteenth Census of the United States, 1930,* vol. 5, *General Report on Occupations.*

26. Mrs. A. M. Diaz, *A Domestic Problem* (Boston: James Osgood & Co., 1875), p. 16.

27. Addie Gregory, *A Greatgrandmother Remembers* (Chicago: A. Krich & Sons, 1940), pp. 4, 41.

28. Anna Clary, *Reminiscences* (Los Angeles: Printed by B. McCallister at the Adcraft Press, 1937), pp. 21, 50-51.

29. Belinda Jelliffe, *For Dear Life* (New York: Charles Scribner's Sons, 1936), p. 19. The incident described probably occurred during the 1880s.

30. U.S., Department of Commerce and Labor, Bureau of the Census, *Statistics of Women at Work: Based on Unpublished Information Derived from the Schedules of the Twelfth Census: 1900* (1907), p. 56; U.S., Department of Commerce, *Women in Gainful Occupations, 1870-1920*, p. 35; U.S., Department of Commerce and Labor, Bureau of the Census, *Thirteenth Census of the United States, 1910*, vol. 10, *Manufactures: Reports for Principal Industries*, p. 887.

31. Valerie Kincade Oppenheimer, "The Female Labor Force in the United States: Factors Governing Its Growth and Changing Composition" (Ph.d. dissertation, University of California, Berkeley, 1966), pp. 40-41.

32. E. M. Pelton, "New Aids to Housework," *Illustrated World*, April 1916, pp. 215-19.

33. For descriptions of household tasks, available appliances, and so on, in urban areas see the following: *Daily Oklahoman*, May 8, 1894, January 14, 1904, September 4, 1904, November 12, 1914, and July 11, 1914; *Chicago Times*, July 19, 1885; *Morning Oregonian*, May 1, 1900; *Detroit Free Press*, November 2, 1905; *Kansas City Star*, January 9, 1901, and May 24, 1914; *New Orleans Times Picayune*, October 9, 1880; Rubinow, "Women and Economic Dependence," pp. 614-19; Harold Barger, *Distribution's Place in the American Economy Since 1869* (Princeton, N.J.: Princeton University Press, 1955); Clary, *Reminiscences;* Marie Thérèse (de Solms) Blanc, *The Condition of Women in the United States*, trans. Abby Langdon Alger (Boston: Roberts Bros., 1895; reprint ed., New York: Arno Press, 1972); Amelia Neville, *The Fantastic City* (Boston: Houghton Mifflin Co., 1932), p. 94; Gregory, *A Greatgrandmother Remembers*, pp. 57-58; Busbey, *Home Life in America;* Estelline Bennett, *Old Deadwood Days* (New York: J. H. Sears & Co., 1928); Elsie Robinson, *I Wanted Out* (New York: Farrar & Rinehart, 1934); Isabella Alden, *Memories of Yesterday* (Philadelphia: J. B. Lippincott Co., 1933), pp. 256-60; George Woodward, *Diary of a "Peculiar" Girl* (Buffalo: Peter Paul Book Co., 1896), p. 90; Harbert Collection, Harbert Diary, 1880s (U 12 F4), Huntington Library, San Marino, California. For rural areas see the following: Paul Pierce, *Social Survey of Three Rural Townships in Iowa*, University of Iowa Monograph Series, vol. 5, no. 2 (Iowa City: The University of Iowa Press, 1917); Helen M. Doyle, *A Child Went Forth* (New York: Gotham House, 1934); Jelliffe, *For Dear Life,* pp. 5-20; Mary C. Brooke, *Memories of Eighty Years* (New York: Knickerbocker Press, 1916), pp. 16-22; David M. Cohn, *The Good Old Days* (New York: Simon

& Schuster, 1940); Busbey, *Home Life in America;* Martha F. Crowe, *The American Country Girl* (New York: Frederick A. Stokes Co., 1915).
    34. William Goode, *World Revolution and Family Patterns* (New York: Free Press of Glencoe, 1963), p. 15, and Ruth Schwartz Cowan, "The 'Industrial Revolution' in the Home: Household Technology and Social Change in the 20th Century," *Technology and Culture* 17 (January 1976): 1-23, both question whether "labor-saving" devices actually eased the house-cleaning burden or if along with the appearance of such devices came a rise in the level of expected cleanliness with the net result that women did not save any time. Although the general level of cleanliness probably did increase, there still seems little doubt that the time-consuming drudgery of earlier days had diminished. Of course women could continue to extend the time allotted to household tasks, but time and energy that had the potential to be redirected into other channels was becoming increasingly available.
    Cowan bases much of her provocative article on information culled from women's magazines, especially the advertising that increasingly depicts women as worrying about properly cleaning their homes, taking care of their children, and using the "right" product to do the task. However, as Cowan herself points out, she had not taken into account A. Michael McMahon's seminal article, "An American Courtship: Psychologists and Advertising Theory in the Progressive Era," *American Studies* 13 (Fall 1972): 5-18, which deals with the growth of the psychological "sell" technique in American advertising between 1910 and 1920. The technique emphasized selling on an emotional level, where purchase of a particular product assured the buyer that he/she was buying "the good life," whereas failure to buy the product was tantamount to depriving oneself or one's family of the same "good life." Any attempt to assess women's lives as depicted in advertising must take into account the psychological "soft sell," and Cowan has failed to do this. In addition, in her discussion of the decline in the number of household servants, Cowan has failed to take two important factors into account. First, since the middle class was expanding at the time that the number of servants was declining, many households had been or would have been unable to find servants. Thus the supposed disappearance of servants from the home was a "loss" that many families probably never noticed. In addition, although the number of live-in servants declined, there is some indication that women who wanted "help" in the home increasingly hired someone to come in once or twice a week to assist with household chores. See Robert S. Lynd and Helen M. Lynd, *Middletown: A Study in Contemporary American Culture* (New York: Harcourt Brace, 1929), p. 170, regarding this point.
    35. C. V. Rawson, "An Inexpensive Music Room," *Good Housekeep-*

ing, February 1906, p. 175; Emma Paddock Telford, "First Aid to Brides: The Cook Stove," *Good Housekeeping,* February 1906, pp. 196-200; Maria Treadwell, "The Anatomy of the Beef Creature," *Good House-keeping,* February 1906, pp. 215-17; Miriam Bitting-Kennedy, "Modern Methods in Laundry," *Good Housekeeping,* February 1906, pp. 235-36.

36. Anne Higginson Spicer, "How to Furnish a House," *House Beautiful,* December 1903, pp. 28-31; Grace Van Everen Stoughton, "Scientific Training as Applied to the Household," *House Beautiful,* December 1903, pp. 61-63; Ellen M. Henrotin, "The Woman's Forum," *House Beautiful,* December 1903, pp. 44-45.

37. "The Housemother's Problems," *Harper's Bazaar,* February 1909, pp. 44-48; Josephine Grenier, "Yesterday's Dishes Made Over," *Harper's Bazaar,* February 1909, pp. 93-95; "Menus for the Month," *Harper's Bazaar,* February 1909, pp. 228-32; Ida Husted Harper, "What the Suffragists Are Doing," *Harper's Bazaar,* February 1909, pp. 201-3; "The Best Thing Our Club Ever Did," *Harper's Bazaar,* February 1909, pp. 156-57.

5 Women's Organizations

Women's clubs are the natural product of a progressive
sex living in a progressive age. They stand for the home,
for the school, for art and literature and music; for
domestic science and for the intellectual advancement
of the American woman. . . . They are practical; they
act, they do things for the good of society; for the good
of the community and of the country.[1]

In cities and towns of late nineteenth- and early twentieth-
century America, a tremendous growth occurred in the number and variety
of women's organizations. Clubs, self-improvement and social outreach,
temperance societies, suffrage organizations, civic groups, and a myriad of
other associations flourished during the era. Those organizations became
the outside-the-home focus for the energy and talents of an increasing
number of middle- and upper-class women.

Women's participation in voluntary organizations was not a development unique to the late nineteenth century. From at least the early 1800s,
some middle- and upper-class urban women had been active participants
in a variety of different benevolent associations.[2] Many of the early nineteenth-century women's organizations were closely tied to various churches
and focused mainly upon religious concerns. Other groups became more
involved with attempting to alleviate the problems facing the poor in an
urban environment.

Some of the causes urban women of the early nineteenth century became involved with included opening industrial schools for girls; attempt-

ing to find jobs for destitute women; pushing for prison reform; working for various moral reforms; working to reform property laws; and setting up children's and lying-in hospitals. Women were also vital participants in the antislavery movement, at first taking an active role in fund-raising and petition drives; and gradually, amid criticism, they moved into a more visible role as public speakers.[3]

The shared activism of those early nineteenth-century women gave them a sense of their own individuality and self-worth as well as a sharp awareness of their shared oppression in a male-dominated society. From the growing feminist consciousness, the organized women's movement of the mid-nineteenth century arose.[4] At the first official convention of the women's rights movement in Seneca Falls (1848), the women pressed for a range of reforms including control over earnings and property, guardianship of children in case of divorce, equal education and employment opportunities for women, and suffrage.

Although the inspirational thread for women's organizations obviously can be traced back at least to the early 1800s, the massive number of participants, the variety of organizations, and the wide range of projects found during the late nineteenth and early twentieth centuries dwarfed anything seen during earlier years. During the latter decades of the nineteenth century and the opening years of the twentieth, a number of factors meshed, giving rise to an explosion in association formation and activism by women. Part of the activism focused on issues inherited from unfinished struggles engaged in by earlier generations of women. Most prominent were the fight for suffrage, and moral reform battles such as the temperance movement. Although some of the activism reflected a continuation of earlier concerns, new issues, very much products of their day, captured much of women's attention.

The upheaval brought about by the Civil War, the turmoil engendered by the massive physical and social changes in the post-Civil War cities, the explosive industrialization—all had combined to create a climate of excitement and uncertainty. During the decades following the Civil War, huge fortunes were amassed by the new plutocrats of industry such as John D. Rockefeller, Andrew Carnegie, and J. Pierpont Morgan. For the wealthy and fortunate few, life during the Gilded Age was pleasurable and bountiful. For many, the struggle merely to survive was constant. In both country and city, conditions were often harsh, but in the city problems were more concentrated, less escapable. Problems resulting from overcrowding, obsolete services, prostitution, intemperance, epidemics, and corrupt politics confronted the late nineteenth-century urban dweller on a day-to-day basis.

The need to come to grips with, to bring order to the increasingly turbulent urban environment provided the impetus for much of the reform activity of the era. A growing army of urban professionals began to analyze the social and political woes facing the city and the nation. Gradually, the laissez-faire philosophy of earlier years gave way to a new activist philosophy predicated on the idea that, not only could people intervene to change social and economic conditions, but that they were obligated to do so. Urban Protestantism gained new fire and direction with the Social Gospel movement, which called upon its adherents to tend to society's salvation by working to better the urban environment and condition.[5]

The faces of reform were varied. Civic reformers campaigned for clean, efficient government and an end to bossism. Social reformers struggled to ameliorate some of the harshest elements of urban life including overcrowded living quarters, disease, and unbearable working conditions. City planners worked to rationalize and beautify the urban environment in the hopes of bettering the lives of the inhabitants. Many of the efforts at reform emerged first on a local level, and only later evolved into the national campaigns of Progressivism as people became aware of their shared problems and concerns.

It was such a political and social climate that provided a medium conducive to the flourishing of activism by urban middle- and upper-class women. Many of those women were increasingly well educated, and brought up during an era when the challenge to the idea of the propriety of a circumscribed sphere of activity for women was growing. A lightened household burden resulting from a decrease in the number of children, smaller homes, and an increase in labor-saving appliances and commodities provided women of the era with time and energy that could be redirected toward external channels. Since, for married women, societal prohibitions against employment remained exceedingly strong, as had been the case with their sisters earlier in the century, other outlets for energy and talents were sought. Some women found their niche in the social purity and temperance campaigns. Others gravitated toward the suffrage movement. Still others joined one of the many women's clubs that flourished during the era. Many women were active in more than one type of organization.

One of the major causes carried over from the antebellum era was the fight for women's suffrage. Following the Civil War, the women's rights

movement had split into two sections, each differing in its reaction to the
Fourteenth Amendment, focuses for the future, and tactics to be used.
The National Woman Suffrage Association was organized by Susan B.
Anthony and Elizabeth Cady Stanton in May 1869, and the American
Woman Suffrage Association by Lucy Stone in November of the same year.
Anthony and Stanton were outraged at a constitutional amendment that
gave the vote to Black men while denying it to women. Stone was willing
to accept the moment as belonging to the Black man. In addition, Stanton
and Anthony believed in a wide-ranging women's movement, one that
would tackle issues such as divorce reform, organizing workingwomen,
as well as working to secure women's suffrage through a federal amendment. In contrast, Stone advocated focusing solely on the question of
women's suffrage, fearing that all other issues would harm the cause.
The American Woman Suffrage Association, though paying lip service to
a federal amendment, directed its energies toward working for suffrage on
a state-by-state basis. Not until 1890, when many of the differences that
had caused the original split had been smoothed over, did the two wings
of the women's rights movement merge into the National American
Woman Suffrage Association. Although the suffrage movement remained
numerically small until the second decade of the twentieth century, its
pressure and presence kept the issue of women's role and women's rights
in the public eye. Full suffrage, which in 1870 had been limited to Wyoming and Utah, was finally extended to all women by the Nineteenth
Amendment, ratified in 1920.[6]

Many women who never would have dreamed of working for anything so "radical" as women's suffrage felt perfectly comfortable joining
one of the many Woman's Christian Temperance Union (WCTU) chapters,
or one of the thousands of women's clubs that mushroomed in cities and
towns in the decades following the Civil War. In "The Attitude of the
Typical Southern Woman to Clubs," Hannah Robinson Watson explained
that many southern women had at first been antagonistic toward clubs,
which they had equated with prosuffrage sentiment.[7]

With the organizing in 1874 of the WCTU under the leadership of
Frances E. Willard, the temperance movement took on revived strength.
Temperance work had a greater respectability in the eyes of most women
than did suffrage, for unlike suffrage, the temperance movement in its
narrowest focus neither questioned nor threatened the political subjuga-
tion of women. Oftentimes, temperance societies did not confine them-

selves strictly to working toward the elimination of "demon rum," but instead involved themselves in a wide range of causes, including child welfare issues, kindergarten legislation, and working among the Indians.[8]

One of the most remarkable developments in post-Civil War women's association history was the growth of a massive network of women's clubs. The two organizations that vied for the distinction of being first appeared almost simultaneously in New York and Boston in 1868. Sorosis of New York was organized by Jenny Croly, a New York journalist, as a response to her exclusion from a New York Press Club dinner for Charles Dickens. Sorosis had a more literary flavor to it than did Boston's New England Woman's Club, but both organizations were, almost from their inception, involved with matters of social concern. In 1869, Sorosis set up a committee to investigate infant mortality in homes for foundlings, while, during the same year, the New England Woman's Club pushed for the state of Massachusetts to establish a horticulture school for women.[9]

Both Sorosis and the New England Woman's Club were formed with the idea that women should organize in order to assist one another *and* to be of use to the world. The majority of clubs that came into existence during the late 1860s and early 1870s, however, tended to focus almost exclusively upon programs of "self-improvement" for their own members.[10] In towns and cities scattered across the nation, women began to organize clubs that served as forums for the exchange of information regarding various aspects of literature, art, history, and so on.

Women of the era were quite conscious of the relationship between the reduction in the amount of time needed for household tasks and the growth of the club movement. Alma A. Rogers, author of "The Woman's Club Movement: Its Origins, Significance and Present Results," summed it up as follows: "Verily, the march of mechanical invention has been the emancipation of women. The freeing of their hands has led to the freeing of their minds."[11] Rogers pointed out that it would have been impossible for her grandmother to think of having time for clubs, but ready-made clothing, prepared food, the gas stove, and telephones had given more free time to women.

Not surprisingly, the woman's club movement of the late nineteenth and early twentieth centuries was almost exclusively an urban movement, for only in the cities and towns was leisure time becoming a reality for a growing number of middle- and upper-class women. In 1889 Sorosis had issued an invitation for individual clubs to unite into a single federation.

An 1893-94 list of clubs belonging to the General Federation of Women's Clubs revealed that virtually all were located in towns and cities, with the larger cities such as Chicago, Boston, and New York having a dozen or more clubs.[12]

Although the women's club movement ultimately penetrated the rural areas, it never became as widespread as in the urban sector. In 1909, an author of an article appearing in *Harper's Bazaar* urged countrywomen to follow the example of the city and start the "civilizing influence" of clubs.[13] As late as 1915, Caroline Burrell, in *The Complete Club Book for Women*, described letters she received from rural women regarding the possibility of starting clubs, clearly indicating the slower growth of outside activities for women in the countryside.[14]

Not only the club movement had its roots planted in urban areas; other organizations exhibited a similar pattern. The National Household Economic Association, organized in 1890 for the "purpose of arousing public interest in regard to matters of sanitation, dietetics, sound art and architecture, in short, wholesome and sensible living," drew its direction from urban women. The 1895-97 list of officials of the organization revealed that most came from urban areas, including cities such as Chicago, Milwaukee, New Orleans, and Philadelphia and towns like Oskaloosa, Iowa, and Manhattan, Kansas.[15] Elizabeth Boynton Harbert and other reform-minded women founded the Illinois Social Science Association, dedicated to the "practical application of social science," in Chicago in 1877. According to the annual report of the secretary of the American Social Science Association read at Cincinnati, May 20, 1878, Illinois was the first state to organize an association of women for the promotion of social science, and within six months the organization had over two hundred members.[16] Its leadership was drawn mainly from the Chicago area and scattered small towns, and a listing of women elected to membership in the association in 1878 followed the same pattern.[17]

Even the WCTU, at least in its early years, drew upon the urban sector, especially small towns, for much of its leadership. According to the 1884 list of national and state officials, fifty-seven came from towns of less than 10,000 population, twelve from towns of 10,000-25,000, seventeen from cities of 25,000-100,000, and twenty-two from cities of over 100,000.[18] Much of the strength of the women's suffrage movement also came from urban areas.[19] Address books belonging to Elizabeth Boynton Harbert, a midwestern leader in the suffrage movement, revealed the urban residence of many of the supporters. A large number of women lived in Chicago; others came from places such as Rockford, Moline, Belvidere, Minneapolis, Racine, Indianapolis, Kewanee (Illinois), Waukegan, Manitee (Michigan), Prairie City (Iowa), Bloomington, Salt Lake City, New York City, and Boston.[20]

If the women's club movement gained its momentum from the increased free time of urban women, it also gained its focus from the types of problems that were part of the urban scene of the period. Although the strictly "self-improvement" type of club remained, it became increasingly common for women's clubs to turn their attention outward and grapple with some of the social problems confronting the communities to which they belonged. Typical of this progression was the Fortnightly Club of Winchester, Massachusetts. Founded in 1881, it originally focused upon self-improvement and offered classes in history and literature for its members. From 1886 on, the club became involved in "outreach" projects, working for adult education, industrial training, and public kindergartens.[21]

Numerous clubs appeared to have been established originally to deal with a specific problem, but once organized, they turned their energy toward a variety of issues. In 1884, in New York City, eleven women organized the Women's Health Protective Association to combat "foul odors emanating from a huge pile of manure." With that problem resolved, they turned their attention toward the elimination of other "noxious" industrial odors, seeing to it that city streets were kept clean, and that stores and street vending places operated under "hygienic" conditions.[22] In Indianapolis, an 1893 outbreak of cholera prompted women to organize the Indianapolis Sanitary Association. The women soon became involved with other areas of concern: hospitals, schools, parks, food preparation.[23]

The involvement of women in a variety of civic improvement projects was widespread, especially from the 1890s on. A 1912 comment from the General Federation's chairman of civil service reform that she had not heard of a town that was undergoing "civic awakening" without also having an active woman's club illustrated the ubiquitous nature of the women's club movement.[24]

The outreach orientation of the club movement was illustrated by the development and function of specific committees in the General Federation. In "The Woman's Club Movement," Mary I. Wood described the function of the eleven federation committees. The Art Committee provided traveling art galleries and established municipal art commissions;

the Literature and Library Extension Committee encouraged the study of "good literature"; and the Education Committee worked to arouse the interest of the public in education. The Legislative Committee offered information about a variety of issues; the Civics Committee undertook a wide range of projects to benefit the community such as providing noonday restrooms for employed women and working for city beautification; and yet another committee focused upon civil service reform. In addition, the Forestry Committee attempted to see that natural resources were preserved; and the major concern of the Health Committee was the control of tuberculosis. Other committees included Food and Sanitation, which worked for the passage of the 1906 Pure Food Bill; Household Economics, which attempted to get domestic science taught in the schools and encouraged the study of household care; and Industrial and Child Labor Conditions, which investigated working conditions and attempted to better them.[25]

A further indication of the civic activism of women appeared in the journal *The American City*. Between 1909, when the first issue was published, and 1920, more than one hundred articles detailed the "civic work" of women. The majority of articles appeared between 1909 and 1917, prior to U.S. entry into World War I.[26]

Women's clubs were involved with a phenomenal range of projects. Some of the projects focused upon educational concerns and attempted to set up trade schools for girls, libraries, university extension courses, college fellowships, schools for handicapped children, and vacation schools for school-age children; to improve the physical environment of the public schools; to acquaint the public with "household economics"; and to place women on school boards. Other projects attempted to help the workingwoman in various ways: establishing workingwomen's clubs and "Les Crèches" where working mothers could leave their babies; improving working conditions for women; eliminating sweatshops; and getting women factory inspectors. A variety of "sanitary reforms," including the installation of drinking fountains, and public baths, and working for "hygienic conditions in stores," clean streets, and improved water and sewage reforms, made up another set of projects. A related group of projects included tenement house reform, the establishment of playgrounds, and the beautification of parks. Still other projects focused upon redressing inequities in the criminal justice system and worked to reform the prison system and the law's treatment of juveniles, to provide equal parental guardianship of minors, and to get female matrons assigned to jails.[27]

A recent study of the Progressive movement in Wisconsin during the 1890s revealed that women were involved in a wide range of social reforms, especially after the upheaval of the economic depression of 1893-94. In urban areas throughout Wisconsin women worked to make schools more accessible to the poor by providing clothing when needed. Women also pushed for the establishment of kindergartens and manual-training programs. In 1897 the women's clubs began to investigate the exploitation of women and children in factories. In 1899 the clubs organized a Comsumer's League and led a boycott of stores selling "exploitative" products. Also in 1899, led by the Woman's Club of Madison, women worked with the Wisconsin Federation of Labor for strict factory inspection bills.[28]

A number of other organizations, many of them middle class in origin, sought to provide material and moral support for working girls and women. The middle- or upper-class genesis of many of the societies was illustrated by the comment of a New York woman regarding how unusual a group of workingwomen's clubs in New York was because it was run by the workingwomen rather than by "wealthy women."[29] In 1866 the first American Young Women's Christian Association (YWCA) was formed in Boston to aid the "temporal, moral, and religious welfare of young women who had to support themselves."[30] The YWCA had originated in England. Emma Roberts organized the first YWCA in London in 1855 to serve as the woman's counterpart to the Young Men's Christian Association, which had been organized in 1844 under the guidance of George Williams, a London draper's assistant. Both the YMCA and the YWCA combined a deep religiosity with a desire to be of service to the community. In addition to the ubiquitous prayer meetings, the American YWCAs usually offered lodging, recreation, employment services, and job training to young women.[31] By 1871 thirteen cities contained YWCAs, and by 1891 the number had risen to 225.[32] During the late 1870s, the Women's Educational and Industrial Union was organized in Boston. It provided a place for noon lunches and an outlet where unemployed women could make and sell items. Similar organizations soon appeared in a number of other cities.[33] Meanwhile, in 1884, under the aegis of Grace Dodge, Working Girls Societies were set up in New York City, while in Philadelphia, the New Century Guild of Working Girls appeared, offering manual arts training to those who needed it.[34]

Another association to emerge during this era, but one that placed middle-class "ladies" and workingwomen on a more equitable footing, was the National Women's Trade Union League (WTUL). Founded at the 1903 American Federation of Labor convention in Boston by Mary Kenny O'Sullivan, herself a union organizer, the WTUL was to assist those unions that already had women members and to aid in the formation of new unions.[35] Further middle- and working-class alliance came through the National Consumer's League, organized by Josephine Shaw Lowell in 1899 from a merger of four local leagues: New York, Philadelphia, Boston, and Chicago. Middle-class women organized consumer support for better working conditions for workingwomen and children and a boycott of those establishments that failed to meet the specified standards. By the early 1900s there were sixty-four branches of the league.[36]

Although never exclusively a women's undertaking, the settlement house movement provided yet another link between middle-class women and men and members of the working class. Growing out of the same spirit of reform and moral outreach that characterized many of the women's club activities, from the 1890s on, "settlements" sprang up in many of the major American cities, especially in the Northeast and Middle West. Hull House, founded by Jane Addams and Ellen Gates Starr in Chicago (1889), and College Settlement, established by Vida Scudder in New York (1889), served as models for similar establishments in other cities. In 1891 only six settlements existed, but by 1910 the number had jumped to more than four hundred.[37] The vast majority of women who worked in the settlement houses came from a middle-class background and had attended college.[38] In contrast to the club movement with its preponderance of married women, the settlement houses, due to the intensity of involvement demanded, for the most part attracted single women.

How widespread was involvement in the many organizations that proliferated during this era? The participation of many women in more than one club rendered total membership figures unreliable—one Boston woman was reported to have belonged to 22 clubs[39]—but the General Federation of Women's Clubs provided a rough estimate. In 1898 total federation membership was somewhere around 160,000. By 1902 the number had risen to 220,000, by 1905 to 500,000, and by 1910 to more than 1 million.[40] The federation, however, during any given year, contained only a small portion of the total number of women's clubs. For example, in Wichita, Kansas, in 1891, only 2 out of the 42 clubs in the city belonged to the federation.[41] Similarly, an 1893 survey made by the Massachusetts State Federation of Women's Clubs found a total of 726 women's organizations present in the state, but only 37 of those belonged to the General Federation.[42]

Another indication of the extent of women's involvement in organizations came from an estimate of the membership of the National Council of Women, a union of national women's organizations. The National Council, organized in 1888, was the brainchild of May Wright Sewall, educator, suffragist, and active clubwoman, who envisioned an international association of women's groups united under the auspices of suffragists, but not limited to those who supported suffrage.[43] The council's 1902 membership was reported to be over 1 million—all exclusive of the General Federation of Women's Clubs![44] One woman in 1898 commented upon the proliferation of women's clubs, summing up the situation as follows: "In Puritan days the test of right living was church membership, now the test seems to be club membership."[45]

Married women, women in the midst of taking care of homes and raising families, dominated the club movement. Of 615 women listed as either presidents or recording secretaries for the member clubs of the General Federation, from 1893 to 1894, 479, or 78 percent, were married.[46] Commentators from the era seemed generally to agree that the vast majority of women involved with club work were married. De Blanc noted that most clubwomen were "good wives and mothers." Mary Boyce, herself a clubwoman, confirmed de Blanc's assertion, while May Wright Sewall described the women who attended the 1892 convention of the General Federation of Women's Clubs in Chicago as "home staying, church-going women with no career and no [desire] for one."[47]

The preponderance of married women also appeared among the 1878 leadership of the Illinois Social Science Association, where, out of twenty women, eighteen were married, while among the twenty-seven women elected to membership in January 1878, twenty-one were married.[48] Similarly, in the National Household Economic Association, of the leadership during the mid-1890s only two women were unmarried.[49] In the WCTU, the 1884 listing of national and state officials revealed eighty-two married and sixteen single women.[50] In the suffrage movement, too, married women seemed to comprise a considerable portion of the membership and leadership, at least in the Midwest. According to two address books listing suffrage workers, one from the late 1870s or early 1880s and the other from the early 1890s, the greatest percentage of workers were married.[51]

In a certain respect, the involvement in either self-improvement clubs or social outreach organizations was a compromise between the pressure to remain in the home and the attractions offered by a career. Volunteer work was more flexible in terms of time demand and, for most women, could more easily be combined with family life than could a career. More importantly, although the clubs and associations did bring many women out of the home and undoubtedly enhanced their feelings of self-assurance and self-worth, they did not, in general, affect the family structure in the same way as a career could, since, financially, the family still relied upon the earnings of the husband.

Nonetheless, even with this nonpaying activity, women still felt a tension and the need to reassure themselves and their critics that involvement had not come at the expense of their families. Mrs. A. O. Granger, a Georgia clubwoman, insisted that although southern clubwomen had broadened their scope of interest and become a "recognized force," it was done "without neglecting their homes." May Alden Ward, editor of the official publication of the General Federation of Women's Clubs, stressed the positive influence that clubs had had upon home life through the development of domestic science.[52]

Even the justification of the types of projects that the clubs and other women's associations undertook revolved around their relationship to the home. The women pointed out that it was "natural" for them to be concerned with all aspects of the development of children—home environment, education, play, and so on—just as it was "natural" for them to become involved with making their towns and cities clean and safe, since all of those were but extensions of women's traditional concerns within the home. After all, what was civic improvement but the "larger housekeeping," and what were women but "the city's housekeepers."[53] Similarly, journalist and feminist Rheta Childe Dorr argued that "woman's place is in the home" but "Home is the Community" and "The City full of people is the Family," and "The Public School is the real Nursery."[54] In the same vein, Josephine Shaw Lowell studiously pointed out the propriety of the Woman's Municipal League of New York City, formed in 1894 to work against Tammany Hall. Lowell contended that since the "questions were moral and not political [they were] essentially [as much] the concern of women as of men."[55] Although, to a certain extent, such justifications and reassurances were a response to critics who railed against any outside activity for women, they also reflected the tension created by contradictory role demands.

Many members of the women's groups realized the significance of having organizations exclusively for females. Those women readily recognized the tendency for men to dominate groups that contained both men and women, thereby depriving women of invaluable organizational and administrative experience. In 1897 the president of the General Federation of Women's Clubs asserted that the purpose of clubs was:

> To make women a practical power in the great movements
> that are directing the world and for giving her the ability to
> serve the highly developed and complex civilization that is
> awaiting her influence.[56]

The visiting de Blanc noted a similarity between the salons of Paris and the clubs of the United States, except in the salons the men were "allowed to shine," whereas in the United States the clubs closed their doors to men. One clubwoman, commenting upon de Blanc's observation, stated: "Oh as for that, we don't care; we prefer to shine on our own account."[57] Similarly, some women members of press clubs in southern states disapproved of having both women and men in the same club, observing that "in such organizations, women are apt to become auxiliaries."[58] Another woman author emphasized that the value of clubs came especially through the feeling of identity with other women and a growing sense of self-worth and equality with men.[59]

Members of women's clubs consciously recognized their organized endeavors as an important development. A strong feeling that women had come into their own as a potent force in history peppered comments from the era. One clubwoman, writing in the 1890s, characterized the nineteenth century as the "Woman's Century," pointing out that for the first time organizations of women espoused the purpose of "bearing the burden, lessening the ills, and doing the work of the world."[60] In 1906 Sarah S. Platt Decker, a clubwoman and civic reformer, expressed the hope that the General Federation of Women's Clubs,

> May become a mighty factor in the civilization of the century if
> wielded as a whole—an army of builders . . . not only potent in

this generation, but transmitting to the next a vigor and strength
which have never been given by any race of women to their in-
heritors.[61]

The strength of the club movement manifested itself clearly when
Harper's Bazaar in 1909 sponsored a contest regarding noteworthy club
ventures and noted, "In every state, nowadays, the woman's clubs are a
factor, and an important one in the making of public opinion."[62] For
women of the era, especially for middle-class, married ones, the club movement of late nineteenth- and early twentieth-century America offered a
tremendous opportunity for involvement in a whole range of new activities.
Small wonder, then, that in 1902 Winifred Harper Cooley hopefully pre-
dicted that clubs would enlarge woman's sphere "until it is co-existent
with the globe . . . and we venture to prophesy optimistically of the work
of women in the twentieth century."[63]

In addition to the abundance of often multipurpose organizations to
which married women flocked, an array of associations emerged to meet
the needs of the growing number of working professional women. Between
1890 and 1920, women in a number of professions formed associations
along occupational lines. For nurses, two organizations emerged during
the 1890s, one becoming the National League of Nursing Education and
the other the American Nurses Association. Between 1900 and 1920, a
half-dozen other associations for professional women came into existence:
the Women's Homeopathic Fraternity (1904), the International Association
of Policewomen (1915), the Medical Women's National Association (1915),
the National Association of Deans of Women (1916), and the National
Federation of Business and Professional Women's Clubs (1919), the last a
union of 105 existing clubs.[64]

Between 1870 and 1920 women's associations, ranging from the most
esoteric of literary clubs to civic action groups, multiplied rapidly. The
projects undertaken by many of the groups were shaped by the urban
environment to which they belonged. The women's groups drew their
membership mainly from middle- and upper-class urban women, many
of whom were married. Increased free time coupled with a desire to become more active participants in the world outside the home had encouraged many women to seek outside activities. However, inner conflicts
plus societal pressures tended to inhibit most married, middle-class women
from pursuing careers. For many women of the era, the multitude of

voluntary associations provided an important outlet for creative and social talents that otherwise would have been limited to the boundaries of the home.

Notes

1. W. L. Bodine, Superintendent of Compulsory Education in Chicago, quoted in May Alden Ward, "The Influence of Women's Clubs in New England and in the Middle-Eastern States," *Annals of the American Academy of Political and Social Science* 28 (September 1906): 205.

2. Keith Melder, *Beginnings of Sisterhood: The American Woman's Rights Movement, 1800-1850* (New York: Schocken Books, 1977); Barbara J. Berg, *The Remembered Gate: Origins of American Feminism: The Woman and the City, 1800-1860* (New York: Oxford University Press, 1978). Both Melder and Berg discuss the organizational activity of women in the early 1800s. Melder sees the impetus for female voluntary organizations of that period as growing out of the religious revivalism of the era, while Berg, in a provocative and thoughtful study, views urban life of the era as providing the stimulus for such organizations.

3. Berg, *Origins of American Feminism;* Melder, *Beginnings of Sisterhood.*

4. Ibid. Berg emphasizes the importance of the benevolent association; Melder places more emphasis on abolitionist involvement.

5. See Chapter 2, note 31, for a discussion of studies about the Progressive movement.

6. For details regarding the women's rights movement see: Aileen S. Kraditor, *The Ideas of the Woman Suffrage Movement, 1890-1920* (New York: Columbia University Press, 1965); Eleanor Flexner, *Century of Struggle: The Woman's Rights Movement in the United States* (Cambridge, Mass.: Harvard University Press, 1959; reprint ed., New York: Atheneum, 1971). Suffrage for women in Utah was temporarily lost in 1887 and not regained until 1896.

7. Hannah Robinson Watson, "The Attitude of the Typical Southern Woman to Clubs," *Arena,* August 1892, pp. 363-88.

8. Inez Haynes Irwin, *Angels and Amazons* (New York: Doubleday, Doran & Co., 1933). Irwin, p. 201. Willard herself backed suffrage, but temperance always remained the primary goal. The temperance movement was considerably more successful than the suffrage organizations in attracting members. Andrew Sinclair, *The Better Half: The Emancipation of the American Woman* (London: Jonathan Cape, 1966), p. 222, estimated

that by 1900 the temperance movement had ten times as many members as did suffrage societies, and he put the 1912 WCTU membership at 250,000.

9. Irwin, *Angels and Amazons,* pp. 215-20; Sophonisba P. Breckinridge, *Women in the Twentieth Century* (New York: McGraw-Hill Book Co., 1933), p. 18. The New England Woman's Club was founded by Julia Ward Howe, Caroline Severance, and other women of Boston. See Flexner, *Century of Struggle,* p. 180.

10. Mrs. A. O. Granger, "The Effect of Clubwork in the South," *Annals of the American Academy of Political and Social Science* 28 (September 1906): 248; Mrs. John Dickinson Sherman, "The Club in the Midwest States," *Annals of the American Academy of Political and Social Science* 28 (September 1906): 228; Martha E. D. White, "The Work of the Woman's Club," *Atlantic,* May 1904, p. 614.

11. Alma A. Rogers, "The Woman's Club Movement: Its Origins, Significance, and Present Results," *Arena,* October 1905, p. 347. The recognition of the importance of free time was also commented upon by Winifred Harper Cooley, "The Eternal Feminine: The Future of the Woman's Club," *Arena,* April 1902, p. 380.

12. Harbert Collection, "The New Cycle" (list of federated clubs, 1893-94) (Box 12), Huntington Library, San Marino, California.

13. Marcie Howe, "Self Help for the Country Woman," *Harper's Bazaar,* March 1909, pp. 269-72. Howe suggested combining culture with outreach and emphasized the need to have many books available. See also, "The Best Thing Our Club Ever Did," *Harper's Bazaar,* June 1909, pp. 614-15, which discusses the setting up of a club in rural North Carolina.

14. Caroline Frances Burrell [Caroline French Benton], *The Complete Club Book for Women* (Boston: Page Co., 1915), pp. 119-25. Burrell suggested starting with the reading of books for self-improvement and then moving into outreach programs. The urban base of the club movement is pointed to by both Sinclair, *The Better Half,* pp. 319-20, and Anne Firor Scott, *The Southern Lady: From Pedestal to Politics, 1830-1930* (Chicago: University of Chicago Press, 1970), pp. 134-63.

15. Harbert Collection, "National Household Economic Association" (two manuscript notebooks) (U 12 F4).

16. Harbert Collection, "Reprint of valuable report of Honorable Frank Sanborn in regard to Social Science." Box 11 (See Illinois Social Science).

17. Harbert Collection, "Illinois Social Science Journal, February 1878," pp. 10-11 (Box 11).

18. Harbert Collection, printed lists of WCTU leaders, 1884-85. The size of the city is based on population figures from the 1880 census.

19. Howard Furer, "The City as a Catalyst for the Women's Rights Movement," *Wisconsin Magazine of History* 52 (Summer 1969): 285-305, has documented the urban roots of the major leadership of the movement.

20. Harbert Collection, address books belonging to Elizabeth Boynton Harbert. The books appear to date from the late 1870s or early 1880s.

21. Massachusetts State Federation of Woman's Clubs, *Progress and Achievement: A History of the Massachusetts State Federation of Woman's Clubs, 1890-1931* (Boston: n.p., 1932), p. 218.

22. Mary E. Trautman, "Woman's Health Protective Association," *Municipal Affairs* 2 (September 1898): 439-46.

23. Hester M. McCluny, "Women's Work in Indianapolis," *Municipal Affairs* 2 (September 1898): 523-26.

24. "Woman's Work for Better Cities," *Literary Digest,* July 13, 1912, pp. 49-50.

25. Mary I. Wood, "The Woman's Club Movement," *Chautauquan,* June 1910, pp. 36-39.

26. *The American City,* 1909-1920, vols. 1-5; 8-22. Following World War I, articles describing women's civic activism were almost nonexistent. Only four appeared between 1920 and 1925. The decline may have in part reflected an editorial decision made by the publishers of the magazine, which after World War I appeared to focus more heavily upon the activities of urban professionals. It probably also reflected a real decrease in the civic activism of women's groups.

World War I had deflected activism away from local concerns to international ones. In addition, the types of problems that had sparked the formation of many of the local women's civic groups were increasingly being handled by professionals hired by expanding government bureaucracies. For example, the number of cities having public health departments grew rapidly during the late nineteenth and early twentieth centuries. Following the 1901 example of New York's Tenement Law, other cities moved to tighten up their building codes. Cities increasingly took over services such as playgrounds and kindergartens.

Some women took up professional careers, and indeed the 1920s saw an upsurge in professional women's organizations. (See J. Stanley Lemons, *The Woman Citizen: Social Feminism in the 1920s* [Urbana, Ill.: University of Illinois Press, 1973], pp. 41-62 regarding this point.) Many other women probably either shifted the focus of their activism or became less active. Although during the early 1920s social feminists continued to pursue a wide variety of progressive causes (Lemons, *The Woman Citizen,* pp. 117-80), many women's groups, especially women's clubs which had been involved in social activism prior to World War I, retreated from their activism during the 1920s (see Lois Banner, *Women in Modern America: A Brief History* [New York: Harcourt Brace Jovanovich, Inc., 1974], pp. 132-41 regarding this point).

27. Alice Hyneman Rhine, "The Work of Women's Clubs," *Forum,* December 1891, pp. 519-28; Julia Holmes Smith, "The Woman's Club as an Agent of Philanthropy," *Arena,* August 1892, pp. 382-84; Margaret Polson Murray, "Women's Clubs in America," *Living Age,* June 1900, p. 561; Trautman, "Protective Association," pp. 439-46; Edith Wetherill, "The Civic Club of Boston," *Municipal Affairs* 2 (September 1898): 480; Jane Addams, "Woman's Work for Chicago," *Municipal Affairs* 2 (September 1898): 502-8; McCluny, "Women's Work in Indianapolis," pp. 523-26; Mary M. Pierson, "What a Few Women in New London, Iowa, Have Accomplished," *American City* 8 (May 1913): 512-13; Sarah S. Platt Decker, "The Meaning of the Woman's Club Movement," *Annals of the American Academy of Political and Social Science* 28 (September 1906): 200; Mary Beard, *Women's Work in Municipalities* (New York: D. Appleton & Co., 1915).

28. David P. Thelen, *The New Citizenship: Origins of Progesssivism in Wisconsin, 1885-1900* (Columbia: University of Missouri Press, 1972), pp. 86-126.

29. Hester M. Poole, "Club Life in New York," *Arena,* August 1892, p. 369.

30. Breckinridge, *Women in the Twentieth Century,* p. 76.

31. Grace H. Wilson, *The Religious and Educational Philosophy of the Young Women's Christian Association* (New York: Columbia University Press, 1933), pp. 4-8.

32. Breckinridge, *Women in the Twentieth Century,* pp. 15-16; Rhine, "Work of Women's Clubs," p. 537.

33. Furer, "Women's Rights Movement," p. 293.

34. Blanc, *Condition of Women,* pp. 242-44, 253-54.

35. Gladys Boone, *The Women's Trade Union League* (New York: Columbia University Press, 1942), p. 44.

36. Breckinridge, *Women in the Twentieth Century,* p. 25; Frank Chapin Bray, "The National Consumer League," *Chautauquan,* June 1910, pp. 106-15.

37. Allen F. Davis, *Spearheads for Reform* (New York: Oxford University Press, 1967), p. 12. Davis offers an excellent study of the settlement house movement.

38. Ibid., pp. 33-35. Davis estimates that over 90 percent of the men and women who volunteered to work in the settlements had attended college.

39. *Daily Oklahoman,* May 12, 1894.

40. The 1898 estimate comes from Breckinridge, *Women in the Twentieth Century,* p. 21. Furer's estimate for that year was 500,000 ("Women's Rights Movement," p. 297), but that is out of line with later estimates from other sources and is probably incorrect. The 1902 estimate is from Cooley, "Future of the Woman's Club," p. 374, the 1905 from Decker, "Meaning of the Woman's Club Movement," p. 199, and the 1910 estimate from Wood, "The Woman's Club Movement," pp. 36-39.

41. Rhine, "Work of Women's Clubs," p. 522. Cooley, "Future of the Woman's Club," p. 374, also contended that the federation contained only a portion of the clubs in existence. See also "Best Thing Our Club Ever Did," pp. 156-57, for further confirmation.

42. *Progress and Achievement,* p. 23. Of the 726 mentioned, 333 were WCTU, 166 were women's clubs, 162 were Women's Relief Corps, 28 were suffrage, and the rest were assorted other organizations.

43. Irwin, *Angels and Amazons,* p. 230.

44. Cooley, "Future of the Woman's Club," pp. 374-75.

45. Martha E. D. White, "The Case of the Woman's Club," *Outlook,* June 25, 1898, p. 479.

46. Harbert Collection, "The New Cycle." Marital status was determined by the designation on the list as "Miss" or "Mrs."

47. Blanc, *Condition of Women,* p. 89; Mary Boyce, "The Club as an Ally to Higher Education," *Arena,* August 1892, pp. 379-83; May Wright Sewall, "The General Federation of Women's Clubs," *Arena,* August 1892, p. 365.

48. Harbert Collection, "Illinois Social Science Journal, February 1878," pp. 10-11.

49. Harbert Collection, manuscript notebooks containing list of leaders of National Household Economic Association (U 12 F4).

50. Harbert Collection, printed list of WCTU leaders, 1884.

51. Harbert Collection, address books belonging to Elizabeth Boynton Harbert. Book I (1870s or 1880s): Twenty-eight of the women were married and three were single. Book II (possibly early 1890s): Eighty-nine were married, twenty-three were single, and the conjugal status of twenty-four could not be determined. See also Sinclair, *The Better Half,* p. 237, who contends that most of the suffrage workers were married and mothers.

52. Granger, "Effect of Club Work in the South," p. 255; Ward, "The Influence of Women's Clubs," p. 206.

53. Burrell, *Complete Club Book,* p. 119; Olivia H. Danbar, "The City's Housekeepers," *Harper's Bazaar,* June 1909, pp. 594-96.

54. Rheta Childe Dorr, *What Eight Million Women Want* (Boston: Small,

Maynard & Co., 1910), p. 327.

55. Josephine Shaw Lowell, "Woman's Municipal League of New York City," *Municipal Affairs* 2 (September 1898): 465.

56. Helen M. Wood, "The Unquiet Sex," *Scribner's,* October 1897, p. 487.

57. Blanc, *Condition of Women,* pp. 43-45.

58. Watson, "Attitude of Typical Southern Woman to Clubs," p. 378.

59. "As to Woman's Clubs," *Atlantic,* January 1909, pp. 135-36.

60. Boyce, "Club as an Ally to Higher Education," p. 378. The depiction of the nineteenth century as the "woman's century" was found in other articles. See, for example, Wood, "The Unquiet Sex," p. 490, and Murray, "Women's Clubs in America," p. 561.

61. Decker, "The Meaning of the Woman's Club Movement," p. 204.

62. "The Best Thing Our Club Ever Did," p. 156.

63. Cooley, "Future of the Woman's Club," p. 377.

64. Breckinridge, *Women in the Twentieth Century,* pp. 24-25, 34-35, 39, 67.

6   Employment

> One has only to stand during the early morning hours in the waiting room of a station in a large city and observe the thousands of young working-women who arrive on every incoming train, to be impressed with the fact that much of the work of that great city is in the hands of these competent-looking young girls.[1]

The preceding observation, made in 1913, points to a major social and economic change that had its roots in the cities and towns of late nineteenth- and early twentieth-century America. For the first time, a significant number of middle-class women and girls ventured forth beyond their traditional sphere of the home and into the working world. That development was an important one, one that had a marked influence upon women's feelings of self-worth and their relationship with other members of their families.

Between 1870 and 1920 a growing army of women entered the working world. During the era, the overall female labor force increased by more than 63 percent. In 1870 only 14.7 percent of all females sixteen or older were employed. By 1920, 24 percent were working.[2] However, significant differences existed between the urban and rural sectors of the nation. For both the aggregate population and NWNP the percentage of wage-earning women was considerably higher in urban areas than in the countryside (Table 7). In addition, for both the aggregate population and NWNP, the difference between the percentage of women working in the two sectors appeared to increase over time[3] (Table 7).

TABLE 7. Percentage of Females, Ten Years or Older, Working in Urban and Rural Areas, Aggregate Population and Native Whites of Native-Born Parents, 1870-1920

	1870[a]	1880[a]	1890	1900	1910	1920
Aggregate population						
Urban	15.9	17.8	25.5	26.0	b	28.1
Rural	9.8	10.4	15.7	16.0	b	16.1
Percent urban greater than rural	62.2	71.2	62.4	62.5	—	74.5
Native whites of native-born parents						
Urban	c	c	17.7	d	b	25.3
Rural	c	c	10.7	d	b	14.1
Percent urban greater than rural	—	—	65.4	—	—	79.4

112

Table 7 continued

SOURCES: U.S., *Censuses, 1870-1920.*

NOTE: For 1870, 1880, 1900, and 1920, urban = cities of 25,000+. For 1890, urban had to be calculated on the basis of cities of 50,000+.

[a] For 1870 and 1880, employment data were available only for the total female population.

[b] Urban/rural female employment figures for native whites of native-born parents are not available for 1910, and the data for the aggregate population are a source of much dispute. The 1910 census was taken in April, which would tend to elevate the number working in seasonal, agricultural work, rather than in January as was done in 1920. Moreover, the 1910 census was the only one from the period that specifically instructed the census taker to make serious inquiry as to whether or not a woman was employed. Thus as Robert Smuts argues, the 1910 census may indeed be a more accurate count, but its comparability to other censuses is questionable. See Robert Smuts, "The Female Labor Force: A Case Study in the Interpretation of Historical Statistics," *Journal of the American Statistical Association* 55 (March 1960): 77-79. For a full discussion of the problems posed by the 1910 female labor force statistics, see the Smuts article cited previously, and John Durand, *The Labor Force in the United States, 1890-1960* (New York: Social Science Research Council, 1948); Oppenheimer, "Female Labor Force in the United States," pp. 2-5. Although not included in this table, the percentage of the aggregate, ten-or-older population working in 1910 in urban areas was 28.5 percent, whereas that in rural areas was 20.2 percent. See also, U.S., Department of Commerce, *Women in Gainful Occupations, 1870-1920.*

[c] Data for native whites of native-born parents were not available for 1870 or 1880.

[d] For 1900, data for native whites of native-born parents were only available for females sixteen or older in cities of 50,000+. For that year, the percentage working in urban areas was 19.2 percent and that in rural areas was 10.9 percent. Since these data are not comparable to those for other years, they have not been included in the table.

For both urban and rural areas, however, the percentage of employed NWNP women increased more sharply than did the overall percentage of employed women (Appendix A, Table 17). Indeed, the sharp increase between 1890 and 1920 in the percentage of employed NWNP women considerably narrowed the divergence between the percent working in the aggregate population and that working among NWNP. In 1890, the percentage of employed women in the aggregate population was greater than the percentage of NWNP who worked by 44.1 percent in urban areas and 46.7 percent in rural areas. By 1920 that difference had dropped to 11.1 percent and 14.2 percent respectively.

For females of all nativity and racial groups, the percentage of employed women was higher in urban than in rural areas. However, the overall percentage of women employed and the time period of entrance into the labor force varied considerably from group to group. In 1890, Black women had the highest percentage with jobs, followed by NWFP women, then FW women. NWNP women had the lowest percentage. In 1900, although the order of the groups in terms of percentage working stayed the same, NWNP women showed the biggest increase (Appendix A, Table 18).

In 1900 and 1920, the census distinguished between cities with a population of 100,000 or larger and all communities with a smaller population (including rural areas). NWNP women again showed the greatest percentage increase of any group, with the increase in cities of 100,000 or more people outstripping the gains in the lesser populated areas. Although the percentage of employed Black women remained higher than for other groups throughout the era, NWNP in larger cities experienced the most marked increases (Appendix A, Table 19). Indeed, by 1920 in cities of over 100,000 population, the gap between the percentage of NWNP and NWFP women who were employed had narrowed, and a considerably higher percentage of NWNP than FW women were in the labor force.

The factors that tended to draw women into the labor force probably differed from group to group. The degree of economic necessity, types of occupations available and acceptable, existing attitudes within the group regarding employment for women—all undoubtedly played a part in determining employment patterns. More detailed research is needed before a definitive analysis of the participation of different groups of women in the labor force can be offered. However, it is evident that although NWNP women tended to enter the work force later than did other racial and nativity groups, by 1920 in larger cities NWNP women had almost "caught up" with all other groups except Black women.

What was drawing such record numbers of NWNP women into the labor force? One important factor was the tremendous growth in white-collar positions, and to a lesser extent, professional employment. Between 1870 and 1920 the number of women in clerical positions rose dramatically.[4] One indicator of the growth in the clerical field was its treatment in the census. Prior to 1910, clerical occupations were included under the general category of trade and transportation. From 1910 on, a separate clerical category was used. In 1870 slightly more than 10,000 women, fewer than 1 percent of all women ten years or older in nonagricultural jobs, were employed in clerical occupations. In 1900 the number had risen to almost 400,000, or 9.1 percent of the nonagricultural female labor force. By 1920, 2 million women, or more than 25 percent of all women, ten years or older, in nonagricultural jobs worked in clerical positions.[5] During the same time period, the number of women in occupations designated as "professional" rose from a little less than 92,000 in 1870, 6.4 percent of the nonagricultural female labor force, to 400,000 (10 percent) in 1900, to almost 1 million, or 13.3 percent, by 1920.[6]

The burgeoning fields of white-collar and professional work were dominated by NWNP women. In 1890 those women, though making up only 34.7 percent of the total female work force, comprised 51 percent of all female clerical workers and 68 percent of all female professionals.[7] In 1920 NWNP women comprised 44.5 percent of the female work force, but more than 55 percent of all female clerical workers and 64.5 percent of all female professionals.[8] While the growth in white-collar and professional fields provided a new set of occupational opportunities for middle-class women, the availability of employment opportunities had to be coupled with the desire or need, and time to enter the working world.

Although most middle-class women married, and at an increasingly younger age, they entered into marriage with mixed feelings. On the one hand, society condoned marriage as the proper goal for women. Yet many women realized, and often verbalized, the limitations on independence that marriage would bring. In 1905 Margaret E. Sangster devoted her column in *Woman's Home Companion,* "Mrs. Sangster's Home Page," to the question "Shall Wives Earn Money?" She discussed the "hundreds of married women" who "look back with a tender regret at days before marriage," when they were self-supporting workingwomen. One married woman described by Sangster gave the following reasons for deciding to return to the business world. "I should greatly enjoy the work [and] I am weary of the daily grind [of housework]."[9] Employment, with the making of money and contacts that it brought, loomed as a desirable, if generally temporary option, to many women.

The same revolution in caring for the household that had provided the urban, middle-class housewife with a growing amount of free time, had also provided increased free time to her daughters. Numerous sources indicated an urban/rural dichotomy with respect to the time devoted by daughters to household chores. In the cities, daughters did not appear to help much with household work, and one father expressed his concern that homemaking skills were no longer being acquired by young women.[10] A number of urban women commented upon how little they had learned about cooking prior to marriage, and the *New Orleans Times Picayune* of January 1897 even had an advertisement for a cooking school for brides.[11] In contrast to city girls, daughters in the rural areas seemed uniformly to help around the home.[12]

A growing number of girls were obtaining lengthier and better educations and were thus more prepared to handle a wider range of jobs than had previously been the case. Educational opportunities for women expanded rapidly during the era. In part, this was but one segment of the more general growth in the nation's educational system, but it also indicated a shift in attitude regarding the propriety of education for women. During the decades following the Civil War, the secondary school system grew rapidly. From at least as early as 1890, females outnumbered males both in the overall student body and as graduates of the nation's high schools. Between 1890 and 1920, females comprised approximately 55 percent of all high school students and 60 percent of all high school graduates.[13] In 1880 women had comprised only 19.3 percent of those attending colleges, universities, and technical schools, but by 1910, 30.4 percent of those enrolled were women.[14]

In 1911, one author, writing about the "passing of the home daughter," spoke of a "restlessness" that was spreading throughout the "mighty middle class of American society," a restlessness characterized by young women's unwillingness to stay at home and await marriage but instead to go out and seek the independence of a career.[15] Although many of those young women probably planned ultimately to marry, the growing number of white-collar and professional jobs provided a desirable and respectable alternative to staying at home.

The question of what makes a particular occupation respectable in the eyes of society, and another one not, is difficult to answer. During the late nineteenth century, many opponents of employment for women cited the constant contact with men and the possibility of "illicit liaisons." Sales work, at least at its inception, was considered suspect. In his classic study of New York in the late 1860s, George Ellington described the tendency of the "dollar stores" to hire attractive young women in those stores frequented by men, with the suggestion that many affairs started at such stores.[16] Later authors, although pointing to the attempt of department store owners to provide better working conditions for their employees, reaffirmed the problem facing saleswomen regarding advances from men. One store even hired a detective to protect its female employees from "mashers."[17]

Proponents of employment for women felt obliged to address themselves to the quesiton of the morality of the workingwoman. Carroll Wright, the first U.S. Commissioner of Labor, asserted in his 1884 study, *The Working Girls of Boston,* that most workingwomen were respectable. Similarly, Helen Campbell in 1891 felt obliged to assure her readers that most workingwomen were not prostitutes.[18]

Office work, in particular, and telephone work to a lesser extent provided what could be considered an ideal employment opportunity for apt, middle-class young women. The pay for office work was relatively high, ranging from $5 to $8 per week for starting typists up to $25 to $30 for experienced stenographers. Pay for telephone operators was considerably lower, with $8 being about the top salary. Despite the lower wages for telephone operators, an effort was made to assure a comfortable work setting: A dining room, a reading room, and an infirmary were sometimes provided.[19] Reasonable working hours, good pay, at least for office work, generally pleasant working conditions, and nonstrenuous activity, made such work acceptable to middle-class morality. Critics of sales work, who viewed its low wages and loose supervision as a very real threat to a woman's reputation, seemed to express less concern that office employment might lead a young woman into "sin," despite the obvious interaction with males. One author in 1890 aptly illustrated the high acceptability of clerical work when she asserted that young ladies who wanted to earn their own living could find no more "agreeable or profitable" employment than shorthand or typewriting.[20] That sentiment was echoed by later authors. Eleanor Martin and Margaret Post in their 1914 book,

Vocations for the Trained Woman, contended that secretarial work was "dignified and not so physically tiring as teaching."[21] In 1919 Helen C. Hoerle and Florence B. Saltzberg assured their readers of *The Girl and the Job* that "next to teaching, stenography may be said to be the most generally acceptable occupation for girls. . . . It is considered respectable and ladylike."[22]

Prior to the late nineteenth century, men had dominated office work. The question of why employers began to hire women for clerical and telephone work will require more detailed studies to provide a definitive answer. Some employers, at least, seemed to believe that young women made much more satisfactory workers than did young men. One author pointed out how he had no trouble placing young women he had trained; they "could readily supplant inefficient office boys and young men who depended upon their sex to hold their own as against women of whatever qualification."[23] Most employers who hired women for office work explained their preference with reasons such as neatness, quickness, clear handwriting, and precision.[24] Telephone officials contended that young men had originally been used but they were not always "civil or accurate." Young women were "reluctantly" tried, and their politeness and accuracy assured the female domination of the field.[25] For both office and telephone work, the fact that women workers received lower wages was most probably a significant factor in their being hired. An 1895 study put forth by the commissioner of labor revealed that male stenographers in a life insurance firm averaged $27.65 a week. For women stenographers, the average weekly salary was $13.46. The situation was similar for telephone work, where the men averaged $12 a week, whereas the women made only $6.22.[26]

With each passing decade, the proportion of women in the clerical field grew: 2.3 percent in 1870, 4.4 percent in 1880, 16.4 percent in 1890, 25.4 percent in 1900, and 45.7 percent in 1920.[27] The growing importance and acceptability of clerical work for women was reflected in the proliferation of technical schools and courses geared to train office workers, especially stenographers and typists. In the 1880s, classes in stenography, typing, and bookkeeping opened at the New York City YWCA and Cooper Union, and by 1900 clerical courses had attracted more than 19,000 girls in the public schools and 24,000 in commercial and business schools.[28]

Although the most impressive increases in employment opportunities for middle-class women during the era came in the clerical field, signifi-

cant growth also appeared in other areas. Between 1870 and 1920, while
the total number of women working rose almost 400 percent, the number
of women in the major professions grew from 91,963 to 992,638, an increase of more than 900 percent. Those employed as teachers increased
from 84,047 to 652,500; the number employed as "physicians, surgeons,
etc." rose from 527 to 16,784; and the number working as lawyers, judges,
notaries, and the like jumped from 5 to more than 3,000. Other professional occupations that saw large gains during the era included nursing,
which grew in membership from 11,119 to 143,664 between 1900 and
1920, and library work, which rose from 3,122 to 14,714 during the
same time period.[29]

During the late nineteenth and early twentieth centuries, an important
pattern of female employment became firmly established. On the one
hand, a growing number of middle-class women were entering a wider
variety of occupations. On the other hand, the vast majority of women
employed in white-collar and professional occupations were increasingly
concentrated in clerical work. In 1900, 23 percent of all such women
were in clerical occupations, but by 1920 the concentration had risen to
almost 50 percent.[30]

The growing concentration of women in clerical work can be accounted
for by a phenomenal expansion of jobs in that occupational field. Between 1900 and 1920 the percentage of females ten or older employed
in nonagricultural pursuits increased by more than 3 million, a rise of 72
percent (Appendix A, Table 20). During the same time period, a little
more than 1.5 million women entered clerical occupations. The growth
in the clerical component of the female labor force was the equivalent of
almost one out of every two women entering the labor force between
1900 and 1920 going into a clerical job. Although the number of women
employed as servants, waitresses, or the like declined by 72,000 during
the same period of time, that small decline of about 5 percent could in
no way explain the tremendous increase in the clerical sector. The growth
of the clerical field did not appear to come at the expense of the servant
sector, but came instead as a consequence of a continued growth in the
female labor force, in general, and an especially pronounced increase in
office work.

During the entire period studied, the female labor force was composed
primarily of young, single women. However, significant shifts in both the
age composition and marital status of members of the female labor force

did occur. Between 1890 and 1920, although the female work force remained a youthful one, the proportion of those between sixteen and twenty-four declined, and the proportion of those between twenty-five and forty-four rose. In 1890, 49.9 percent of all female workers fifteen or older were between the ages of fifteen and twenty-four. By 1920 only 39.3 percent of those sixteen or older were in the sixteen- to twenty-four-year-old age bracket. During the same period, the proportion of the female labor force between twenty-five and forty-four years of age rose from 33.7 percent to 41.7 percent of the total.[31]

The decrease in the percentage that sixteen to twenty-four year olds were of the sixteen-or-older female labor force may have been due to a decline in the proportion of females in that age group. Between 1900 and 1920, there was a 13.2 percent decrease in the proportion that females sixteen to twenty-four were of all females sixteen or older (Appendix A, Table 21). During the same time period, the proportion that females sixteen to twenty-four were of all sixteen or older employed females declined by 11.1 percent. But the shifting age composition of the female labor force was not solely a product of the changing age structure of the female population. Between 1890 and 1920 the percentage distribution that females twenty-five to forty-four were of all sixteen-or-older females rose by only 5.2 percent. The corresponding increase for employed females twenty-five to forty-four was 23.7 percent. An aging of the female labor force was occurring: Either women were staying on longer in their jobs or more older women were entering the working world, or both.[32]

Between 1900 and 1920, except for the age group that was sixty-five or older, the female labor force of both the aggregate population and NWNP showed continued growth (Appendix A, Table 22). However, significant differences existed between the patterns of growth exhibited by the two groups. Although overall the growth shown by the NWNP female labor force was greater than that of the aggregate population, the largest increases for NWNP occurred in the age groups sixteen to twenty-four and twenty-five to forty-four, with comparatively little growth among forty-five to sixty-four year olds. In contrast, the female labor force of the aggregate population increased more slowly, and all age groups, except for those sixty-five or older, showed about the same rate of growth (Appendix A, Table 22).

As women entered the working world, one would expect first to see the younger women, the very group that would be least bound by old traditions. Once having joined the labor force, a certain percentage of women would remain. Thus a gradual "aging" of the female labor force would occur.[33]

As was the case for the female labor force in general, the occupations of middle-class women were dominated by the young. Between 1890 and 1920, however, with respect to the professional categories the percentage of fifteen to twenty-four year olds declined and that of twenty-five to sixty-four year olds increased (Appendix A, Table 23).

Not only was the female labor force predominantly youthful, it was also predominantly single. In both 1890 and 1900, almost 70 percent of the total number of employed females ten or older were single. Although married women always composed a smaller percentage of the female labor force than did single women, the proportion of married women in the female work force did increase in the early twentieth century. In 1890, 12.1 percent of all women sixteen or older, and employed in nonagricultural work, were married. In 1900, 13.3 percent were married. By 1910 the percentage of married women had jumped to 19.7 percent, and in 1920 it rose to 21.2 percent.[34] Moreover, between 1890 and 1920, the proportion of married women who worked almost doubled for the aggregate population and more than doubled for NWNP (Appendix A, Table 24).

For all age groups in both the aggregate population and for NWNP, the percentage of employed, married women increased. Among the former, the percentage of employed, married women increased at about the same rate for all age groups, but for the latter the increase was most pronounced among those under forty-five (Appendix A, Table 25).

A variety of factors appeared to be involved with increasing the proportion of married women in the labor force during the early twentieth century. As with the female labor force in general, patterns of employment of married women varied according to social class. The employment patterns reflected differences in economic need, different attitudes toward the propriety of work for married women, and types of available jobs.[35]

For working-class women, the economic survival of the family often necessitated the wife's employment. Such women generally had odious jobs, and retirement from the working world often came as soon as was economically feasible. In addition, some women believed that jobs should be left to those women who needed the money to survive.[36] Economic necessity had probably propelled working-class married women into the working world at an earlier date than their middle-class counterparts. In addition, in 1890, domestic service and mill and factory work comprised more than 60 percent of all the nonagricultural jobs held by women.[37] Such jobs tended not to appeal to middle-class women. By 1920 the tremendous increase in white-collar occupations, which had helped to draw so many single, middle-class women into the labor force, was probably also influential in attracting a growing number of married, middle-class women.

Among the middle class, actual and aspiring, economic factors also were important in drawing married women into the working world. A working wife meant that marriage need not be delayed until the husband's wages alone could support a family.[38] In particular, what seemed to prompt employment for at least some middle-class, married women was the desire for a higher standard of living. Anna Steele Richardson, writing in 1920 of "The Lure of the Double Salary," described the warning given to a young woman about to be married.

> Her cousin [warned] "now Marjorie, hang on to your job.
> You don't see me wearing silk stockings and filet collars
> these days. Of course I wouldn't give up Junior for any salary
> on earth, but if I had it to do over again, I'd stay in the office
> at least two years and get something ahead."[39]

Another woman began working to put her husband through medical school and decided to continue work after the husband began his medical practice. Since his starting income was low, her employment gave them "the opportunity and means . . . to enjoy the good things of life and a few of its luxuries."[40]

The early twentieth-century, urban trend toward younger marriages was quite possibly related to the increased presence of married women in the labor force. A wife's employment often made an earlier marriage possible. In addition, the growing number of young, married women might have encouraged employers to keep their female workers on even after they married. One woman described how her boss urged her to continue working after she had married. "It had taken several years to transform her from a raw business-school graduate to an efficient personal secretary. He preferred raising her salary to training a new girl."[41] For many married women, employment was maintained only until the arrival of the first child. Employment, however, often meant a decision to delay having children.[42]

For middle-class, married women, an important motivating factor for maintaining or retaking a job often was the desire for economic independence. One woman, returning to work after several years of marriage and two children, asserted, "I mean to take up my business life again and secure a measure of independence."[43]

Noneconomic factors also played a role in drawing the middle-class, married woman into the working world. In 1905, Margaret Sangster in her *Woman's Home Companion* column discussed a woman's need to have interests beyond the home.

If a woman can take a job *without detriment to or neglect of her family* and her duty, should she not take some share in the larger interests outside the home, the interests that impart flavor and zest to life and keep a woman young and fresh, because they are so agreeable and absorbing that they take her out of herself and lift her from the danger of stagnation?[44]

The idea that a woman who limited herself to the domestic sphere would grow narrow and uninteresting was reiterated throughout the era. One author even addressed herself to the problems that had developed because the domestic duties of the wife had, in reality, diminished. Fewer children and more household conveniences meant a greater amount of free time for most middle-class women. She urged her readers not to cut themselves off from contact with the working world, warning of the development of "the woman of capability, with her hands empty from the time she is forty."[45]

Related to the idea of the narrowness of a solely domestic existence was the attitude that the working world offered a variety of interesting and worthwhile experiences. One woman spoke of the "keen pleasure" her job gave her.[46] Another described her years spent in the business world as "delightful."[47]

Thus between 1890 and 1920, a number of factors combined to draw more married women into the working world. Although the percentage of married women in the labor force rose sharply between 1890 and 1920, single women still predominated (Appendix A, Table 26). For women who wished to pursue a career, one which they did not wish to give up, the societal prohibitions against employment for married women posed a difficult dilemma. In the mid-1890s Martha Rayne, author of *What Can*

a Woman Do, surveyed the marital status of female physicians. Four
hundred seventy questionnaires were sent out. Seventy-five percent of the
respondents were single.[48] Although some women did manage to combine
a professional career with marriage, the majority of women who pursued
careers were single.

Young women in increasing numbers appeared to fill the myriad of
jobs that were opening in cities and towns across the nation. Where did
they come from? Were they already urban residents, or were they drawn
from the countryside by the prospects of a better, or at least a less isolated,
life in the city? Observers from the era commented upon the migration
from countryside to city of young women who were seeking employment.
The United States Department of Census speculated that the "excess of
female workers, especially in the younger age groups, may be due to the
cityward migration of females seeking work."[49] Opportunities for outside
employment in the rural areas were generally limited to domestic work
or teaching. In contrast, the cities offered a wide assortment of occupations with an expanding number of positions. Thus it was not surprising
to find young, rural women drawn to the city because of greater job possibilities. In addition, the city offered a host of other desirable options:
social contact, escape from the isolation of the farm, and a variety of
places for recreation.

In 1900 and 1920, the United States censuses reported upon the distribution, by family relationship, of workingwomen in selected, large
cities.[50] The fact that more than one-third of the employed white women
of native-born parents were either boarding or living with relatives other
than parents at least suggested the presence of newcomers to the cities.
It must be remembered that some city women would have chosen to
board rather than to run their own homes, so that the percentage of
women boarding cannot be equated with the percentage of rural migrants.[51]
But the highest percentage of workingwomen, at least in the larger cities,
seemed to have come from the cities themselves.

In both 1900 and 1920 the vast majority of working girls and women
lived at home, many of them with their fathers or mothers. In 1884 Carroll
D. Wright conducted a survey among the working girls of Boston and found
that 58 percent lived at home with their parents.[52] In fact, for 1900 and
1920, in the white-collar occupations and the major professional occupation, teaching, slightly more than half of the women lived at home with
either father or mother (Appendix A, Tables 27 and 28).

Within the cities and towns of late nineteenth- and early twentieth-century America, significant numbers of middle-class women began to enter the working world. As with fertility and marriage patterns, the question arises as to the existence of similarities or differences in female employment patterns among cities. Did factors such as city size, economic function, or sex ratio tend to cause significant divergence, or did cities tend to be much alike in the way they affected women's propensity to enter the working world?

Population size, one of the major differentiators among cities, appeared to bear little relationship to the percentage of employed women (Appendix A, Table 29). Only for 1920 was there a slight, positive association between city size and the percentage of women employed.[53] What appeared to exist was a large gap between urban and rural areas, with little differentiation between cities of different sizes.[54] However, as was pointed out in the discussion regarding female marriage and fertility rates, a size-related gradation may have existed below a population of 25,000, whereas over 25,000 city size did not noticeably affect the percentage of women employed.

In contrast to size, the economic function of a city was strongly related to the percentage of women working.[55] As the percentage of the total labor force engaged in manufacturing and mechanical occupations increased, so did the percentage of women employed (Table 8). Cities with a higher proportion of their labor force engaged in trade and transportation occupations showed the opposite pattern: As the percentage in trade and transportation jobs grew, the percentage of employed women dropped. And as can be seen for 1920, both trade and transportation occupations were negatively related to the percentage of women who worked (Table 8). For those cities that inclined toward manufacturing and mechanical occupations and for those more heavily trade and transportation oriented, the strength of their respective correlations with the percentage of women employed appeared to diminish between 1870 and 1920 (Table 8).

A definitive analysis of why a city's economic function appeared to be related to the proportion of employed women cannot be put forth at this time. However, tentative explanations, which relate to the kind of employment opportunities for women in the cities, and the change in opportunities with time, can be posited. For the 1870-1920 time period, cities that inclined most heavily toward either trade and transportation or manufacturing and mechanical occupations were examined. The top 10 percent in

TABLE 8. Correlation Between Economic Function and Percentage of Women Employed, Aggregate Population and Native Whites of Native-Born Parents, 1870-1920

	TRADE AND TRANSPORTATION VS. PERCENT EMPLOYED		MANUFACTURING AND MECHANICAL VS. PERCENT EMPLOYED	
	Agg	*NWNP*	*Agg*	*NWNP*
1870[b]	$r = -0.54$[f] $N = 49$	a	$r = 0.37$[e] $N = 49$	a
1880[b]	$r = -0.49$[f] $N = 50$	a	$r = 0.35$[e] $N = 50$	a
1890[c]	$r = -0.37$[e] $N = 58$	$r = -0.41$[e] $N = 58$	$r = 0.30$[e] $N = 58$	$r = 0.60$[f] $N = 58$
1900	$r = -0.21$[e] $N = 158$	$r = -0.28$[d,e] $N = 79$	$r = 0.04$ $N = 158$	$r = 0.54$[d,f] $N = 79$
1920	Trade $r = 0.04$ $N = 285$ Transp. $r = -0.15$[e] $N = 285$	Trade $r = -0.25$[f] $N = 285$ Transp. $r = -0.34$[f] $N = 285$	$r = 0.04$ $N = 285$	$r = 0.33$[f] $N = 285$

Table 8 continued

SOURCES: U.S., *Censuses, 1870-1920.*

NOTE: Percentage of employed women and percentage of the total labor force in manufacturing and mechanical occupations and trade and transportation ones were computed for each city for each census year. The correlation between economic function (i.e., percent of total labor force in manufacturing and mechanical or trade and transportation) was then calculated. Unless otherwise indicated, calculations were made on the basis of all cities 25,000+. Agg = Aggregate population. NWNP = Native whites of native-born parents. Transp. = Transportation. r = the correlation coefficient; N = the number of observations.

[a]Data not given.

[b]In 1870 and 1880, the percentage of women employed was calculated on the basis of all females. For all other years (except 1900), calculations were made on the basis of females 10+. For 1880, data were available for selected (by census) cities of 25,000+.

[c]In 1890, data given for cities of 50,000+.

[d]In 1900, data for native whites of native-born parents were given for females sixteen or older in cities of 50,000+.

[e]Significant at the 0.01 level.

[f]Significant at the 0.001 level.

each category were chosen from each census year. Each city included in
the sample for a census year met the cutoff criteria for either strong manufacturing and mechanical or strong trade and transportation for that
particular year (Table 9).

Cities with a larger proportion of their total labor force in manufacturing
and mechanical occupations had a greater percentage of employed women
than did cities that inclined toward trade and transportation occupations
(Table 9). Between 1870 and 1920 the difference in the percentage of
workingwomen between the two types of cities declined (Table 9). Significant changes occurring in the kinds of employment opportunities available
to women appeared to be related to the diminishing difference between
the two types of cities.

Between 1870 and 1920 important alterations occurred in the occupational structure of the female labor force. In 1870 domestic work had
provided more than 60 percent of the jobs to women employed in nonagricultural occupations. By 1890 that proportion had dropped to 40.3
percent. Between 1870 and 1890, mill and factory work comprised the
only other sizable occupational category for women workers: 17.6 percent in 1870 and 20.3 percent in 1890. In contrast, white-collar occupations (clerical work plus the professions) contributed only 7.2 percent in
1870 and 13.5 percent in 1890. By 1920 substantial restructuring had
occurred. The proportion in domestic work had dropped to 18.2 percent.
A dramatic increase had come in the white-collar category, which had
jumped to include 38.9 percent of all women employed in nonagricultural
occupations. The percentage in factory and millwork remained virtually
unchanged, inching up slightly to 23.8 percent.[56]

Prior to 1900, strong manufacturing and mechanical cities appeared
to have a distinct advantage over trade and transportation cities in the
types of occupational options open to women. Jobs in mills and factories
as well as jobs in domestic service were available in manufacturing and
mechanical cities. Not surprisingly, such cities had a much higher proportion of employed females engaged in manufacturing occupations than
was the case in trade and transportation cities, where domestic service
provided jobs to the highest percentage of women (Table 9).

The explosive growth in the number of white-collar occupations that
occurred between 1900 and 1920 appeared to be especially important to
trade and transportation cities, where an entire new set of jobs other than
domestic work became available to women. It was as if trade and trans-

portation cities had been "skipped over" at the time when the factory jobs in the manufacturing and mechanical cities opened up a new field of employment to women. With the coming of large numbers of white-collar positions, the trade and transportation cities began to catch up. As a greater number of women in trade and transportation cities were drawn into the labor force, the negative relationship between cities oriented toward trade and transportation occupations and the percentage of women employed declined (Table 8). Conversely, as cities inclining toward manufacturing and mechanical jobs lost their initial advantage with respect to female employment, the positive association between percentage manufacturing and mechanical and the percentage of women employed also declined. As was discussed in Chapter 3, changes in employment opportunities for women in cities with differing types of economic activity tended to be reflected in marriage and fertility patterns.

As was seen in Table 8, the positive relationship between cities with a higher proportion of manufacturing and mechanical jobs and the percentage of women employed was stronger for NWNP than for the aggregate population. The continued stronger correlation for NWNP women may have been related to an increase in cities that tended toward heavy rather than light industry.

In 1870 through 1900, the majority of those cities with a high percentage of their total labor force in manufacturing and mechanical occupations were light-industry cities such as Woonsocket, Lowell, Lynn, and Pawtucket. By 1920, although the light-industry towns were still well represented, more heavy-industry cities had joined the list of strong manufacturing and mechanical cities. Included among the heavy-industry cities were a number of iron- and steel-producing cities such as Racine, Scranton, Chester, Johnstown, and East Chicago. The inclusion of heavy-industry cities in the roster of strong manufacturing and mechanical cities was probably reflected in the higher proportion of men found in such cities in 1920 (Appendix A, Table 30).

A city that had heavy rather than light industry probably had fewer manufacturing jobs for women, and at least after 1900, proportionally more white-collar occupations. Compare Lowell, which in 1920 had 68 percent of its female work force in manufacturing occupations and only 22.5 percent in white-collar jobs, with Johnstown, where the corresponding percentages were 14 percent and 60.3 percent. In Lowell the major industry was textiles, whereas in Johnstown it was steel. For NWNP women, more

TABLE 9. Certain Differences Between Strong Trade and Transportation Cities and Strong Manufacturing and Mechanical Cities, 1870-1920

	1870	1880	1890	1900	1920
Percent employed					
Agg					
Strong M&M	22.8	24.1	29.3	29.0	31.1
Strong T&T	12.1	15.0	22.8	22.7	25.3
Percent M&M greater than T&T	88.4	60.7	28.5	27.8	22.9
NWNP					
Strong M&M	a	a	21.7	24.2	29.7
Strong T&T	a	a	17.2	19.4	25.7
Percent M&M greater than T&T	—	—	26.1	24.7	15.6
Percent women employed as servants					
Strong M&M	b	18.8	20.9	16.4	6.1
Strong T&T	b	41.8	38.2	26.1	13.8
Percent T&T greater than M&M	—	122.3	82.8	59.1	126.2

130

Table 9 continued

Percent women employed in manufacturing
and mechanical jobs

Strong M&M	52.8	67.7	58.1	55.7	54.8
Strong T&T	19.5	35.1	27.5	26.4	13.9
Percent M&M greater than T&T	170.8	92.9	111.3	111.0	294.2

Percent women in white-collar jobs[c]

Strong M&M	b	9.6	17.4	23.5	31.1
Strong T&T	b	16.9	26.2	36.2	52.8
Percent T&T greater than M&M	—	76.0	50.6	54.0	69.8

SOURCES: U.S., *Censuses, 1870-1920.*

NOTE: Sample cities were selected according to the following criteria. The cutoff for those cities considered to be strong trade and transportation was 25.7 percent in 1870 ($N = 8$); 26.3 percent in 1880 ($N = 10$); 29.7 percent in 1890 ($N = 12$); 32.3 percent in 1900 ($N = 34$); and 30.0 percent in 1920 ($N = 29$). For strong manufacturing and mechanical cities, the cutoffs were as follows: 1870, 55.2 percent ($N = 8$); 1880, 50.3 percent ($N = 10$); 1890, 47 percent ($N = 12$); 1900, 51 percent ($N = 30$); and 1920, 63.1 percent ($N = 33$). Agg = Aggregate population; NWNP = Native whites of native-born parents. M&M = Manufacturing and Mechanical; T&T = Trade and Transportation.

[a]Data not available.

[b]Incomplete data.

[c]White-collar occupations = professional, clerical, hotel keepers, nurses, restaurant keepers, agents, bankers, merchants, bank officials, saleswomen, telephone operators, and miscellaneous appropriate categories.

131

of whom gravitated toward white-collar occupations, the comparative decline in light-industry, strong manufacturing and mechanical cities was
probably not as significant as for the aggregate population. Thus the increase in white-collar occupations appeared to be related both to a reduction in the negative relationship between cities with a high proportion of
their labor force in trade and transportation jobs and the percentage of
employed women, and the more gradual decline in the positive correlation
between cities with a high manufacturing and mechanical component and
the percentage of employed NWNP women.

As was the case with marriage and fertility, a city's sex ratio was closely
related to women's employment patterns. A strong and significant negative
association prevailed throughout the era between sex ratio and the percentage of employed women for both the aggregate population and
NWNP (Table 10). The evidence suggests that the tendency for women
to seek employment was strongly related to the availability of men and
therefore the possibility of marriage. The correlation, however, was not
nearly as strong for NWNP women as it was for the aggregate population.
Indeed, NWNP women, those women who had the greatest chance of
finding themselves in a relatively interesting and pleasant occupation,
would most likely consciously have decided to seek employment for the
job itself, rather than having had financial necessity push them into an
odious job because marriage was not available.[57]

Throughout the era a sharp separation existed between woman's traditional domestic role and her newly developing one in the working world.
A graphic illustration of that demarcation appeared in the relationship
between marital status and childbearing and employment. Among cities,
there was a strong and significant negative relationship between the percentage of women married and the percentage of women employed, while
between the percentage of single women and the percentage of women
working the relationship was strong and positive[58] (Appendix A, Table 31).

Given the strong, negative association between marriage and employment, the relationship between employment and fertility also was predict-
ably negative. For all of the years studied and for both the aggregate population and NWNP, the negative relationship between the percentage of
employed women and the child/woman ratio remained strong and highly
significant[59] (Appendix A, Table 32).

Thus, for the most part, a separation existed between employment for
women and the pursuit of the more traditional roles of wife and mother.

TABLE 10. Correlation Between Sex Ratio and the Percentage of
Employed Women in Urban Areas, Aggregate Population
and Native Whites of Native-Born Parents, 1870-1920

	Aggregate Population	Native Whites of Native-Born Parents
1870	$r = -0.54^d$, $N = 49$	[a]
1880[e]	$r = -0.46^d$, $N = 50$	[a]
1890[b]	$r = -0.47^d$, $N = 58$	$r = -0.20$, $N = 58$
1900	$r = -0.44^d$, $N = 158$	[c]
1910	$r = -0.54^d$, $N = 231$	[a]
1920	$r = -0.42^d$, $N = 285$	$r = -0.23^d$, $N = 285$

SOURCES: U.S., *Censuses, 1870-1920*.

NOTE: Percentage of women working and sex ratio was calculated for each city
for each census year. Correlations then were computed. Unless otherwise indicated
calculations were made on the basis of all cities, 25,000+. In 1870 and 1880, the
percentage of employed women was calculated on the basis of all females, and sex
ratio was calculated on the basis of all males and females. For later years, calculations regarding employment were made on the basis of females ten or older, and
sex ratio was calculated on the basis of males and females fifteen or older. r = the
correlation coefficient; N = the number of observations.

[a] Data not given.

[b] In 1890, data available for cities of 50,000+.

[c] In 1900, data regarding employment of native white women of native-born
parents were available only for females sixteen or older in cities of 50,000+. No
correlation was found between sex ratio and percentage employed.

[d] Significant at the 0.001 level.

[e] For 1880, data were available for selected (by census) cities of 25,000+.

Despite an increase in the proportion of older women and married women
who worked, the female labor force of the late nineteenth and early twentieth centuries remained predominantly single and young.

As more and more women joined the working world, opposition to such
a development grew. Outside employment differed in significant ways from
the traditional work that women had long performed within the context
of the family. It removed women from the protective pale of the home
where each member's work had had its value, yet where the structure of
the family hierarchy had remained unthreatened. Volunteer work, although

it took women outside of the home, was less threatening than employment because it was nonremunerative. The structure and functioning of the mid-nineteenth century, middle-class family was predicated upon the dependence of women. Outside employment meant that a woman, too, could derive status and recognition from her occupation and thus the husband's high position in the family hierarchy could be challenged.[60] Thus, not surprisingly, the strongest opposition to employment for women was leveled against employment for married women. Work for single women, however, also encountered unfavorable reactions.

Even during the mid-nineteenth century, at the height of the "Cult of True Womanhood," a limited number of women had been employed: It had been considered acceptable, if unfortunate, for "gentlewomen in reduced circumstances" to support themselves. However, if they wished to stay within the bounds of respectability, the options open to such women were rather carefully prescribed and generally limited to occupations such as opening boardinghouses; managing stores; especially millinery, fancy goods, or candy shops; or becoming teachers.[61] Working because it was an economic necessity had long been the lot of poorer women whose wages were essential for the survival of their families. The idea of women from middle-class homes working because they wanted to rather than because they had to was a new, and for many, unsettling development.

Not surprisingly, precisely during the time period when large numbers of middle-class women began to enter the labor force, the loudest hue and cry against employment for women appeared. Arguments of all kinds emerged: Working was unhealthy, it could deplete a woman's strength and adversely affect her ability to bear children, and it put her in situations in which her virtue could be compromised.[62] All of the arguments had a grain of truth. Many women worked in dismal, unhealthy surroundings: long hours, poor ventilation, inadequate heat in the winter and excessive heat in the summer. Low wages undoubtedly led some working girls and women to turn to prostitution. However, for the white-collar and professional occupations that middle-class women were entering, oppressively long hours and unhealthy working conditions were probably much less of a problem than was the case for blue-collar or unskilled female workers.[63] In addition, the wages in the white-collar and professional occupations generally were relatively high. An 1898 study revealed that starting typists averaged $5 to $8 a week and skilled stenographers received $25 to $30. Librarians averaged $50 to $75 a month, teachers in New York $50 a month, and trained nurses $100. The wages of factory workers varied greatly, but the highest monthly salary averaged around $40 to $50 for the most skilled, with the least skilled making less than $25 a month.[64]

The heart of the opposition to employment for middle-class girls and women apparently rested on the independence that it could bring; both advocates and foes of work for women emphasized that point. One author wrote of the tendency among middle-class, young women to seek out the independence of careers. Another writer described "a new thing under the sun, an awakening of the desire for economic independence." Yet another worried that work would make women too independent, too conscious of themselves, and unwilling to give up the contacts and excitement of urban employment for marriage.[65] A woman capable of providing her own livelihood did not need to view marriage as her only means for support. She could marry if and when she pleased. Even if societal opposition to combining marriage with employment were too strong to combat, she did not need to stay trapped within a tormented marriage as her only means of support. In short, the idea of a woman who was capable of supporting herself was antithetical to the idea of a woman who was protected, dependent, and subservient.

Clearly woman's emergence from the home into the working world came with a struggle. The myriad of articles debating her nature, her sphere, the attempts to glorify her traditional role within the home, all indicated the upheaval that was occurring.[66] In earlier ages, few women had had the time or energy to think of undertaking more than the traditional domestic functions. With few alternatives available, little question regarding fulfilling one's "proper role" existed.

With the new options that were opening up for women in the cities and towns of late nineteenth- and early twentieth-century America came a dilemma: a conflict between the demands to fulfill, above all, the roles of wife and mother, and the growing desire to play an active part in the "outside" world. On the one hand, throughout the nineteenth century, as woman's traditional functions within the home had contracted, the emphasis upon her importance vis-à-vis the nurturing and "shaping" of good children had grown. Moreover, since a man's serving as the sole breadwinner in the family became a status symbol, employment for a woman, especially a wife, posed a threat to the status of all members of the family.[67] On the other hand, many women chafed under the limitations and dependence of a strictly home-centered life and longed for the variety and independence that a career could bring.

In a book published in the early 1920s, Lorine Pruette documented the "home vs. career" conflict. In a series of interviews with more than three hundred girls, most of them from New York City or Chattanooga, Pruette found that although 61 percent of the girls listed white-collar or professional occupations as goals, if they were forced to choose between home and career, the home-centered life won. Pruette found that the "home woman" remained the ideal, but since the more immediate rewards went to the career woman, a conflict developed.[68]

The tension that women felt because of the contradictory role demands was clearly indicated by the reassurances they offered regarding the positive relationship between outside involvement and family life. Those who advocated careers for women justified their position on the grounds that employment allowed an unmarried woman the economic independence to choose a husband wisely, whereas for the married woman a career permitted "growth," a sense of personal fulfillment, and thus a greater satisfaction within the marriage.[69]

Increased employment opportunities for women in urban areas appeared to be one factor in the rising tide of divorce during the late nineteenth and early twentieth century. Writing in 1909, sociologist Edward Alsworth Ross concluded that "it is safe to say that the majority of [divorces] would not be sought but for the access of women to the industrial field. . . . More and more we live in cities, and the city gives the woman her chance."[70]

Between 1870 and 1890, although the frequency of divorce was greater in urban than in rural areas, the rate of increase in the two sectors was about the same for the total United States and greater in the rural sectors of some of the regions (Appendix A, Table 33). However, a substantially greater number of divorced women resided in urban than in rural areas, suggesting that cities probably offered a more comfortable milieu for divorced women (Appendix A, Table 34). Moreover, in sharp contrast to the divorce rate, the percentage of divorced women residing in urban areas was, for the most part, growing more rapidly than the percentage in the rural sector (Appendix A, Table 35). In fact, the general trend was toward a growing divergence between urban and rural areas with respect to the proportion of divorced women who lived in each sector (Appendix A, Table 36).

Rural women possibly had a greater tendency to hide the fact that they were divorced than did urban women. Divorced women in rural areas also might have tended to remarry more quickly than their urban counterparts. Unless one or both of those possibilities grew in importance between 1890 and 1920, it appears likely that for divorced women the tendency was to gravitate toward the city. Thus although urban life itself did not seem exclusively to predispose its female inhabitants toward a trip to the divorce court, the presence of cities, cities that offered employment opportunities, simpler housing, a degree of anonymity, in short an "out" from an unwanted marriage, seemed to be an important factor.

Alimony statistics also seemed to support the idea of a relationship between employment possibilities and the increasing number of divorces. During the late nineteenth and early twentieth centuries, the majority of divorces were granted to the wife, with the percentage increasing only slightly during a sixty-year period. Between 1867 and 1871, 64.5 percent of all divorces were granted to the wife. In 1916 the percentage stood at 68.9 percent.[71] Between 1887 and 1906 only a small percentage of wives asked for alimony and an even smaller proportion received it[72] (Appendix A, Table 37). Although the percentage of women receiving alimony varied from region to region, in no section of the nation did even one-fifth of the divorced women receive alimony.

For divorced women, most of whom appeared not to receive alimony, the possibility of employment became of critical importance. In 1890, in all regions of the nation, a substantial proportion of divorced women were employed: 50 percent in the North Atlantic states, 60.2 percent in the South Atlantic, 42.7 percent in the North Central, 59.6 percent in the South Central, and 45.9 percent in the western states.[73] Of all marital classes, the highest percentage of employed women was found among divorcees (Appendix A, Table 38).

Other factors, such as more demanding expectations of marriage and a brief period of more liberal divorce laws, undoubtedly contributed to the increase in the divorce rate during the late nineteenth and early twentieth centuries.[74] The city, however, with its greater employment opportunities, numerous conveniences, and anonymity, certainly seemed linked to the rising number of divorces during the era.

The closing decades of the nineteenth century and opening years of the twentieth were a time of much ferment and high hopes for women. For the first time, significant numbers of urban, middle-class women were stepping forth beyond their traditional sphere of the home and becoming active participants in the "outside" working world. But along with impressive progress came the genesis of problems. A growing number of women were entering the labor force, but they were becoming increasingly concentrated in a small number of occupations, most of which placed women in positions of limited authority and leadership. In addition, although the percentage of married women and older women who were employed increased, the female labor force of 1920, like that of 1890, was still composed primarily of young, single women. For most women, the inner conflict plus societal pressure proved too strong a force to withstand, and at least after marriage, most middle-class women did not pursue careers. But in spite of the limitations, the day had passed when home and marriage were the only viable options open to middle-class, urban women.

Although World War I is sometimes depicted as a critical factor in breaking down barriers to women's employment,[75] it is evident that a movement of large numbers of women into the working world had been well under way for at least a generation in cities and towns throughout America. The war undoubtedly did draw women into the labor force as men left their jobs to join the armed forces.[76] World War I also opened up some new fields of employment to women, such as the celebrated cases of streetcar conductors and munitions workers; but the gains were often temporary, with women workers laid off or demoted when men returned home from the war.[77] For the most part, women found themselves in the same occupations after the war that they had been in prior to the war. In addition, there did not appear to be a great upsurge of women entering the labor force following the war.[78] For the American women, the breakthrough into the working world had not followed in the wake of World War I, but had instead come in cities and towns across America during the late nineteenth and early twentieth centuries.

Notes

1. Mary A. Laselle and Katherine E. Wiley, *Vocations for Girls* (Boston: Houghton Mifflin Co., 1913), p. 1.

2. U.S., Department of Commerce, Bureau of the Census, *Women in Gainful Occupations, 1870-1920,* by Joseph A. Hill, Census Monograph No. 9, Washington, D.C., Government Printing Office, 1929, p. 19. In 1880 16.0 percent of all women sixteen or older were employed; in 1890, 19.0 percent; in 1900, 20.6 percent; and in 1910, 25.5 percent. (See Table 7 in Chapter 6 for a discussion of the reliability and comparability of 1910 data.)

3. For 1870 and 1880 urban and rural employment figures were available only for the *total* female population; for 1890-1920 data were given

for the female population, ten or older. Therefore, for the aggregate population, the 1870 and 1880 figures should be looked at and compared as one set, and the 1890-1920 figures as another.

4. Other authors have discussed the growth of clerical occupations and the influx of women into the labor force. See in particular Elizabeth F. Baker, *Technology and Women's Work* (New York: Columbia University Press, 1964); Margery Davies, "Woman's Place Is at the Typewriter: The Feminization of the Clerical Labor Force," *Radical America* 8 (July-August 1974): 1-28.

5. U.S., Department of Commerce, *Women in Gainful Occupations, 1870-1920*, p. 40. See also p. 45, where "clerical" is defined so as to include saleswomen so that comparisons with earlier censuses could be made. Between 1870 and 1920, the number of women employed in clerical and sales positions rose from 10,798 to 1,910,695.

6. Ibid., pp. 41-42. Of these, almost two-thirds were teachers.

7. U.S., Department of the Interior, *Eleventh Census, 1890*, vol. 1, *Population*, pt. 2, Ages and Occupations, pp. cxix, cxvii.

8. U.S., Department of Commerce, *Fourteenth Census, 1920*, vol. 4, *Population: Occupations*, p. 341.

9. Margaret E. Sangster, "Shall Wives Earn Money?" *Woman's Home Companion*, April 1905, pp. 32, 42-43. For other discussions regarding the limitations of marriage and the desirability of employment see: Lorine Pruette, *Women and Leisure: A Study of Social Waste* (New York: E. P. Dutton & Co., 1924), pp. 118-87; Suzanne Wilcox, "The Unrest of Modern Woman," *Independent*, June 8, 1909, pp. 62-66; Marion Harland, "The Passing of the Home Daughter," *Independent*, July 13, 1911, pp. 88-90; Interview with Ruth Davidson, April 14, 1970, Pasadena, California; Mary Humphreys, "Women Bachelors in New York," *Scribner's*, November 1896, pp. 626-35.

10. Pownall Papers, PW 577 Joseph Pownall to Joseph Benjamin Pownall and Lucy Senger, October 7, 1877.

11. See Isabella Alden, *Memories of Yesterday* (Philadelphia: J. B. Lippincott Co., 1931), p. 135; Helen M. Doyle, *A Child Went Forth* (New York: Gotham House, 1934), p. 92; Harland, "Passing of the Home Daughter," pp. 88-90; Edgar Schmiedeler, *The Industrial Revolution and the Home* (n.p.: By the Author, 1927), pp. 19-20; *New Orleans Times Picayune*, January 1, 1897. However, Richard Sennett, *Families Against the City* (Cambridge, Mass.: Harvard University Press, 1970), p. 101, did find that daughters in the Union Park area of Chicago helped in the home prior to marriage.

12. Martha F. Crowe, *The American Country Girl* (New York: Frederick A. Stokes Co., 1915); Schmiedeler, *Industrial Revolution and the*

Home, p. 3; Doyle, *A Child Went Forth,* pp. 30-33; Marie Thérèse (de Solms) Blanc, *The Condition of Women in the United States,* trans. Abby Langdon Alger (Boston: Roberts Bros., 1895; reprint ed., New York: Arno Press, 1972), pp. 205-6.

13. Thomas Woody, *History of Women's Education in the United States,* 2 vols. (New York: Science Press, 1929; reprint ed., New York: Octagon Books, 1966), 1:546. Willystine Goodsell, *The Education of Women: Its Social Background and Its Problems* (New York: Macmillan Co., 1924), p. 23, observed that "for forty years or more the enrollment of girls in American High Schools has outnumbered that of boys. In 1915-1916, 54.6 percent of the total was comprised of girls, and in 1917-1918 the percentage of girls was more than 57." Neither Goodsell nor Woody offers an explanation for the higher proportion of female students. Perhaps families may have been more likely to allow daughters to stay in school longer than sons because working sons, even without a high school education, could make more money than daughters. In addition, there may have been a tendency to not want young daughters to go out into the "unprotected" working world.

14. Earl Barnes, *Woman in Modern Society* (New York: B. S. Huebsch, 1912), p. 91.

15. Harland, "Passing of the Home Daughter," pp. 88-89.

16. George Ellington, *Women of New York: Underworld of the Great City* (New York: New York Book Co., 1869), p. 343.

17. Katherine Busbey, *Home Life in America* (New York: Macmillan Co., 1910), pp. 116, 165-66.

18. Massachusetts, Bureau of Statistics of Labor, *Fifteenth Annual Report of the Massachusetts Bureau of Statistics of Labor: The Working Girls of Boston,* by Carroll Wright (1884; reprint ed., New York: Arno Press, 1967), p. 118; Helen Campbell, "Working Women of Today," *Arena,* August 1891, pp. 329-39.

19. Grace H. Dodge et al., *What Women Can Earn: Occupations of Women and Their Compensation* (Boston: Frederick A. Stokes Co., 1898), pp. 145-69.

20. Martha L. Rayne, *What Can a Woman Do: Or, Her Position in the Business and Literary World* (Detroit: F. B. Dickerson & Co., 1883; reprint ed., Petersburg, N.Y.: Eagle Publishing Co., 1893), p. 123.

21. Eleanor Martin and Margaret Post, *Vocations for the Trained Woman* (New York: Longmans, Green & Co., 1914), p. 142.

22. Helen C. Hoerle and Florence B. Saltzberg, *The Girl and the Job* (New York: Henry Holt & Co., 1919), p. 11.

23. Dodge et al., *What Women Can Earn,* p. 142.

24. Ibid., pp. 142, 159; Rayne, *What Can a Woman Do,* p. 123. For a study of women's entry into clerical work see Davies, "Woman's Place Is

at the Typewriter," pp. 1-28. Davies suggests that educated women constituted a pool of unused labor that fit the needs of the expanding business world of the late nineteenth century. Typing, since it was a new development, was "sex-neutral" and therefore open to domination by women.

25. Dodge et al., *What Women Can Earn,* p. 164.

26. U.S., Department of Commerce and Labor, *Work and Wages of Men, Women and Children,* Eleventh Annual Report of the Commissioner of Labor (1897), p. 582. See also Scott Nearing, *Wages in the United States, 1908-1910* (New York: Macmillan Co., 1914), p. 106, for additional information regarding male/female wage differentials for clerical work.

27. U.S., Department of Commerce, Bureau of the Census, *Sixteenth Census of the United States, 1940: Comparative Occupational Statistics for the United States, 1870-1940,* pp. 121, 129.

28. Baker, *Technology and Women's Work,* pp. 71-73; Laselle and Wiley, *Vocations for Girls,* p. 15; David M. Cohn, *The Good Old Days* (New York: Simon & Schuster, 1940), p. 249; Booth Tarkington, *Alice Adams* (New York: Doubleday, Page & Co., 1926), pp. 139-40, 191, 433-34.

29. U.S., Department of Commerce, *Women in Gainful Occupations, 1870-1920,* pp. 42, 45.

30. U.S., Department of Commerce and Labor, *Statistics of Women at Work: 1900,* p. 32; U.S., Department of Commerce, *Women in Gainful Occupations, 1870-1920,* pp. 64-65.

31. U.S., Department of Commerce and Labor, *Women at Work: 1900,* pp. 162, 168; U. S., Department of Commerce, *Women in Gainful Occupations, 1870-1920,* p. 67.

32. U.S., Department of Commerce, *Women in Gainful Occupations, 1870-1920,* p. 23, points to the aging of the female population.

33. John S. Durand, *The Labor Force in the United States, 1890-1960* (New York: Social Science Research Council, 1948), pp. 122-36, postulated a similar progression. See also William Ogburn and M. F. Nimkoff, *Technology and the Changing Family* (Boston: Houghton Mifflin Co., 1955), pp. 153-56.

34. U.S., Department of Commerce, *Women in Gainful Occupations, 1870-1920,* p. 77.

35. For particular case studies see: Barbara Klaczynska, "Why Women Work: A Comparison of Various Groups—Philadelphia, 1910-1930," *Journal of Labor History* 17 (Winter 1976): 74-87; Virginia Yans McLaughlin, "Patterns of Work and Family Organization: Buffalo's Italians," in *The Family in History,* ed. Theodore K. Rabb and Robert Rotberg (New York: Harper & Row, 1973), pp. 111-26.

36. Rebecca August, interview, April 14, 1970, Los Angeles, California.

August was a blue-collar worker and union organizer in the early 1900s. Sangster, "Shall Wives Earn Money?" p. 32.

37. U.S., Department of Commerce, *Women in Gainful Occupations, 1870-1920,* p. 45.

38. A. S. Richardson, "Lure of a Double Salary," *Woman's Home Companion,* May 1920, p. 12.

39. Ibid.

40. "Helping My Husband Earn a Living," *Illustrated World,* April 1916, p. 251.

41. Richardson, "Lure of a Double Salary," p. 12.

42. John Martin, "The Married Woman in Industry," *Survey,* March 11, 1916, p. 697.

43. Sangster, "Shall Wives Earn Money?" p. 32. See also Martin, "Married Woman in Industry," p. 695.

44. Sangster, "Shall Wives Earn Money?" p. 32.

45. Harriet Brunkhurst, "The Married Woman in Business," *Collier's,* February 26, 1910, p. 20.

46. "Helping My Husband Earn a Living," p. 251.

47. Sangster, "Shall Wives Earn Money?" p. 32.

48. Rayne, *What Can a Woman Do,* pp. 77-78. Although Rayne's sample may have been somewhat skewed in favor of single women–married women may have been too busy to respond–it nonetheless appears that single women dominated the field.

49. U.S., Department of Commerce and Labor, *Women at Work: 1900,* p. 18. See also Schmiedeler, *Industrial Revolution and the Home,* p. 4; Crowe, *American Country Girl,* p. 182; Caroline Latimer, *Girl and Woman* (New York: D. Appleton & Co., 1910), p. 155.

50. The twenty-seven sample cities looked at in 1900 were: Atlanta, Baltimore, Boston, Buffalo, Chicago, Cincinnati, Cleveland, Detroit, Fall River (Massachusetts), Indianapolis, Jersey City, Kansas City (Missouri), Louisville, Lowell, Milwaukee, Minneapolis, New Orleans, New York, Newark, Paterson, Philadelphia, Pittsburgh, Providence, St. Louis, St. Paul, Washington, D.C., and Rochester (U.S., Department of Commerce and Labor, *Statistics of Women at Work: 1900,* p. 56). The eleven sample cities studied in 1920 were: Fall River (Massachusetts), Providence, Rochester, Paterson, Louisville, Cincinnati, Indianapolis, St. Paul, Kansas City (Missouri), Atlanta, and New Orleans (U.S., Department of Commerce, *Women in Gainful Occupations, 1870-1920,* p. 124).

51. Blanc, *Condition of Women,* p. 248; John Modell and Tamara K. Hareven, "Urbanization and the Malleable Household: An Examination of Boarding and Lodging in American Families, *Journal of Marriage and the Family* 35 (August 1973): 467-79. Modell and Hareven in their study

of boarding in Boston in the late nineteenth century found that boarding was most common among single, native white migrants to the city.

52. Massachusetts, Bureau of Statistics of Labor, *Working Girls of Boston*, p. 20.

53. $r = 0.2, p < 0.0005, N = 285$.

54. Otis Dudley Duncan and Albert J. Reiss, *The Social Characteristics of Urban and Rural Communities, 1950* (New York: John Wiley & Sons, 1956), p. 92, emphasized the inverse relationship between size of city and the percentage of women working. However, what they really found was that for cities of 25,000 or more people there was little or no difference with respect to the percentage employed, but once one dropped below a population of 25,000, there was a decrease in the percentage of employed women until one reached a low of 16 percent in the rural-farm category: U.S., Department of Commerce, *Women in Gainful Occupations, 1870-1920*, pp. 8-11, also notes that the greatest difference with respect to the percentage of women who were employed was between urban and rural areas, with not much difference existing among cities of more than 25,000 population.

55. One would think that this point would have been explored by other researchers. However, no other studies were found.

56. Figures for the percentage of employed women came from U.S., Department of Commerce, *Women in Gainful Occupations, 1870-1920*, p. 45.

57. Specific reference was made regarding working-class girls and women who looked upon marriage as a release from the drudgery of a job. See Miriam Finn Scott, "Factory Girl's Danger," *Outlook*, April 15, 1911, pp. 817-21; The Bachelor Maid [pseud.], "Work for Women," *Independent*, June 25, 1912, pt. 1, pp. 182-86.

58. In rural areas a similar relationship between marital status and employment was found. In 1890 the correlation between percent single and percent employed was $r = 0.33, N = 34, 0.05 > p > 0.025$, for the aggregate population, and in 1920 it was $r = 0.42, N = 41, p < 0.0005$, for the aggregate population, and $r = 0.28, N = 41, 0.05 > p > 0.025$ for native whites of native-born parents. In 1890 the correlation between percent married and percent employed was $r = -0.57, N = 34, p < 0.0005$, for the aggregate population, and in 1920 it was $r = -0.60, N = 41, p < 0.0005$, for the aggregate population, and $r = -0.62, N = 41, p < 0.0005$, for native whites of native-born parents.

59. Other authors have pointed to this negative relationship between employment and fertility. See the following: Antonella Pinnelli, "Female Labour and Fertility in Relationship to Contrasting Social and Economic Conditions," *Human Relations* 24 (December 1971): 603-10; Andrew

Collver, "Woman's Work Participation and Fertility in Metropolitan Areas," *Demography* 5, no. 1 (1968): 55-60; Sultan H. Hashmi, "Factors in Urban Fertility Differences in the United States," in *Contributions to Urban Sociology,* eds. Ernest Burgess and Donald J. Bogue (Chicago: University of Chicago Press, 1964), pp. 48, 56; William Bowen and T. Aldrich Finegan, *Economics of Labor Force Participation* (Princeton, N.J.: Princeton University Press, 1969), pp. 205-6. Sheldon Haber, "Trends in Work Rates of White Females, 1890-1920," *Industrial Labor Relations Review* 26 (July 1973), pp. 1122-34, contends that, when looked at over time, the strength of the relationship declines sharply. He concludes that changing fertility patterns have not exerted a strong influence upon female labor force participation. See also Durand, *Labor Force in the United States,* pp. 81-82, regarding this point. As in the urban areas, the rural areas exhibited a negative relationship between female employment and fertility. In 1890 $r = -0.74, N = 34, p < 0.0005$, and in 1920 $r = -0.60, N = 41, p < 0.0005$.

60. Sennett, *Families Against the City,* pp. 122-23, 147, found that only a small percentage of wives worked, since their employment might upset the balance of authority in the home. He found that husbands in white-collar occupations were more likely than those in blue-collar positions to have working wives because the wife's income would not form as large a proportion of her husband's wages nor would she be as likely to end up in a higher-status job than her husband. See also, McLaughlin, "Buffalo's Italians," pp. 111-26, in which she points out that employment for wives did not, in all cases, threaten the male dominance in the family hierarchy.

61. Caroline H. Woods [Belle Otis], *The Diary of a Milliner* (New York: Hurd & Houghton, 1867), p. 3; Ellington, *Women of New York,* pp. 584, 592; Albert Rhodes, "Women's Occupations," *Galaxy,* January 1876, p. 48; Amelia Neville, *The Fantastic City* (Boston: Houghton Mifflin Co., 1932), p. 148; Annie Dumond, *The Life of a Book Agent* (Cincinnati: By the Author, 1868), pp. 162, 167.

62. For the effects of employment upon health see: Dr. Lyman Abbott, "Effect of Modern Industry upon Women," *Outlook,* May 22, 1909, pp. 137-38; "Women in Industry: A Racial Evil," *Literary Digest,* April 12, 1913, p. 826. For discussions regarding the tendency of workingwomen to turn to prostitution see: Helen Campbell, "Working Women of Today," *Arena,* August 1891, pp. 329-39; *Four Years in the Underbrush: Adventures as a Working Woman in New York* (Charles Scribner's Sons, 1921), p. 28.

63. Dorothy Richardson, "The Long Day," in *Women at Work,* ed. William O'Neill (New York: Quadrangle Books, 1972), offers vivid descriptions of employment in different types of blue-collar occupations at the turn of the century.

64. Dodge et al., *What Women Can Earn*, pp. 3, 142, 144, 149, 159, 169, 203, 277, 336.

65. Crowe, *American Country Girl*, p. 182; Schmeideler, *Industrial Revolution and the Home*, pp. 29-30; Harland, "Passing of the Home Daughter," p. 88.

66. See the following: T. Cave-North, "Woman's Place and Power," *Westminster Review*, September 1908, pp. 264-67; Lucas Malet, "Threatened Re-subjection of Women," *Living Age*, June 17, 1905, pp. 705-15; Cardinal Gibbons, "Pure Womanhood," *Cosmopolitan*, September 1905, pp. 559-61; Charles W. Eliot, "The Normal American Woman," *Ladies' Home Journal*, January 1908, p. 15; Bachelor Maid, "Work for Women," pp. 182-86; Josephine K. Henry, "The New Woman of the South," *Arena*, February 1895, pp. 353-62; Ouida [pseud], "The New Woman," *North American Review*, May 1894, pp. 610-19; Suzanne Wilcox, "The Unrest of Modern Woman," *Independent*, June 8, 1909, pp. 62-66; Lillian Betts, "The New Woman," *Outlook*, October 12, 1895, p. 587.

67. *Four Years in the Underbrush*, p. 307; Thorstein Veblen, *The Theory of the Leisure Class* (New York: Macmillan Co., 1899; reprint ed., New York: Mentor Books, 1953), pp. 229-32; Annie M. MacLean, *Women Workers and Society* (Chicago: A. C. McClurg & Co., 1916), pp. 5, 39.

68. Pruette, *Women and Leisure*, see especially pp. 123-24, 150-51. The more immediate rewards discussed by Pruette included greater activity, recognition for a job well done, and more fame.

69. Arnold Bennett, *Our Women: Chapters on the Sex Discord* (New York: Cassell & Co., 1920); see especially pp. 41-46. Florence G. Tuttle, *The Awakening of Women: Suggestions from the Psychic Side of Feminism* (New York: Abingdon Press, 1915), pp. 148-59; Bachelor Maid, "Work for Women," pp. 182-86.

70. Edward Alsworth Ross, "The Significance of the Increasing Divorce Rate," *Century Magazine*, May 1909, p. 150.

71. U.S., Department of Commerce and Labor, Bureau of the Census, Special Reports, *Marriage and Divorce, 1867-1906* (1909), 2 vols., 1:21; U.S., Department of Commerce, *Statistical Abstract of the United States, 1923*, p. 73.

72. The authors of U.S., Department of Commerce and Labor, *Marriage and Divorce, 1867-1906*, pointed out that they took into account only those cases in which alimony had been secured as part of a divorce bill. It was possible for alimony to be secured in a separate action following the granting of the divorce (p. 33). However, it seems unlikely that separate actions would have radically altered the alimony picture. See Joel P. Bishop, *Marriage and Divorce*, 2 vols. (Boston: Little, Brown & Co., 1881), 2:325, where he writes that it was common practice for divorce and alimony to

be asked for in one bill. Ross, "Increasing Divorce Rate," p. 150, also contended that only a small percentage of divorcees received alimony.

73. U.S., Department of the Interior, *Eleventh Census, 1890,* vol. 1, *Population,* pt. 2, p. cxxviii.

74. The following books offer detailed information regarding the growth of divorce and divorce laws in the United States: Nelson Blake, *The Road to Reno* (New York: Macmillan Co., 1962); James Barnett, *Divorce and the American Novel, 1858-1937* (New York: Russell & Russell, 1939); Arthur Calhoun, *A Social History of the American Family from Colonial Times to the Present,* 3 vols. in one (Cleveland: A. H. Clark, 1917-19; reprint ed., New York: Arno Press, 1973); George Elliot Howard, *A History of Matrimonial Institutions* (Chicago: University of Chicago Press, 1904); James P. Lichtenberger, *Divorce: A Study in Social Causation* (New York: Columbia University Press, 1909); James P. Lichtenberger, *Divorce: A Social Interpretation* (New York: Whittlesey House, 1931); Alfred Cahen, *Statistical Analysis of American Divorce* (New York: Columbia University Press, 1932); William O'Neill, *Divorce in the Progressive Era* (New Haven, Conn.: Yale University Press, 1967). For a discussion of the incidence of divorce rising as expectations of marriage were heightened, see Christopher Lasch, "Divorce American Style," *New York Review of Books,* February 17, 1966, pp. 3-4.

75. Frederick Lewis Allen, *Only Yesterday* (n.p.: Harper & Bros., 1931; reprint ed., New York: Bantam Books, 1957), p. 68.

76. Mrs. Henry Wade Rogers, "Wanted—the Woman's Land Army," *Forum,* May 1918, pp. 621-29, contended that since 1914, 1,413,300 women had taken over men's jobs. In contrast, another study, based on a survey of 160 large employers, found little substitution, and pointed out that women had already formed a more important source of workers than was commonly thought. "Are Women Replacing Soldiers in Industry?" *Current Opinion,* January 1918, pp. 60-61.

77. According to the U.S. census, female streetcar conductors numbered 253 in 1920 and 17 in 1930. See U.S., Department of Commerce, Bureau of the Census, *Fifteenth Census of the United States, 1930: Abstract,* p. 314.

78. U.S., Department of Commerce, *Fifteenth Census, 1930, Abstract,* pp. 306-20; U.S., Department of Commerce, Bureau of the Census, *Fourteenth Census of the United States, 1920: Abstract,* pp. 483-97. In 1890, 18.2 percent of all females fourteen or older were employed. In 1900 the percentage was 20.2; in 1920, 22.7; and in 1930, 23.6. See U.S., Department of Commerce, Bureau of the Census, *Historical Statistics of the United States, Colonial Times to 1970,* 2 pt., pt. 2, p. 132.

7 Conclusions

In America of the late nineteenth and early twentieth centuries women's lives, in particular those of the urban middle class, began to undergo a far-reaching transformation. During that era, in cities and towns across the nation, the unidimensional woman whose life was expected to focus solely upon home and family was being challenged by the appearance of a growing number of recognizably modern women whose varied and active life-styles reflected the expanding array of options opening up to them. Although most women continued to marry, bear children, and tend to the running of the home, significant changes were occurring in these traditional areas of activity. More important, a growing number of urban, middle-class women moved outside of a strictly home-centered existence, some entering the labor force for at least a period of time, others becoming members of the myriad of women's associations and clubs that flourished during the era.

Within the traditional sphere of the home, changes took place that resulted in an expansion of the free time potentially available to women. In the latter decades of the nineteenth century, the development and the dissemination of information about effective birth control methods were spreading. Those developments had their first impact upon middle- and upper-class urban women, with the information more slowly reaching other sectors of the female population. The ability to limit effectively the number of children one had appeared to be linked directly to the development of a trend, particularly pronounced in urban areas, toward more youthful marriages coupled with a reduced number of children. Fewer children and a growing period of time spent by children in schools meant the potential for reduced child-rearing obligations for many women.

Also, in the urban areas a variety of factors converged to make the running of a home a potentially less time-consuming operation. For those who were interested, apartments or apartment-hotels joined the long-present boardinghouse in offering a simpler alternative to the single-family dwelling, and restaurants and laundries presented options to those who wished to eliminate certain household chores. In addition, prepared foods, ready-made clothing, and a variety of labor-saving devices first began to lighten the burden of the day-to-day running of the household in cities and towns of late nineteenth-century America.

Just as the time needed to run the urban, middle-class household was diminishing, the number and variety of employment opportunities deemed respectable underwent a phenomenal expansion. Between 1890 and 1920, white-collar and professional occupations exhibited considerable growth; during those years NWNP women, especially in the urban areas, entered the labor force in record numbers. However, at the very time that a growing number of women found their way into a greater selection of occupations, women workers also tended to concentrate in those sectors of the professional and white-collar fields that had the least power and prestige. Although most young women terminated their employment when they married, the experience of working, with the contacts and independence that a job brought, had a positive impact upon feelings of self-esteem and self-reliance.

Even women who did not themselves work were affected by the changes brought by expanded employment opportunities for women. The more that women deviated from the pattern of a life that revolved solely around the home, the more readily other women could follow suit. For those women, who in an earlier era would have felt compelled to remain married, no matter what, the possibility of supporting themselves plus the greater variation in acceptable life-styles were probably important factors with respect to the rising incidence of divorce during the late nineteenth and early twentieth centuries. Although urban and rural divorce rates were similar, the majority of divorced women lived in cities and a high percentage of divorcees were employed.

During the era, although the percentage of employed, married women did increase, opposition to employment for married women remained so strong that women generally were forced to choose between marriage and a career. Most women ultimately opted for marriage, but that decision did not necessarily imply satisfaction with the choice. Indeed, the era saw the development of a powerful inner conflict in women between the tremendous pressure to fulfill, above all else, one's role as a wife and mother, and the attraction of the working world with its varied contacts and the chance for autonomy and independent status. Many women never resolved the conflict between the two role choices.

Cities and towns of the era saw a tremendous upsurge in the growth of all sorts of associations for women. Not only did the increased free time of urban, middle-class women allow these organizations to flourish, but the focus of activities often was shaped by problems common to urban areas. In a way, the associations and clubs, self-improvement or outreach, were a compromise between a traditional home-centered life and the pursuit of a career. The myriad of voluntary organizations in which urban women became involved offered both a chance for self-improvement and a sense of doing something of use without threatening the family hierarchy and thus was less subject to criticism than employment. But even the voluntary organizations posed an inner conflict between the demands of the home role and the desire to be an active participant in the "outside" world, and women felt compelled to justify their involvement on the basis of its having a positive effect upon their roles as wives and mothers.

Certain aspects of an urban environment appeared to have the greatest impact upon women and the types of lives they led. Interestingly, population size did not seem to play an important role. At least in cities of 25,000, or possibly as little as of 2,500, conditions appeared to be conducive to the development of an expanded sphere of activity for women. An increase in city size, with few exceptions, did not appear to alter dramatically women's marriage, fertility, or employment patterns. This does not mean that city size was always unimportant, but rather that for the particular variables studied, it did not appear to be significant.

The evidence also suggests that researchers must carefully assess what size places should be considered urban and what rural, and not arbitrarily set too high a cutoff for the urban category. In 1920, with at least two of the variables, child/woman ratio and marital status, places with a population of between 2,500 and 25,000 appeared to function more as urban places than as rural ones, whereas for all of the variables, towns between 25,000 and 50,000 manifested urban behavior patterns. The failure to consider places of 2,500 to 25,000 in population as urban could have masked differences or the magnitude of differences between the urban and rural sectors.

More generally, attention could be directed to the following two questions. What functional differences between the urban and rural sectors exist for other variables? Does a functional definition of "urban" (with respect to particular variables) differ according to the time period studied? Such questions can only be answered by further investigation, but hopefully the material presented in this book will have at least pointed to the need to refine our concepts of urban and rural.

In contrast to city size, the economic orientation of a city was closely related to the propensity of women to remain single and to be employed. In those cities leaning more heavily toward manufacturing and mechanical activities, more single women were present and a higher percentage of women were employed. Conversely, in cities where the proportion of people involved in trade and transportation was higher, both the percentage of single women and the percentage of employed women declined.

Between 1890 and 1920, the strength of both the positive relationship between manufacturing and mechanical occupations and the percentage of employed NWNP women, and the negative association between trade and transportation jobs and the percentage of employed NWNP women decreased. During the same time period, the positive correlation between cities inclining toward trade and transportation occupations and the percentage of married NWNP women declined, and the negative relationship between cities oriented toward manufacturing and mechanical jobs and the percentage of married NWNP women disappeared. Similarly, the negative association between manufacturing and mechanical occupations and the native white child/woman ratio shifted to positive, whereas the positive relationship between trade and transportation jobs and native white child/woman ratio became negative.

Cities with a higher component of their total labor force in manufacturing and mechanical occupations appeared to have had an early advantage in offering employment opportunities to women. In such cities manufacturing jobs as well as domestic work were available to women. Prior to 1890, cities that inclined more heavily toward trade and transportation activities had limited job possibilities for women. With the post-1890 boom in white-collar occupations, the female labor force in trade and transportation cities grew rapidly and the earlier advantage held by manufacturing and mechanical cities appeared to diminish. As employment opportunities in the two types of cities changed, so did the marital and fertility patterns of the female residents. In particular, the increased percentage of employed NWNP women in trade and transportation cities appeared to be linked with the decline in the percentage of married NWNP women and with the lower native white child/woman ratio.

As with economic function, the sex ratio of a city was strongly related to the marital and employment patterns of women: The more men there were, the higher the percentage of married women and the lower the percentage of employed women. The positive association between sex ratio and female employment was especially strong for the aggregate population. Among the aggregate population, women seemed more likely to be "pushed" into often unwanted, disagreeable jobs because of the lack of other options; for NWNP women, however, entrance into the labor force appeared more a result of the "pull" exerted by the positive aspects of being employed.

Although the general behavior patterns in urban areas differed significantly from what was found in the rural sector, the presence of significant variation among cities indicates that caution must be used in making generalizations from single-city studies. Hopefully, the scope of this study has aided in the development of generalizations whose applicability and ways of functioning can be further analyzed and tested in studies of individual cities.

Within each region, as well as in the entire United States, the urban sector offered women both increased autonomy within the traditional sphere of the home and an extension of their activities into the "outside" world. (See Appendix B for a discussion of regional variation.) No longer were the home and its functions deemed to be the sole proper focus of activity for women. Indeed, what was considered to be women's proper sphere underwent considerable expansion during the era. In short, in the cities and towns of the late nineteenth and early twentieth centuries, a recognizably modern woman, with an expanded number of options to choose from and new conflicts to cope with, first began to emerge.

Appendix A. Census Data: Collection, Methodology, and Tables

      This appendix discusses how the census data used in this book were gathered and the methods used in data reduction. It begins with a brief description of certain problems associated with the use of nineteenth-century census data, outlines the general procedure followed in this study, and then provides a more detailed discussion of each of the census years considered.

      Despite the advantages of working with census data, there are certain limitations. First, the conclusions derived from the data are clearly only as reliable as the data themselves. Especially with the earlier census years, less sophisticated and precise data-gathering techniques probably led to errors in the final report. Such errors would become particularly crucial if a historian chose to base a study upon a relatively small sample.

      The large number of inconsistencies in the presentation of data presented another problem, especially with the earlier censuses. For example, employment figures were generally given for those ten or older, but for 1870 and 1880, corresponding figures for the entire ten-or-older population were not given. For most years, employment figures were given for all cities 25,000 population or larger. However, for 1890 the figures applied to cities of 50,000 or more people, whereas for 1880 the figures pertained to selected cities of 25,000 or more people. In addition, for the purposes of this study, the pre-1890 censuses contained limited information: Only employment figures for the aggregate population and the aggregate sex ratio were available. In general, the more recent the year, the greater the amount of available data.

      Prior to 1910, the data were generally not divided into urban and rural categories. For those years, for each variable for which information was given, I derived an urban and rural total from raw census data. For 1910 and 1920, the censuses contained relatively detailed information regarding urban and rural areas for most of the variables. The 1910 and 1920 censuses, designated urban as all places of 2,500 or more people. However, employment figures were given only for those cities of 25,000 population or larger. For most of the years studied and for most of the variables, information was given for cities of 25,000 or more people. Therefore, unless otherwise specified, in this study "urban" is equivalent to cities of 25,000 population or larger, and rural anything less.

The variables for which information was collected were as follows: (1) child/woman ratio: the number of children under age five per 1,000 women twenty to forty-four; (2) employment: percentage of women, generally ten or older, who were working; (3) sex ratio: the number of men per 100 women. Since the impact that availability of men had upon the marriage rate for women was of particular interest, when possible, the sex ratio for the fifteen-or-older population was calculated; (4) conjugal condition: the percentage of females fifteen or older, who were single, married, or divorced. Until 1910, data regarding the number of single females fifteen or older were not always available for every city. In order to arrive at a relatively accurate estimate of this number for each city, I totaled the numbers of married, widowed, and divorced women, with the assumption that most would be fifteen or older, and then subtracted that sum from the total number of females fifteen or older to get the number of single females who were fifteen or older.

The following procedure was used for each census year to arrive at the urban and rural totals. For each state that had at least one city of 25,000 population or larger, information regarding the variables was obtained for the state as a whole and for each of the cities having 25,000 or more people. By using only those states with cities of 25,000 or larger, sufficient information was obtained about the differences between the urban and rural United States, while still following the state-by-state variation regarding differences between the city and the surrounding countryside. For each variable, I obtained the overall urban average for a state by taking the mean of the city values for that state. Each city was weighed equally when making the calculation, since the "city" was really the unit under investigation. In this way very large cities such as New York, Philadelphia, and Chicago were not, despite the great numbers of inhabitants, given dominance in their respective state totals. The rural average for each

state was arrived at by subtracting the urban total from the state total
for each variable and then calculating the mean. Then all of the state urban
means and the state rural means for each variable were added separately
and divided by the total number of states to obtain national averages. In
order to ascertain that the differences between the urban and rural means
were statistically significant, a t-test for paired variates was performed,
pairing each state's urban and rural means for the calculation.[1]

A t-test for paired variates is a statistical test used to determine whether
the different means seen for two related samples (in this case, population)
can be attributed solely to chance or if the difference between the two
population means is statistically significant. This significance is expressed
by p. The closer to 1 that p is, the weaker the significance and the more
likely the difference is due to chance. For example, $p = 0.05$ means that
there is one chance in twenty that the results have occurred due to chance,
whereas $p = 0.01$ means that there is only one chance in a hundred that
the results are due to chance.

In addition to overall urban/rural differences, I studied differences
among cities in an attempt to detect aspects of city life that influenced
roles for women in society. Size of city according to population was one
variable examined. The cities were grouped into the following size categories: 25,000-50,000; 50,000-100,000; 100,000-500,000; and 500,000
or more. For each size grouping, the mean, the standard deviation, and
the variance were calculated.

The impact of certain types of economic activity upon the variables
was also examined. The original plan had been to classify each city for
each census year according to major economic activity, but most of the
censuses contained inadequate information to permit precise enough categories to be developed.[2] Moreover, even relatively precise categories had
the disadvantage of lumping together cities that really exhibited significant
differences in economic activity. For example, the category manufacturing
would have included cities with as little as 35 percent of their work force
in manufacturing or as much as 75 percent. Therefore, in order to detect
more subtle variations among cities, the category approach was rejected.

The calculation of the Pearson Correlation Coefficient was selected as
a much more sensitive and desirable approach for analyzing the impact
of economic activity. For each census year except 1910, the percentages
of the total work force in each city engaged in (1) manufacturing and
(2) trade and transportation[3] occupations were calculated. The percentages

derived from those calculations were used as indicators of a city's economic activity. Then a Pearson Correlation Coefficient was calculated to determine whether a significant relationship existed between economic activity (the percentage of the total work force in the preceding categories) and each of the variables. The correlation coefficient, r, gives one an estimate of the strength of a linear relationship between two sets of observations. The closer to 1 or -1 that r is, the more highly correlated, either positively or negatively, the two sets of observations are. The significance of the correlation is expressed by p. The closer to 1 that p is, the weaker the significance and the more likely the correlation is due to chance. For example, $p = 0.05$ means that there is one chance in twenty that the results have occurred due to chance, whereas $p = 0.01$ means that there is only one chance in a hundred that the results are due to chance.

An examination was then made of how the sex ratio of a city affected the remaining variables: child/woman ratio, employment, and conjugal condition. The same procedure was followed for employment and conjugal condition where in each instance an investigation was made of how each of the remaining variables was affected. In all of the preceding calculations, Pearson Correlation Coefficients were calculated.

Next, an investigation of the effects of regional differences on the different variables was made. The more inclusive census regional division, which designated five major regions, was followed.[4] Especially for the earlier years, there were too few states with cities of 25,000 or more people in some of the regions to make a more detailed division of regions possible. For each region, separate totals of state urban and rural means were made and regional urban and rural means were calculated. A check was made to see how the degree of urbanization within a region affected the difference between the urban and the rural means of a particular variable. The percentage difference between the urban and rural means for each variable was calculated; for example, what percent greater was urban female employment than rural in the North Central region. Next, the degree of urbanization of each region was obtained. For 1890 through 1920, the census provided figures for the percent of the total population in each region living in places of 2,500 or more people. For 1870 and 1880, it was possible to calculate the percentages.

After completing the preceding analysis for each census year, an analysis, spanning the entire 1870-1920 period, was made for the urban and rural totals for the entire United States. Each variable was plotted with respect to time, so that temporal trends in urban and rural values could be detected. The effect of urbanization upon the difference between the urban and rural means for each of the variables, for the United States as a whole and for each of the five regions, was analyzed for the entire time period. (See Appendix B for the results of the analysis.)

As mentioned earlier, each census year presented different limitations regarding data collection. In 1870 and 1880 the amount of data available was small. For 1870 two major sources of data were used: the 1870 census and the U.S. Department of Commerce and Labor, Special Reports, *Marriage and Divorce: 1867-1906*, volumes one and two. From the 1870 census, it was possible to obtain information regarding the aggregate male and female population plus the total number of employed females ten or older for all cities of 25,000 population or larger except Nashville. Sex ratios were derived from the total number of males and females. Unfortunately, there was no information regarding the total number of females ten or older who lived in the cities. Therefore, the female employment rate was arrived at by ascertaining what percent employed females ten or older were of all females.

The calculation of 1870 and 1880 urban and rural divorce rates presented a number of problems. Since divorce laws differed widely from state to state, the overall U.S. urban and rural rates had to be computed without having the legal differences between states mask the significant urban and rural differences that existed in virtually every state. The censuses did not contain information regarding the number of divorced persons residing in a particular area. So, an estimation of urban and rural divorce rates was arrived at by using divorce figures from the U.S. Department of Commerce and Labor, Special Reports, *Marriage and Divorce 1867-1906*, and population figures from the censuses.

Divorce figures were given for the number of divorces registered in each county of each state for every ten-year period starting in 1867. Designated as urban was any county that had at least one city of 25,000 people within its boundaries. Then for each state the total female population for the entire state and for each of its urban counties was obtained, and the urban county totals were subtracted from the state totals to get the total number of females in the rural portion of the state. Total number of females was used rather than total population, since the interest was in the female divorce rate. Also, because there generally were more females in the cities than in the surrounding rural area for almost every state, it seemed that this approach made overstating the female urban divorce rate less likely than if the entire population were used. Next a calculation was made of the average number of divorces to occur in a one-year period for each state as a whole and for each urban county within the state. The sum of the urban county divorces was subtracted from the state divorce total to obtain the total number of rural county divorces. Then the divorce rate for the rural county total and for each urban county within each state was computed using the female population figures from the census and the divorce figures from the U.S. Department of Commerce and Labor, Special Reports, *Marriage and Divorce: 1867-1906*. The average urban divorce rate for each state was then obtained by taking the mean of the urban county divorce rates.[5] Then total U.S. urban and rural averages were calculated by taking the mean of the state totals. In order to ascertain that the difference was statistically significant, a *t*-test for paired variates (using the urban and rural totals from each state) was performed.

Since the divorce figures for 1870 refer to divorces granted in an area rather than the residence of divorced persons, there may well have been some inaccuracy in the urban/rural difference as a result of people taking up residence in a particular city and then leaving after their divorce was granted. In addition, since the divorce figures were given for counties rather than specific cities, the urban/rural difference may be somewhat diluted by the inclusion of some rural areas in the urban total. Despite the lack of complete accuracy in the 1870 divorce figures, it was still possible to obtain valuable information.

Overall urban and rural differences, impact of city size and economic activity, and regional differences were calculated for each of the variables. The effect that regional differences in degree of urbanization had upon the urban/rural difference found for each variable also was analyzed. The urbanization of each of the five regions was calculated by using a table from the 1880 census that listed all places with a population of 4,000 or more in 1880 and also gave their populations for 1870.[6] This table probably picked up most, if not all, of the towns with 2,500 or more people in 1870.

For 1880 much the same information for the same variables as were found for 1870 was available. The one unfortunate difference was that information about female employment was given only for fifty selected cities rather than for all cities of 25,000 or more people. This meant that twenty cities between 25,000 and 35,000 population were omitted. Thus the 1880 urban/rural employment figures are somewhat less accurate than the 1870 ones. The same procedures described for 1870 were followed for the 1880 data. As with the 1870 divorce statistics, certain states had to be eliminated because of missing or incomplete records.[7] The degree of urbanization for each of the five regions was calculated as follows: The 1880 table that listed all places having 4,000 or more people was supplemented by an 1890 table that gave all places that had a population of 1,000 or more with the corresponding population figures for 1880.

By 1890, considerably more information was available. For cities of 25,000 or more people, there were data regarding the total number of males and females fifteen or older, for both the aggregate and the NWNP populations. Employment data were given for females ten or older for both the aggregate population and NWNP, but only for cities of 50,000 or more people. Thus the difference between the urban and rural working rate was somewhat masked by the need to include those cities between 25,000 and 50,000 population in the rural category. For the first time there were data for the child/woman ratio and conjugal status.[8] Information about the aggregate and the native white child/woman ratios appeared for all cities of 25,000 or more people.[9] The conjugal status of the fifteen-or-older, aggregate female population in all cities of 25,000 population or larger was given. Unfortunately, information regarding the conjugal status of native white females of native-born parents fifteen or older was only given for cities of 100,000 or more people, which limited the usefulness of any urban/rural comparison for this variable.

Some, but not all of the 1890 data, were present in ready-to-use form in the census: employed females ten or older, aggregate population, and NWNP; females ten or older, aggregate population, for cities of 50,000 or more; females and males fifteen or older, aggregate population, and NWNP for cities of 100,000 or more; and the conjugal condition for female fifteen or older, for both the aggregate population and NWNP, for cities of 100,000 or more. Other data needed for the variables had to be calculated, with the tables of ages providing a great deal of information. The tables were used to obtain the child/woman ratio for both the aggregate and native white populations, the number of NWNP females who were ten or older in cities of 50,000 or more, and the number of males and females fifteen or older in cities of less than 100,000. The tables giving conjugal status were used to obtain the number of single, married, and divorced females of the aggregate population according to the method described in the general procedure section at the beginning of this appendix. The percentage of females fifteen or older who were married or single was computed on the basis of all females who were fifteen or older. The percentage of divorced females was computed on the basis of all women who could have been divorced—married plus divorced females—rather than on the basis of all females. I also calculated the urban county versus rural county divorce rate as I had done for 1870 and 1880.

The 1900 census contained approximately the same amount of information that had been available in 1890. The only differences were that employment data were given for the ten-or-older, aggregate female population for cities of 25,000 population or larger, whereas, for NWNP, employment figures were given for females sixteen or older. Information regarding the employment of NWNP females came from the U.S. Department of Commerce, *Statistics of Women at Work: 1900.* In order to keep the 1900 employment figures of native white females of native-born parents comparable to those of preceding and succeeding years, the employment rate was derived by using the number of NWNP females who were ten or older as the population base rather than those who were sixteen or older. Since most employed females were over sixteen, this approach allowed for a reasonable degree of accuracy. The same procedure used to collect and reduce the data in 1890 was followed for 1900.

For 1910 the amount of information regarding the conjugal condition of females increased: For all cities of 25,000 or more people, the conjugal condition of the aggregate female population and for NWNP females was given. Data for males and females fifteen or older, for both the aggregate population and NWNP, were available. However, there was less information than had been present in either the 1890 or the 1900 censuses regarding female employment and the child/women ratio. Employment data were given only for the aggregate population for cities of 25,000 or more people. Sufficient data were unavailable for NWNP females.[10] For the child/woman ratio, not enough information was given to calculate a ratio for native white women. Since the child/woman ratio of native and foreign-born white women differed significantly, it was pointless to calculate a separate ratio for white women in nonsouthern cities that would have lumped together these two very different groups of women. Therefore, only an aggregate child/woman ratio was computed. Because of these limitations and because of questions raised regarding the accuracy of the 1910 female employment data,[11] the analysis of the 1910 data was more limited than that done for other years.

By 1910 many of the data were presented in ready-to-use form. The tables of conjugal condition provided information about the conjugal status of both the aggregate female population and NWNP females, and the total number of males and females fifteen or older, for the aggregate population and NWNP. The age tables contained the data for constructing the child/woman ratios. Occupation tables provided figures both for the number of females of the aggregate population, ten or older, and the number of employed females.

Only for 1920 was information available for all of the variables, and all of it was presented in immediately usable form. As with the 1910 census, information regarding the number of males and females fifteen or older, and the conjugal status of females came from the tables of conjugal condition. Information regarding females ten or older and their employment came from the tables of occupations. Most of the data were contained in the 1920 census. The one exception was the information about the child/woman ratio found in the U.S. Department of Commerce, *Ratio of Children to Women.* In addition to containing data for cities of 25,000 population for all of the variables, the 1920 census also presented a breakdown for the child/woman ratio and conjugal condition into an urban (2,500 or more people) and a rural (2,500 or fewer people) category. Thus for these variables, a determination of whether places between 2,500 and 25,000 in population size were more urban or more rural was made. Unfortunately, since comparable information regarding employment in places 2,500 or more and 2,500 or less was not given, it was not possible to determine whether places 2,500-25,000 in population were more urban or more rural with respect to female employment.

Each census posed a slightly different set of problems. But in spite of the difficulties presented by the inconsistencies and limitations of the data, the U.S. census and related special reports offer a rich source of material for the historian that can provide valuable new insights into the history of the city.

The remainder of Appendix A consists of thirty-eight tables referred to in the text portion of this book.

TABLE A.1. Percentage of Women Married in Each Age Group and Percentage Increase, 1890-1920, by Age Groups, for the Aggregate Population and Native Whites of Native-Born Parents

| | AGGREGATE POPULATION | | | | | NATIVE WHITES OF NATIVE-BORN PARENTS | | | | |
Age Group	1890	1900	1910	1920	Percent Increase 1890-1920	1890	1900	1910	1920	Percent Increase 1890-1920
15-19	9.5	10.9	11.3	12.5	31.6	10.8	12.2	12.5	13.3	23.2
20-24	46.7	46.5	49.6	52.3	12.0	50.3	49.8	51.8	53.4	6.2
25-29	71.4	68.9	71.8	73.4	2.8	74.0	71.8	} 77.1	74.0	b
30-34	79.8	78.0	79.0	80.1	b	80.8	79.7		80.7	b
35-44	80.6	79.5	80.1	80.3	b	81.5	80.8	81.9	81.6	b
45-54	73.9	73.9	74.8	74.0	b	75.0	75.6	71.7[a]	76.1	b

SOURCES: U.S., Department of the Interior, *Eleventh Census, 1890: Population*, pt. 1, Total Population, Sex, Nativity, Dwellings, and Marital Status, and pt. 2; U.S., Department of the Interior, Office of the Census, *Twelfth Census of the United States, 1900*, vol. 2, *Population: Ages, Marital Status, Occupations*; U.S., Department of Commerce and Labor, Bureau of the Census, *Thirteenth Census of the United States, 1910*, vol. 1, *Population*; U.S., Department of Commerce, *Fourteenth Census, 1920*, vols. 2 and 3.

[a] Ages forty-five to sixty-four.

[b] Less than 1 percent change.

TABLE A.2.   Percentage of Females Fifteen or Older Who Were Married, Aggregate Population and Native Whites of Native-Born Parents, 1890-1920

	AGGREGATE POPULATION			NATIVE WHITES OF NATIVE-BORN PARENTS		
	Urban	Rural	Percent Rural/ Urban Difference	Urban	Rural	Percent Rural/ Urban Difference
1890	52.0	59.3	14.0	a	a	—
1900	52.1	59.3	13.8	a	a	—
1910	54.7	61.3	12.1	53.6	61.0	13.8
1920	57.9	63.2	9.2	56.5	62.1	10.3

SOURCES: U.S., *Censuses, 1890-1920*.

NOTE: The overall percent married in urban areas and rural areas for each of the census years was calculated as follows. For each state that had at least one city of 25,000+, information regarding the variable was obtained for the state as a whole and for each of the 25,000+ cities. The overall, urban state average was computed by taking the mean of the city values. The state rural average was arrived at by subtracting the urban total from the state total and then calculating the mean. All of the state urban means and state rural means were added separately and divided by the total number of states to obtain the national averages.

[a]Data regarding the marital status of native whites of native-born parents in urban and rural areas were incomplete prior to 1910.

TABLE A.3. Percentage of Women Married in Each Age Group and the Percentage Change in the Proportion Married, for the Aggregate Population and Native Whites of Native-Born Parents in Urban and Rural Areas, 1910-20

	Aggregate Population						Native Whites of Native-Born Parents					
	1910		*1920*		*PERCENT INCREASE 1910-1920*		*1910*		*1920*		*PERCENT INCREASE 1910-1920*	
Age Group	*Urban*	*Rural*	*Urban*	*Rural*	*Urban*	*Rural*	*Urban*	*Rural*	*Urban*	*Rural*	*Urban*	*Rural*
15-24	25.1	35.9	30.4	34.6	21.1	-3.6	25.6	36.5	30.5	34.5	19.1	-5.5
25-34	69.6	81.4	72.6	82.0	4.3	0.7	69.9	82.3	71.4	82.6	2.1	0.4
35-44	75.4	85.6	76.2	85.8	1.1	0.2	75.4	86.4	76.0	86.5	0.8	0.1

SOURCES: U.S., *Censuses, 1910 and 1920.*

TABLE A.4. Percentage Rural/Urban Difference in Women Married, Aggregate Population and Native Whites of Native-Born Parents, 1910 and 1920

Age	1910		1920	
	Agg	NWNP	Agg	NWNP
15-24	43.0	42.6	13.8	13.1
25-34	17.0	17.7	13.0	15.7
35-44	13.5	14.6	12.6	13.8

NOTE: The percentage difference was calculated as follows:

$$\frac{\text{percent married in rural areas}}{\text{percent married in urban areas}} - 1 \times 100$$

Agg = Aggregate population. NWNP = Native whites of native-born parents.

TABLE A.5. Percentage of People Favorable Toward Birth Control as Reflected in Magazines of the Era

Time Period	Percent Favorable
1905-14	86[a]
1915-18	50
1919-21	87
1922-29	64

SOURCE: Harnell Hart, "Changing Social Attitudes and Interests," in *Recent Social Trends in the United States* (New York: McGraw-Hill, 1933), p. 416.

[a] Figures on which this index are based are too small to make the index reliable.

TABLE A.6.   Mean Age at Marriage for Women Married Between
1900 and 1905

Occupation of Husband	Mean Age at Marriage
Professional	24.8
Proprietor	23.3
Clerk	22.9
Skilled worker	21.8
Semiskilled worker	21.2
Unskilled worker	21.4

SOURCE: Frank Notestein, "Differential Age at Marriage According to Social
Class," *American Journal of Sociology* 37 (June 1931): 40.

TABLE A.7.   Average Age at Marriage According to Number of
Years Married, College-Educated (A) and Non-
College-Educated (B) Women, 1900

	MARRIED 10 YEARS OR LESS		MARRIED 10-20 YEARS		MARRIED 21 YEARS OR MORE	
	A	B	A	B	A	B
Average age at marriage	26.8	25.9	26.1	24.2	24.2	21.6

SOURCE: Mary Roberts Smith, "Statistics of College and Non-college Women,"
American Statistical Association 49 (March 1900): 8.

NOTE: The women in category B, that is, non-college-educated women, had
generally received their education in the following: private schools, high schools,
public schools, seminaries, and/or academies; some had partial college, art or music
study, or private teachers.

TABLE A.8. The Percentage of Married Women by Size of City, 1890-1920

	POPULATION OF CITY			
	25,000-50,000	*50,000-100,000*	*100,000-500,000*	*500,000+*
1890	52.8 ± 5	51.4 ± 5	51.3 ± 4	51.5 ± 4
Agg	*N* = 66	*N* = 30	*N* = 24	*N* = 4
1900	53.6 ± 5	51.9 ± 5	52.0 ± 3	50.6 ± 3
Agg	*N* = 81	*N* = 38	*N* = 31	*N* = 8
1910	52.7 ± 6	54.1 ± 5	51.1 ± 5	48.2 ± 3
NWNP	*N* = 122	*N* = 59	*N* = 42	*N* = 8
1920	56.2 ± 6	56.6 ± 5	54.8 ± 6	52.6 ± 5
NWNP	*N* = 144	*N* = 74	*N* = 55	*N* = 12

SOURCES: U.S., *Censuses, 1890-1920*.

NOTE: The mean percentage of married women was calculated from census data (1890-1920) for all cities in the United States in each given size category. ± Standard deviations are shown. For 1890 and 1900, calculations were made using the aggregate population because data were not available for all size categories for native whites of native-born parents. N = Number of observations. Agg = Aggregate population; NWNP = Native whites of native-born parents. The correlation coefficients for years other than 1910 were as follows: 1890, $r = -0.07$; 1900, $r = 0.02$; 1920, $r = 0.04$.

TABLE A.9. Native White and Aggregate Child/Woman Ratios by Size of City, and Correlation Coefficients for Native Whites, 1890-1920

	POPULATION OF CITY					Correlation Coefficient
	25,000-50,000	50,000-100,000	100,000-500,000	500,000+		
1890 NW	357 ± 82 N = 66	359 ± 98 N = 30	334 ± 69 N = 24	311 ± 34 N = 4		r = −0.16[a] N = 124
1900 NW	342 ± 75 N = 81	311 ± 78 N = 39	299 ± 60 N = 31	296 ± 60 N = 8		r = −0.11 N = 158
Agg	481 ± 94 N = 81	455 ± 77 N = 39	471 ± 104 N = 31	471 ± 39 N = 8		—
1910 Agg	446 ± 107 N = 122	457 ± 84 N = 59	416 ± 77 N = 42	456 ± 48 N = 8		—
1920 NW	403 ± 73 N = 144	387 ± 70 N = 74	361 ± 46 N = 55	336 ± 61 N = 12		r = −0.15[b] N = 285

SOURCES: U.S., *Censuses, 1890-1920.*

NOTE: The mean was calculated from census data for all cities in the United States in each given size range. ± Standard deviations are shown. Agg = Aggregate population; NW = Native white population, N = Number of observations. r = the correlation coefficient.

[a] Significant at the 0.05 level.
[b] Significant at the 0.01 level.

TABLE A.10. Percentage Differences Among Communities of Different Population Sizes, 1920

	25,000+	Under 25,000	Percent Difference	2,500+	Under 2,500	Percent Difference
Native white child/ woman ratio	388	643	65.7	415	699	68.4
Percent single						
Agg	28.1	25.7	9.3	27.9	24.8	12.5
NWNP	30.6	27.3	12.1	30.0	26.4	13.6
Percent married						
Agg	57.9	63.2	9.2	58.2	64.5	10.8
NWNP	56.5	62.3	10.3	57.1	63.7	11.6

SOURCE: U.S., Department of Commerce, *Fourteenth Census, 1920.*
NOTE: Agg = Aggregate population; NWNP = Native whites of native-born parents.

TABLE A.11. Correlation Between the Percentage of Catholic Females
or the Percentage of Foreign-Born Females and the
Aggregate Child/Woman Ratio, 1900

	Correlation Coefficient	*Number of Observations*
Percentage of Catholic females vs. child/woman ratio	$r = 0.21^a$	$N = 146$
Percentage of foreign-born females vs. child/woman ratio	$r = 0.39^a$	$N = 158$

SOURCE: U.S., Department of the Interior, *Twelfth Census, 1900.*
NOTE: Cities of 25,000+. Data regarding the number of Catholic women were
missing for some cities.
[a]Significant at the 0.001 level.

TABLE A.12.   Correlation Between Percent of Catholic Women and
              (1) Fertility, (2) Economic Function, and (3) Female
              Employment, 1900

	Correlation Coefficient	Number of Observations
Percent of Catholic women vs. native white child/woman ratio	$r = -0.39^a$	$N = 146$
Percent of total labor force in M&M occupations vs. percent of Catholic women	$r = 0.44^a$	$N = 146$
Percent of total labor force in M&M occupations vs. percent NWNP employed[b]	$r = 0.54^a$	$N = 79$
Percent of total labor force in M&M occupations vs. native white child/woman ratio	$r = -0.28^a$	$N = 158$

SOURCE: U.S., Department of the Interior, *Twelfth Census, 1900*.

NOTE: Cities of 25,000+. Data regarding the number of Catholic women were missing for some cities. Agg = Aggregate population; NWNP = Native whites of native-born parents. M&M = Manufacturing and Mechanical.

[a]Significant at the 0.001 level.

[b]In 1900, data regarding employment of native white women of native-born parents were available for females sixteen or older in cities of 50,000 or larger.

TABLE A.13. Number of Persons Employed as Servants, Waiters, and Housekeepers and Stewards per 1,000 Population, 1870-1920

	Number of Servants, Waiters, Housekeepers, and Stewards of Both Sexes and All Ages per 1,000 Population	Number of Servants of Both Sexes Per 1,000 Population
1870	25.9	a
1880	23.0	a
1890	24.7	a
1900	22.6	19.1
1910	22.4	18.3
1920	17.3	13.0

SOURCE: U.S., Department of Commerce, *Women in Gainful Occupations, 1870-1920*, p. 39.
[a]Data not given.

TABLE A.14. Number and Percent of Employed Females Ten Years or Older Who Worked in Occupations Classified as Domestic or Personal or as Servants

	DOMESTIC AND PERSONAL[a]		SERVANTS	
	Number	Percent of Total Age 10+ Employed	Number	Percent of Total Age 10+ Employed
1890	1,667,698	42.6	1,216,639	31.2
1900	2,099,165	39.4	1,242,192	23.3
1920	2,186,924	25.6	1,012,133	11.8

SOURCES: U.S., Department of Commerce, *Women in Gainful Occupations, 1870-1920*; U.S., Department of Commerce and Labor, Bureau of the Census, *Statistics of Women at Work: Based on Unpublished Information Derived from the Schedules of the Twelfth Census: 1900* (1907).
[a]The category changed over time.

TABLE A.15. Increase in the Number of Establishments and Employees in Selected Food and Clothing Industries, 1850-1910

Industry	1869	1909	Percent Increase
Canning and preserving fruits and vegetables			
Establishments	127	3,369	2552.8
Employees	6,024	50,000	730.0
Slaughtering and meat-packing			
Establishments	768	1,641	113.7
Employees	8,366	89,728	972.5
Bakery and bakery products			
Establishments	3,550	23,926	574.0
Employees	14,126	100,216	609.4
Butter, cheese, condensed milk[a]			
Establishments	3,932[b]	8,479	115.6
Employees	7,903[b]	18,431	133.2
Men's clothing			
Establishments	4,278[c]	96,551	2156.9
Employees	5,584[c]	191,000	3320.5
Women's clothing			
Establishments	188[d]	4,558	2324.5
Employees	5,739[d]	153,743	2579.9

SOURCE: U.S., Department of Commerce and Labor, Bureau of the Census, *Thirteenth Census of the United States, 1910*, vol. 10, *Manufactures: Reports for Principal Industries*.

[a] At the time of the 1849 census there were 8 cheese establishments with 55 employees; in 1859 there were 2 with 7 workers plus 1 condensed-milk establishment. In 1869 there were 1,313 with 4,607 workers. In 1879 the two categories were combined.
[b] Figures are for 1879.
[c] Figures are for 1849.
[d] Figures are for 1859.

TABLE A.16.   Retail Sales by Type of Outlet, 1869-1919
(Millions of Dollars)

Type of Retail Outlet	1869	1879	1889	1899	1909	1919
Grocery, independent	985	1,238	1,668	2,027	2,934	7,602
Grocery, chain	–	–	–	183	751	2,588
Department store	–	–	–	161	676	2,501
Household appliances	44	46	83	113	246	720
Meat markets	128	175	246	374	654	1,616
Restaurants	83	135	200	361	680	2,189

SOURCE: Harold Barger, *Distribution's Place in the American Economy Since 1869* (Princeton, N.J.: Princeton University Press, 1955), pp. 148-49. See Barger for a discussion of how totals were calculated.

TABLE A.17.   The Percentage Increase in the Proportion of Employed Women, Urban and Rural Areas, 1870-80 and 1890-1920, Aggregate Population and Native Whites of Native-Born Parents

	1870-80		1890-1920	
	Urban	Rural	Urban	Rural
Agg	12.0	6.1	10.2	2.6
NWNP	a	a	42.9	31.8

SOURCES: U.S., *Censuses, 1870-1920*.
NOTE: See Table 24 for the percent of women working in different years. For 1870, 1880, and 1920, urban = cities of 25,000+. For 1890, urban = cities of 50,000+. Agg = Aggregate population. NWNP = Native whites of native-born parents.
^aData not available.

TABLE A.18. Percentage of Employed Women Ten Years or Older,
by Nativity Group, 1890 and 1900

	1890	1900	Percent change 1890-1900
NWNP	12.4	14.5	16.9
NWFP	25.3	25.4	a
FW	19.8	19.4	−2.0
Blacks	39.9	43.2	8.3

SOURCE: U.S., Department of Commerce and Labor, *Statistics of Women at Work: 1900*, p. 20.

NOTE: NWNP = Native whites of native-born parents. NWFP = Native whites of foreign-born parents. FW = Foreign-born whites.

[a]Less than 1 percent change.

TABLE A.19. Percentage of Employed Women Sixteen or Older,
by Nativity Group, in Cities of 100,000 Population or
Larger and Smaller-Sized Areas, 1900 and 1920

	100,000+			SMALLER AREAS		
	1900	1920	Percent Increase 1900-1920	1900	1920	Percent Increase 1900-1920
Agg	28.0	32.5	16.1	18.6	20.5	10.2
NWNP	24.6	33.2	35.0	13.4	17.0	26.9
NWFP	32.4	37.4	15.4	21.8	23.6	8.3
FW	23.2	22.4	−3.5	16.1	15.2	−5.6
Black	53.7	53.7	0.0	42.0	41.2	−1.9

SOURCE: U.S., Department of Commerce, *Women in Gainful Occupations, 1870-1920.*

NOTE: Agg = Aggregate population; NWNP = Native whites of native-born parents; NWFP = Native whites of foreign or mixed parentage; FW = Foreign-born whites.

TABLE A.20. Number and Percentage of Females Ten or Older Engaged in Nonagricultural Pursuits, 1870-1920

Year	Total Females Ten or Older in Nonagricultural Work	SERVANTS WAITRESSES, ETC.		CLERKS, SALES-WOMEN, STENOS, TYPISTS, BOOK-KEEPERS, ETC.		MILLS AND FACTORIES		PROFESSIONALS	
		Number	Percent	Number	Percent	Number	Percent	Number	Percent
1870	1,439,285	873,738	60.7	10,798	0.8	252,702	17.6	91,963	6.4
1880	2,052,582	970,273	47.3	38,088	1.9	429,132	20.9	175,351	8.5
1890	3,235,424	1,302,728	40.3	171,712	5.3	657,661	20.3	307,774	9.5
1900	4,341,599	1,430,692	33.0	394,747	9.1	966,167	22.3	433,862	10.0
1910	6,268,271	1,595,572	25.5	930,763	14.8	1,450,151	23.1	724,176	11.6
1920	7,465,383	1,358,665	18.2	1,910,695	25.6	1,777,022	23.8	992,638	13.3

SOURCE: U.S., Department of Commerce, *Women in Gainful Occupations, 1870-1920*, pp. 36, 40-51.

TABLE A.21. Females Sixteen Years or Older, Total and Employed, 1890-1920

Age Group	PERCENT DISTRIBUTION OF ALL WOMEN SIXTEEN OR OLDER BY AGE GROUP				PERCENT DISTRIBUTION OF EMPLOYED WOMEN SIXTEEN OR OLDER BY AGE GROUP			
	1890	1900	1920	Percent Change (1890-1920)	1890	1900	1920	Percent Change (1890-1920)
16-24	30.4	28.8	25.0	−13.2[b]	49.9[a]	44.2	39.3	−11.1[b]
25-44	42.3	43.4	44.5	5.2	33.7	38.2	41.7	23.7
45+	26.9	27.5	30.3	12.6	15.9	17.2	18.8	18.2
Not reported	0.3	0.2	0.2	—	0.5	0.4	0.2	—

SOURCES: U.S., Department of Commerce, *Women in Gainful Occupations, 1870-1920*, pp. 23, 67, 257-58; U.S., Department of Commerce and Labor, *Women at Work: 1900*, pp. 162, 168; U.S., Department of the Interior, *Eleventh Census, 1890*, vol. 1, *Population*, pt. 2, p. cxxi.

[a] In 1890 data were given for the fifteen to twenty-four age group.

[b] For the sixteen to twenty-four age group the percentage change was calculated for 1900-1920 because of lack of comparability of 1890 figures for the percentage employed.

TABLE A.22. Percent of Employed Women in Different Age Groups,
Aggregate Population and Native Whites of Native-
Born Parents, 1900 and 1920

Age Group	AGGREGATE POPULATION			NATIVE WHITES OF NATIVE-BORN PARENTS		
	1900	1920	Percent Increase	1900	1920	Percent Increase
16-24	31.6	37.6	19.0	21.0	30.8	46.7
25-44	18.1	22.4	23.8	12.9	18.5	43.4
45-64	14.1	17.1	21.3	11.3	14.4	27.4
65+	9.1	8.0	−12.1	7.8	6.8	−12.8

SOURCE: U.S., Department of Commerce, *Women in Gainful Occupations,
1870-1920,* pp. 257-58.

TABLE A.23. Percentage That Each Age Group Is of Total Employed in Selected Occupational Categories, Aggregate Population, 1890 and 1920

Age Groups	ALL OCCUPATIONS			PROFESSIONAL			CLERICAL		
	1890	1920	Percent Change	1890	1920	Percent Change	1890	1920	Percent Change
10-14	5.2	2.4	−53.8	0.1	a	—	2.6	0.4	−84.6
15-24	47.3	39.4	−16.7	52.6	37.4	−28.9	63.9	59.0	−7.7
25-44	31.9	40.0	25.4	39.5	48.3	22.3	29.5	36.4	23.4
45-64	12.6	15.8	25.4	6.7	12.8	91.0	3.4	4.0	17.6

SOURCES: U.S., Department of the Interior, *Eleventh Census, 1890*, vol. 1, *Population*, pt. 2, pp. 306, 308, 372, 374; U.S., Department of Commerce, *Fourteenth Census, 1920*, vol. 4, *Occupations*, p. 376.
^aLess than 0.1.

TABLE A.24. Percentage of Married Women Sixteen or Older Who Were Employed, 1890 and 1920, Aggregate Population and Native Whites of Native-Born Parents

	1890	1920	Percent Increase (1890-1920)
Aggregate population	4.6	9.0	95.7
Native whites of native-born parents	2.7	6.3	133.3

SOURCES: U.S., Department of Commerce, *Women in Gainful Occupations, 1870-1920*, pp. 76, 78; U.S., Department of the Interior, *Eleventh Census*, 1890, vol. 2, *Population*, pt. 2, p. cxxiv.

TABLE A.25. Percentage of Married Women Working, by Age Group, 1890 and 1920, Aggregate Population and Native Whites of Native-Born Parents, Total United States

	15-24	25-34	35-44	45+
Agg				
1890	6.4	4.8	4.5	3.6
1920	11.7	9.7	9.5	6.6
Percent increase (1890-1920)	82.8	102.1	111.1	83.3
NWNP				
1890	2.5	2.4	2.3	3.1
1920	7.7	6.6	6.6	5.0
Percent increase (1890-1920)	208.0	175.0	187.0	61.3

SOURCES: U.S., Department of Commerce and Labor, *Statistics of Women at Work: 1900*, p. 16; U.S., Department of the Interior, *Eleventh Census, 1890*, vol. 2, *Population*, pt. 2, p. 750; U.S., Department of Commerce, *Women in Gainful Occupations, 1870-1920*, p. 79.

NOTE: Agg = Aggregate population. NWNP = Native whites of native-born parents.

TABLE A.26. Percentage of Women in Selected Occupations Who Were Married, Aggregate Population, 1890 and 1920

Occupation	1890	1920	Percentage Increase
All occupations	11.6[a]	21.2[b]	82.8
Stenos and typists	2.4	6.6	175.0
Bookkeepers, accountants	4.3	11.5	167.4
Lawyers	21.2	34.2	61.3
Teachers of music	11.9	24.6	106.7
Physicians, surgeons	27.0	32.9	21.0
Professors in colleges and universities	10.9	11.3	3.7
Teachers	4.5	9.7	115.6
Trained nurses	c	7.5	—
Librarians	c	7.4	—

SOURCES: U.S., Department of the Interior, *Eleventh Census, 1890,* vol. 1, *Population,* pt. 2, pp. 306-8, 372-74, 416-17; U.S., Department of Commerce, *Women in Gainful Occupations, 1870-1920,* pp. 77, 83, 182-87.

NOTE: Data from 1890 based on females fifteen or older; 1920 data based on females sixteen or older.

[a]Women fifteen or older in nonagricultural work.

[b]Women sixteen or older in nonagricultural work.

[c]Data not given.

TABLE A.27. Percent Distribution, by Living Situation, of Employed Women for Selected Occupations, Aggregate Population and Native Whites of Native-Born Parents, 1900

Living Situation	AGGREGATE POPULATION				NATIVE WHITES OF NATIVE-BORN PARENTS			
	All Occupations	Stenographer and Typist	Teachers	Clerk and Copyist	All Occupations	Stenographer and Typist	Teachers	Clerk and Copyist
Living at home	64.8	79.3	72.3	82.1	66.2	72.6	69.8	74.4
Heads of homes	11.9	2.3	6.6	4.8	11.5	6.9	3.0	6.4
Living with father or mother	38.5	64.8	51.6	63.8	40.6	50.5	53.5	54.0
Living with other relatives	14.5	12.2	14.1	13.5	14.1	15.2	13.3	13.0
Boarding[a]	35.2	20.7	27.7[b]	17.9	33.8	27.4	30.2[b]	25.6

SOURCE: U.S., Department of Commerce and Labor, *Statistics of Women at Work: 1900*, pp. 25, 101, 108, 121.

[a]Includes living with employer.

[b]It appeared to be common practice, at least in small towns and rural areas, for teachers to board around at the homes of students. See Marie Louise Barrett Chamberlin, *Looking Back from Eighty-five* (Chicago: Federal Printing Co., 1926); Ella M. Doggett Hostetler, *Sketches Along the Way from the Year 1856* (Lincoln, Neb.: Woodruff Printing Co., 1916), pp. 74-77.

TABLE A.28. Percent Distribution, by Living Situation, of Employed Women for Selected Occupations, Aggregate Population, 1920

Living Situation	ALL OCCUPATIONS		AGGREGATE POPULATION				
	Aggregate Population	Native Whites of Native-Born Parents	Stenographers and Typists	Teachers	Telephone Operators	Clerks
Living at home	78.6	76.7	84.6	69.6	83.5	85.8
Heads of homes	15.2	12.1	3.4	9.5	3.6	5.5
Living with father or mother	37.7	42.9	66.5	43.0	64.0	62.7
Living with other relatives	11.4	11.4	11.1	12.8	12.4	12.2
Living with husband	14.3	10.3	3.5	4.3	3.5	5.4
Boarding[a]	21.5	23.3	15.4	30.4	16.5	14.2

SOURCE: U.S., Department of Commerce, *Women in Gainful Occupations, 1870-1920*, pp. 124, 130.
[a]Includes living with employer.

TABLE A.29. Percentage of Employed Women by Size of City, Aggregate Population and Native Whites of Native-Born Parents, 1870-1920

	POPULATION			
	25,000- *50,000*	*50,000-* *100,000*	*100,000-* *500,000*	*500,000+*
1870				
Agg	17.7 ± 8.5 $N = 25$	16.9 ± 4.1 $N = 10$	15.3 ± 3.3[a] $N = 14$	—
1880				
Agg	19.8 ± 7.8 $N = 15$	18.3 ± 6.7 $N = 13$	15.6 ± 3.6 $N = 16$	18.1 ± 3.8 $N = 4$
1890				
Agg	b	25.9 ± 7.2 $N = 30$	23.9 ± 3.8 $N = 24$	25.3 ± 3.8 $N = 4$
NWNP	b	18.5 ± 4.0 $N = 30$	18.1 ± 1.9 $N = 24$	18.3 ± 2.9 $N = 4$
1900				
Agg	24.2 ± 6.0 $N = 81$	26.4 ± 7.1 $N = 39$	25.4 ± 4.9 $N = 31$	26.7 ± 2.7 $N = 8$
NWNP[c]	b	20.3 ± 5.2 $N = 39$	20.2 ± 2.6 $N = 31$	21.7 ± 2.2 $N = 8$
1910[d]				
Agg	26.7 ± 6.3 $N = 122$	27.7 ± 6.7 $N = 59$	29.1 ± 5.2 $N = 42$	29.2 ± 3.4 $N = 8$
1920				
NWNP	24.3 ± 4.7 $N = 144$	25.8 ± 5.0 $N = 74$	27.6 ± 3.5 $N = 55$	29.7 ± 3.1 $N = 12$

SOURCES: U.S., *Censuses, 1870-1920.*

NOTE: Mean and standard deviation (±) were calculated on the basis of the total number of cities in a particular size category. For 1870 and 1880, employment data were available only for the total female population rather than females ten or older. Agg = Aggregate population. NWNP = Native whites of native-born parents. N = Number of observations.

[a]100,000+.

[b]Data not available.

[c]For 1900, data for native whites of native-born parents were available for females sixteen or older.

[d]In 1910, employment data for native whites of native-born parents were not given.

TABLE A.30. Sex Ratio Found in Strong Manufacturing and Mechanical Cities or Strong Trade and Transportation Cities, 1870-1920

	1870	1880	1890	1900	1920
Strong M&M	92.8	90.5	92.1	94.9	109.1
Strong T&T	102.9	106.9	109.1	103.2	101.9

SOURCES: U.S., *Censuses, 1870-1920*.

NOTE: See Table 9 in Chapter 6 for a description of how strong manufacturing and mechanical and strong trade and transportation cities were determined. M&M = Manufacturing and Mechanical. T&T = Trade and Transportation.

TABLE A.31. Correlation Between Conjugal Condition and Percent of Women Employed in Urban Areas, Aggregate Population and Native Whites of Native-Born Parents, 1890-1920

	1890[a]	1900	1920
Married			
Agg	$r = -0.68^c$	$r = -0.65^c$	$r = -0.64^c$
	$N = 58$	$N = 158$	$N = 285$
NWNP[b]	$r = -0.26$	$r = -0.10$	$r = -0.66^c$
	$N = 27$	$N = 30$	$N = 285$
Single			
Agg	$r = 0.52^c$	$r = 0.42^c$	$r = 0.51^c$
	$N = 58$	$N = 158$	$N = 285$
NWNP[b]	$r = 0.17$	$r = 0.18$	$r = 0.62^c$
	$N = 27$	$N = 30$	$N = 285$

SOURCES: U.S., *Censuses, 1890-1920*.

NOTE: Percentage of women married or single and percentage of women employed were calculated for each city for each census year. Correlations were then computed. Unless otherwise stated, calculations were made on the basis of all cities of 25,000+. Marital status was calculated on the basis of females fifteen or older,

Table A.31 Continued

and employment on the basis of females ten or older. Agg = Aggregate population.
NWNP = Native whites of native-born parents. r = Correlation coefficient. N =
Number of observations.

[a] For 1890, employment data were available only for cities of 50,000+.

[b] In 1890 and 1900, marital status for native white women of native-born parents
was only given for cities of 100,000+. Due to reporting error in the census, in 1890,
100,000+ cities in Massachusetts had to be excluded from the calculation; in 1900,
100,000+ cities in Massachusetts, New Jersey, and Rhode Island had to be eliminated
from consideration.

[c] Significant at the 0.001 level.

TABLE A.32.   Correlation Between Percent of Employed Women and
Child/Woman Ratio, Aggregate and Native White
Populations, 1890-1920

	Percent of Employed Women, Aggregate Population Vs. Aggregate Child/Woman Ratio	Percent of Employed Native White Women of Native-Born Parents Vs. Native White Child/Woman Ratio
1890[a]	$r = -0.49^c$, $N = 58$	$r = -0.36^c$, $N = 58$
1900	$r = -0.37^c$, $N = 158$	b
1910	$r = -0.28^c$, $N = 231$	d
1920	–	$r = -0.46^c$, $N = 285$

SOURCES: U.S., *Censuses, 1890-1920.*

NOTE: The percent of employed women ten or older in each city of 25,000+ (unless
otherwise indicated) and the child/woman ratios for the same cities were calculated,
and the strength of the correlation between the two variables was then tested. The child/
woman ratios for native white women rather than for native white women of native-born
parents were computed because data for the latter were not given. r = Correlation coefficient. N = Number of observations.

[a] In 1890, data were given for cities of 50,000+.

[b] In 1900, employment data for NWNP women were only available for females sixteen
or older in cities of 50,000+. The difference in the age group looked at is important, and
the results of the correlation analysis have not been included in the table because of lack
of comparability. The results were $r = -0.61$, $N = 77$, significant at the 0.0001 level.

[c] Significant at the 0.001 level.

[d] Data not given.

TABLE A.33. Divorces per 1,000 Females in Urban and Rural Areas for Total United States and by Region, and Percentage Increase by Decade for Total United States, 1870-90

				PERCENT CHANGE	
	1870	1880	1890	1870-80	1880-90
Total United States					
Urban	0.98	1.39	2.04	42.2	47.2
Rural	0.64	0.97	1.40	52.5	44.1
North Atlantic					
Urban	0.92	1.07	1.08	16.3	a
Rural	0.77	0.86	1.03	11.7	19.8
South Atlantic					
Urban	0.39	0.51	0.70	30.8	37.3
Rural	0.16	0.28	0.56	75.0	100.0
North Central					
Urban	1.52	1.84	2.19	21.0	19.0
Rural	0.89	1.06	1.47	19.0	38.7
South Central					
Urban	0.77	0.93	2.46	20.8	165.6
Rural	0.26	0.55	1.24	111.5	125.5
West					
Urban	2.24	4.17	4.02	86.2	−3.6
Rural	1.64	3.44	2.77	109.8	−19.5

SOURCES: U.S., Department of Commerce and Labor, Bureau of the Census, Special Reports, *Marriage and Divorce: 1867-1906*, 2 vols. (1909); and U.S., *Censuses, 1870-1890*.

NOTE: The following procedure was used to calculate the divorce rate. The number of divorces occurring in a ten-year period (1867-76, 1877-86, 1887-96) was given for every county in every state, and a one-year "average" was calculated for 1870, 1880, and 1890. The number of females residing in each state and the urban counties of that state was obtained from the 1870-90 censuses. Divorce rates were then calculated for each urban county in each state. Then state urban divorce rates (the average of the rate of all urban counties in the state) and state rural divorce rates were computed. Then overall U.S. urban and rural divorce rates were calculated on the basis of state averages. Regional urban and rural rates were also calculated on the basis of state averages. Urban = counties with cities of 25,000 or more people. Only states that had both urban and rural sectors were used in the analysis.

[a] Less than 1 percent.

TABLE A.34. Number of Divorced Women per 1,000 Women Married or Divorced in Urban and Rural Areas, Aggregate Population and Native Whites of Native-Born Parents, 1890-1920

	1890		1900		1910		1920	
	Agg	NWNP[a]	Agg	NWNP[a]	Agg	NWNP	Agg	NWNP
Total United States								
Urban	9.5	11.4	14.0	15.0	15.9	17.8	21.1	23.0
Rural	7.1	8.4	8.7	10.0	9.5	9.7	10.7	11.4
North Atlantic								
Urban	7.2	9.7	8.2	b	9.1	15.4	11.6	19.0
Rural	7.2	6.8	8.6	b	9.3	12.7	10.4	14.7
South Atlantic								
Urban	5.5	6.6	10.7	8.5	10.6	9.8	13.6	13.3
Rural	3.4	2.4	5.8	3.1	6.5	4.8	6.9	5.5

Table A.34 continued

North Central								
Urban	10.3	12.7	13.1	17.5	17.7	21.9	21.8	23.1
Rural	7.6	9.8	8.4	10.8	9.5	11.1	10.4	11.8
South Central								
Urban	13.6	8.3	20.4	11.4	22.2	16.1	29.2	23.5
Rural	6.7	5.2	9.2	6.5	10.8	6.6	12.0	7.9
West								
Urban	13.2	17.3	21.6	21.0	23.0	28.0	32.4	36.1
Rural	10.5	12.2	11.9	14.7	13.5	13.5	16.2	16.7

SOURCE: *United States Censuses, 1890-1920.*
NOTE: Unless otherwise stated, urban = 25,000+. Agg. = Aggregate population. NWNP = Native whites of native-born parents.
[a] Data available only for cities of 100,000+ excluding Massachusetts.
[b] NWNP for the North Atlantic region were omitted because Massachusetts, New Jersey, and Rhode Island had to be excluded from calculation due to errors in the data published in the census.

TABLE A.35. Percentage Increase by Decade of Number of Divorced Women per 1,000 Women Married or Divorced, Urban and Rural Areas, Aggregate Population and Native Whites of Native-Born Parents, 1890-1920

| | 1890 to 1900[a] | | 1900 to 1910 | 1910 to 1920 | |
	Agg	NWNP	Agg	Agg	NWNP
Total					
Urban	47.4	32.4	13.7	32.1	29.2
Rural	21.3	18.5	9.8	13.2	16.7
North Atlantic					
Urban	13.5	b	10.7	27.6	23.4
Rural	20.7	b	7.6	12.7	15.7
South Atlantic					
Urban	95.8	28.6	98.4	28.4	34.7
Rural	70.6	29.2	12.3	6.0	14.6

Table A.35 continued

North Central					
Urban	26.9	37.8	35.4	23.1	5.6
Rural	11.1	10.2	12.6	9.6	6.3
South Central					
Urban	50.6	37.3	8.6	31.5	46.0
Rural	37.0	25.0	16.9	11.3	19.7
West					
Urban	64.3	21.4	6.4	40.6	28.6
Rural	12.7	20.5	13.5	19.9	23.7

SOURCE: U.S., *Censuses, 1890-1920.*

NOTE: Unless otherwise stated, urban = 25,000+. Agg = Aggregate population. NWNP = Native whites of native-born parents.

[a] Urban = 100,000+, excluding Massachusetts for 1890 and Massachusetts, New Jersey, and Rhode Island for 1900.

[b] NWNP for the North Atlantic region were omitted because Massachusetts, New Jersey, and Rhode Island had to be excluded for 1900 due to errors published in the census.

TABLE A.36. Urban/Rural Difference with Respect to Number of Divorced Women per 1,000 Married or Divorced Women, Aggregate Population and Native Whites of Native-Born Parents, 1890-1920

	1890		1900		1910		1920	
	Agg	NWNP[a]	Agg	NWNP[a]	Agg	NWNP	Agg	NWNP
Total United States	33.8	35.7	60.9	50.0	67.3	83.5	97.2	101.8
North Atlantic	0.0	42.6	-4.7	[b]	-2.2	21.3	11.5	29.3
South Atlantic	61.7	175.0	84.5	174.2	63.1	104.2	97.1	141.8
North Central	35.5	29.6	56.0	62.0	86.3	97.3	109.6	95.8
South Central	102.9	59.6	121.7	75.4	105.6	143.9	143.3	197.5
West	25.7	41.8	81.5	42.9	70.4	107.4	100.0	116.2

SOURCE: U.S., *Censuses, 1890-1920.*

NOTE: Urban = 25,000+ unless otherwise stated. Urban/rural − 1 x 100 = urban rural difference.

[a]Urban = 100,000+, excluding Massachusetts for 1890 and Massachusetts, New Jersey, and Rhode Island for 1900.

[b]Data for NWNP for the North Atlantic region were omitted because Massachusetts, New Jersey, and Rhode Island had to be excluded due to errors published in the census.

TABLE A.37. Percentage of Women Asking for and Receiving Alimony in Divorces Granted to Wife, 1887-1906

	US	NA	SA	NC	SC	W
Alimony requested	18.4	14.6	11.4	24.3	8.1	19.0
Granted	12.7	9.3	5.1	17.2	6.1	12.3
Not granted	5.6	—	—	—	—	—
Unknown	0.1	—	—	—	—	—
Alimony not requested	80.2	—	—	—	—	—
Unknown	1.4	—	—	—	—	—

SOURCE: U.S., Department of Commerce and Labor, *Marriage and Divorce: 1867-1906*, 1:33, 99.

NOTE: US = United States; NA = North Atlantic; SA = South Atlantic; NC = North Central; SC = South Central; W = West.

TABLE A.38. Percentage of Employed Women in Each Marital Class, Aggregate Population and Native Whites of Native-Born Parents, 1890-1900

	1890		1900	
	Agg	NWNP	Agg	NWNP
All	19.0	12.4	20.6	14.6
Single	40.5	27.5	45.9	33.8
Married	4.6	2.7	5.6	3.0
Widowed	29.3	23.7	31.5	26.1
Divorced	49.0	42.6	55.3	47.5

SOURCES: U.S., Department of Commerce and Labor, *Statistics of Women at Work: 1900*, p. 16; U.S., Department of Commerce, *Women in Gainful Occupations, 1870-1920*, p. 19; U.S., Department of the Interior, *Eleventh Census, 1890*, vol. 1, *Population*, pt. 2, p. cxxix.

NOTE: In 1890, percentages were calculated on the basis of females fifteen or older, and in 1900 on the basis of those sixteen or older. Agg = Aggregate population. NWNP = Native whites of native-born parents.

Notes

1. All simple calculations were performed on a Texas Instruments SR10 hand calculator. More complicated statistical operations (mean, standard deviation, and variance, t-test for paired variates, and Pearson Correlation Coefficient) were performed on a Wang 600 desk top computer. See M. J. Moroney, *Facts from Figures* (Baltimore: Penguin Books, 1951); H. T. Hayslett, *Statistics Made Simple* (Garden City, N.Y.: Doubleday & Co., 1968); and William Guenther, *Concepts of Statistical Inference* (New York: McGraw-Hill Book Co., 1965), for discussions of these statistical tests.

2. The original plan had been to follow a classification schema somewhat on the order of that proposed by Chauncy Harris, "Functional Classification of Cities in the United States," *Geographical Review* 33 (January 1943): 86-99. The more recent and detailed typologies such as Robert Atchley, "A Size-Function Typology of Cities," *Demography* 4, no. 2 (1967): 721-33, required much more information than was available in the censuses.

3. For most of the years under study, no breakdown between the total engaged in trade and the total engaged in transportation was given. In 1920, trade and transportation figures were presented separately and an analysis of each one's impact was made.

4. The states found in each region are as follows. *North Atlantic:* Maine, New Hampshire, Vermont, Massachusetts, Rhode Island, Connecticut, New York, New Jersey, and Pennsylvania. *South Atlantic:* Delaware, Maryland, Washington, D.C., Virginia, West Virginia, North Carolina, South Carolina, Georgia, and Florida. *North Central:* Ohio, Indiana, Illinois, Michigan, Wisconsin, Minnesota, Iowa, Missouri, North Dakota, South Dakota, Nebraska, and Kansas. *South Central:* Kentucky, Tennessee, Alabama, Mississippi, Louisiana, Texas, Oklahoma, and Arkansas. *Western:* Montana, Wyoming, Colorado, New Mexico, Arizona, Utah, Nevada, Idaho, Washington, Oregon, and California.

5. For 1870, some states with cities of 25,000 population had to be omitted for various reasons: Alabama—the pre-1887 records for Mobile were destroyed by fire; Illinois—Cook County records were destroyed by fire in 1871; South Carolina—divorce was illegal except between 1872 and 1878. Also, Cincinnati was not included in the Ohio total, since its records were destroyed by fire in 1884.

6. There was no list of towns of 2,500 or more people in the 1870 census.

7. Cincinnati and Mobile records were incomplete. (See note 5.)

8. The census itself points out certain limitations in the data regarding conjugal condition: No attempt was made to discover whether or not people who reported themselves as married had previously been widowed or divorced. Also, a person might report himself or herself as married in an effort to conceal a separation from a spouse. (See U.S., Department of the Interior, *Eleventh Census, 1890,* vol. 1, *Population,* pt. 1, p. lxxviii.)

9. Because of limitations in the information available, the child/woman ratio of native-born white women was calculated rather than that of native whites of native-born parents. To arrive at the native-born white rate, figures for native whites of native-born parents for children under five, and native whites of native-born parents plus native whites of foreign-born parents for the women twenty to forty-four were used.

10. Although the number of employed native white females of native-born parents, ten or older, in cities of 100,000 or more people was given, the corresponding number of total native white females of native-born parents, ten or older, was not available.

11. See the following two studies. Robert Smuts, *Women and Work in America* (New York: Columbia University Press, 1959); Robert Smuts, "The Female Labor Force: A Case Study in the Interpretation of Historical Statistics," *Journal of the American Statistical Association* 55 (March 1960): 71-79.

Appendix B. Regional Variation, Urban/Rural Differences, and Urbanization

This appendix briefly explores three issues: (1) regional differences exhibited by some of the variables; (2) the temporal convergence or divergence between rates for the rural and urban areas; and (3) the relationship of such temporal trends to urbanization.

The importance of regional differences has long been recognized by historians, and any study generalizing about urban/rural differences for the entire United States should take these regional variations into consideration. Although it is beyond the scope of this study to explain the variation among regions, it is nonetheless important to determine whether each of the regions followed the general U.S. pattern or if in fact significant variation from the general pattern tended to be present.[1]

Urban/rural differences with respect to the percentage of women who married or remained single, the child/woman ratio, and the percentage of women employed were evident for the United States as a whole. Were similar differences present within each region? As can be seen in the following tables, in all regions the percentage of married women and the child/woman ratio were higher in the rural sector (Tables 2 and 4), whereas the percentage of single women and the percentage of employed women were higher in the urban areas (Tables 1 and 3). Although the degree of difference between urban and rural sectors varied from region to region, the direction of the difference was the same in all.

This book has especially considered whether certain factors, which can be generally characterized as indicative of increased autonomy and an expanded sphere of activity for women, originated in the cities of the late nineteenth and early twentieth centuries. For most of the variables studied, it was found that significant differences did exist between the

TABLE B.1. Percentage of Single Women Fifteen Years or Older, Urban and Rural Areas, Total United States and by Region, Aggregate Population and Native Whites of Native-Born Parents, 1890-1920

	1890[a]	1900[a]	1910		1920	
	Agg	Agg	Agg	NWNP	Agg	NWNP
United States	$N=36$	$N=38$	$N=40$	$N=40$	$N=42$	$N=42$
Urban	34.7	33.8	31.5	33.7	28.1	30.6
Rural	30.0	29.2	27.5	28.7	25.7	27.3
Percent urban/rural difference	15.7	15.7	14.5	17.4	9.3	12.1
North Atlantic	$N=8$	$N=8$	$N=8$	$N=8$	$N=8$	$N=8$
Urban	38.1	36.6	35.7	35.9	32.3	34.9
Rural	32.9	31.6	29.9	29.4	28.3	28.0
Percent urban/rural difference	15.8	15.8	19.4	22.1	14.1	24.6
South Atlantic	$N=7$	$N=8$	$N=9$	$N=9$	$N=9$	$N=9$
Urban	36.0	34.9	31.7	34.2	28.5	30.5
Rural	32.6	30.5	28.3	28.9	26.4	26.8
Percent urban/rural difference	10.4	14.4	12.0	18.3	8.0	13.8

Table B.1 continued

North Central	$N=10$	$N=10$	$N=10$	$N=10$	$N=11$	$N=11$
Urban	34.0	33.0	31.4	34.3	27.7	31.0
Rural	29.3	29.1	28.2	30.4	26.6	29.6
Percent urban/rural difference	16.0	13.4	11.3	12.8	4.1	4.7
South Central	$N=6$	$N=6$	$N=7$	$N=7$	$N=7$	$N=7$
Urban	32.0	32.3	28.7	31.7	26.1	28.6
Rural	28.5	28.3	25.3	25.7	24.4	24.8
Percent urban/rural difference	12.3	14.1	13.4	23.3	7.0	15.3
West	$N=5$	$N=6$	$N=6$	$N=6$	$N=7$	$N=7$
Urban	33.2	31.5	29.8	31.4	25.2	27.3
Rural	26.0	25.7	24.9	27.3	22.3	24.7
Percent urban/rural difference	27.7	22.5	19.7	15.0	13.0	10.5

SOURCES: U.S., *Censuses, 1890-1920.*

NOTE: Urban calculated on the basis of 25,000+. Agg = Aggregate population. NWNP = Native whites of native-born parents. Urban/rural difference = urban/rural − 1 x 100. See Table A.2 for the method of calculation used for entire United States. The same method was used to obtain regional totals using only those states found in the particular region. N = the number of observations.

[a]In 1890 and 1900, data for native whites of native-born parents were available only for cities of 100,000+.

TABLE B.2. Percentage of Married Women Fifteen Years or Older, Urban and Rural Areas, Total United States and by Region, Aggregate Population and Native Whites of Native-Born Parents, 1890-1920

	1890[a]	1900[a]	1910		1920	
	Agg	Agg	Agg	NWNP	Agg	NWNP
United States	N = 36	N = 38	N = 40	N = 40	N = 42	N = 42
Urban	52.9	52.1	54.7	53.6	57.9	56.5
Rural	59.3	59.3	61.3	61.0	63.2	62.3
Percent rural/urban difference	14.0	13.8	12.1	13.8	9.2	10.3
North Atlantic	N = 8	N = 8	N = 8	N = 8	N = 8	N = 8
Urban	49.6	51.0	52.7	50.0	55.4	51.5
Rural	54.7	55.7	57.5	56.6	59.4	57.2
Percent rural/urban difference	10.3	9.2	9.1	13.2	7.2	11.1
South Atlantic	N = 7	N = 8	N = 9	N = 9	N = 9	N = 9
Urban	48.2	48.3	52.7	53.1	56.6	56.7
Rural	56.3	57.5	60.7	61.2	62.1	63.1
Percent rural/urban difference	16.8	19.0	15.2	15.3	9.7	11.3

Table B.2 continued

	$N=10$	$N=10$	$N=10$	$N=10$	$N=11$	$N=11$
North Central						
Urban	55.6	55.5	56.9	54.5	60.0	57.8
Rural	61.6	61.6	62.0	60.2	63.2	61.1
Percent rural/urban difference	10.8	11.0	9.0	10.5	5.3	5.7
	$N=6$	$N=6$	$N=7$	$N=7$	$N=7$	$N=7$
South Central						
Urban	49.8	48.4	54.2	55.2	57.1	58.0
Rural	59.1	58.7	62.1	64.0	64.2	65.4
Percent rural/urban difference	18.7	21.3	14.6	15.9	12.4	12.8
	$N=5$	$N=6$	$N=6$	$N=6$	$N=7$	$N=7$
West						
Urban	56.1	56.6	57.5	55.7	59.9	58.7
Rural	65.2	64.1	64.9	63.7	67.4	65.8
Percent rural/urban difference	16.2	13.3	12.9	14.4	12.5	12.1

SOURCES: U.S., *Censuses, 1890-1920.*

NOTE: Urban calculated on the basis of 25,000+. Agg = Aggregate population. NWNP = Native whites of native-born parents. Rural/urban difference = rural/urban − 1 x 100. See Table A.2 for the method of calculation used for entire United States. The same method was used to obtain regional totals using only those states found in the particular region. N = the number of observations.

[a]In 1890 and 1900, data for native whites of native-born parents were available only for cities of 100,000+.

TABLE B.3.　Percentage of Employed Women, Urban and Rural Areas, Total United States and by Region, Aggregate Population and Native Whites of Native-Born Parents, 1870-1920

	1870[a] Agg	1880[a] Agg	1890 Agg	1890 NWNP	1900[b] Agg	1900[b] NWNP	1920 Agg	1920 NWNP
United States	N = 24	N = 29	N = 36	N = 36	N = 38	N = 38	N = 42	N = 42
Urban	15.9	17.8	25.5	17.7	26.0	19.2	28.1	25.3
Rural	9.8	10.3	15.7	10.7	16.0	10.9	16.6	14.1
Percent urban/rural difference	62.2	72.8	62.4	65.4	62.5	76.1	69.3	79.4
North Atlantic	N = 7	N = 8	N = 8	N = 8	N = 8	N = 8	N = 8	N = 8
Urban	15.4	18.5	26.2	18.8	28.1	21.9	30.2	28.7
Rural	11.3	13.2	20.4	13.6	20.4	15.3	22.9	20.2
Percent urban/rural difference	36.3	40.2	28.4	38.2	37.8	43.1	31.9	42.1
South Atlantic	N = 6	N = 7	N = 7	N = 7	N = 8	N = 8	N = 9	N = 9
Urban	20.0	22.6	31.1	17.2	31.5	18.3	32.5	25.2
Rural	14.0	14.1	19.8	10.6	20.1	9.9	19.0	13.6
Percent urban/rural difference	42.9	60.0	57.1	62.3	56.7	84.8	71.0	85.3
North Central	N = 6	N = 8	N = 10	N = 10	N = 10	N = 10	N = 11	N = 11
Urban	12.0	14.3	21.7	17.9	21.6	20.0	25.0	25.6
Rural	4.1	6.1	10.6	9.9	11.5	10.5	12.7	12.7
Percent urban/rural difference	200.0	134.4	104.7	80.8	87.8	90.5	96.9	101.6

Table B.3 continued

South Central	$N=4$	$N=4$	$N=6$	$N=6$	$N=6$	$N=6$	$N=7$	$N=7$
Urban	15.7	18.4	27.3	16.2	28.6	15.2	29.6	23.3
Rural	11.9	11.3	16.6	7.6	18.6	7.5	16.1	10.7
Percent urban/rural difference	31.9	62.8	64.5	113.2	53.8	102.7	83.9	117.8
West	$N=1$	$N=2$	$N=5$	$N=5$	$N=6$	$N=6$	$N=7$	$N=7$
Urban	15.2	13.0	20.9	17.8	20.5	19.0	23.2	23.4
Rural	2.8	5.9	12.5	10.8	10.7	9.5	13.2	13.2
Percent urban/rural difference	442.9	120.3	67.2	64.8	91.6	100.0	75.8	77.3

SOURCES: U.S., *Censuses, 1870-1920.*

NOTE: For 1870, 1880, 1900, and 1920, urban = 25,000+. For 1890, urban had to be calculated on the basis of 50,000+. Urban and rural means were calculated for each state with at least one city of 25,000+. Regional averages were computed on the basis of state means. Agg = Aggregate population. NWNP = Native whites of native-born parents. Urban/rural difference = urban/rural − 1 x 100. N = Number of observations.

[a]For 1870 and 1880, employment data were available only for the total female population.

[b]For 1900, data were available only for NWNP sixteen or older, in cities of 50,000+.

TABLE B.4. Child/Woman Ratio, Urban and Rural Areas, Total United States and by Region, Aggregate Population and Native Whites, 1890-1920

	1890		1900		1910[a]	1920	
	Agg	NWNP	Agg	NWNP	Agg	Agg	NWNP
United States	N = 36	N = 36	N = 38	N = 38	N = 40	N = 42	N = 42
Urban	489	364	452	333	429	429	388
Rural	753	651	728	628	702	674	643
Percent rural/urban difference	54.0	78.8	61.1	88.6	63.6	57.1	65.7
North Atlantic	N = 8	N = 8	N = 8	N = 8	N = 8	N = 8	N = 8
Urban	442	287	477	279	472	493	360
Rural	502	403	522	391	540	578	469
Percent rural/urban difference	13.6	40.4	9.4	40.1	14.4	17.2	30.3
South Atlantic	N = 7	N = 7	N = 8	N = 8	N = 9	N = 9	N = 9
Urban	458	411	416	368	421	417	421
Rural	838	779	831	791	794	742	745
Percent rural/urban difference	83.0	89.5	99.8	114.9	88.6	77.9	77.0

Table B.4 continued

North Central	N = 10	N = 10	N = 10	N = 10	N = 10	N = 11	N = 11
Urban	561	375	491	329	442	446	397
Rural	765	601	712	558	655	640	614
Percent rural/urban difference	36.4	60.3	45.0	69.6	48.2	43.5	54.7
South Central	N = 6	N = 6	N = 6	N = 6	N = 7	N = 7	N = 7
Urban	488	425	423	407	385	372	388
Rural	948	937	910	.919	870	751	778
Percent rural/urban difference	94.3	120.5	115.1	125.8	126.0	101.9	100.5
West	N = 5	N = 5	N = 6	N = 6	N = 6	N = 7	N = 7
Urban	464	323	435	289	406	394	362
Rural	792	657	729	580	678	681	636
Percent rural/urban difference	70.7	103.4	67.6	100.7	67.0	72.8	75.7

SOURCES: U.S., *Censuses, 1890-1920.*

NOTE: N = Number of states. Agg = Aggregate population. NWNP = Native whites of native-born parents. Rural/urban difference = rural/urban − 1 x 100. See Table A.2 for the method of calculation used for entire United States. The same method was used to obtain regional totals using only those states found in the particular region.

[a]In 1910, data were not given for native whites.

urban and the rural sectors. The differences between the two sectors, however, did not remain static, and the question arises as to whether there was a relationship between the degree of urbanization and the changing extent of difference between the two sectors.

Researchers have pointed to the tendency for differences between the urban and rural sectors of a society to be lowest when the society is either predominantly rural or predominantly urban.[2] When a society first begins to urbanize, differences between the two sectors grow, but the differences begin to diminish after the degree of urbanization has reached a certain level. Between 1890 and 1920, as the degree of urbanization[3] in the United States increased from 35.4 percent to 51.4 percent, did the urban/rural difference for the variables studied increase or decrease? Was there any indication that the increasing degree of urbanization was reflected in the tendency for behavior patterns in rural areas to more closely approximate those of the urban sector?

Both the tendency for a greater proportion of rural women to marry and the propensity for them to have more children than their urban counterparts were long-standing patterns.[4] Numerous authors have discussed the rural/urban differential with respect to the child/woman ratio.[5] These authors have suggested that children in an urban setting were considered a burden, since they did not contribute to the family's economic production. Rearing children cost more in the city: the more children, the lower the obtainable living standard. In addition, the social milieu of the city itself presented problems when it came to child rearing. In short, a number of reasons had long existed in urban areas to account for having fewer children.

A look at the relationship between the degree of urbanization and the rural/urban difference in the child/woman ratio for the native white population shows an overall reduction as the United States became more urbanized[6] (Table 5). Insofar as the tendency for women to marry or remain single was concerned, the rural/urban differences for the two variables were converging (Table 5). However, that convergence resulted not from the rural sector's following the behavior pattern of urban dwellers, but rather from more youthful marriages in cities raising the traditionally lower urban marriage rate and bringing it closer to that of the rural sector. Significantly, the trend toward younger marriages, especially pronounced in urban areas, was accompanied by a continued reduction in the number of children and, as previously discussed, appears to have been linked to the spread of more effective methods of birth control.

TABLE B.5. Degree of Urbanization and Percentage Difference Between the Urban and Rural Sectors, 1890-1920

	1890	1900	1910	1920
Percent of United States urbanized	35.4	40.0	45.8	51.4
Percent difference between urban and rural sectors				
Single: percent urban/rural difference				
Agg	15.7	15.7	14.5	9.3
NWNP	d	d	17.4	12.1
Married: percent rural/urban difference				
Agg	14.0	13.8	12.1	9.2
NWNP	d	d	13.8	10.3
Native white child/woman ratio: percent rural/urban difference	78.8	88.6	b	65.7
Employed: percent urban/rural difference				
Agg[a]	62.4	62.5	c	69.3
NWNP	65.4	76.1	b	79.4

SOURCES: U.S., *Censuses, 1870-1920.*

NOTE: Percentage urbanized calculated on the basis of places 2,500+. Rural urban difference = rural/urban − 1 x 100. Urban/rural difference = urban/rural − 1 x 100. Agg = Aggregate population. NWNP = Native whites of native-born parents.

[a] In 1870, 20.1 percent of the United States was urban and the urban/rural difference was 62.2 percent. In 1880, 24.4 percent was urban and the urban/rural difference was 72.8 percent. For both 1870 and 1880, the percentage of employed women was calculated on the basis of the total number of females.

[b] Data not available.

[c] See Table 7 in Chapter 6 for discussion of problems with 1910 employment data.

[d] Data available only for cities of 100,000+.

Finally, for the percentage of employed NWNP women in urban and rural areas, the rates in fact diverged (Table 5). The divergence most probably resulted from the recent expansion of employment opportunities for women in urban areas. However, some of the difference may have been due to inaccuracies in census reporting. Census takers may have more accurately recorded female employment in urban areas, whereas some farm women who worked were not reported as employed in the census. Of the four variables, only the reduction in the urban/rural difference for the child/woman ratio seemed possibly linked to the impact of increased urbanization.

A study investigating changing rates of employment, marriage, or fertility, at least during the late nineteenth or early twentieth centuries, should take into account the persistence and importance of regional differences. Figures 1, 2, 3, and 4 indicate that the individual regions, with some exception, tended to exhibit the same pattern with respect to convergence or divergence of urban and rural rates as did the entire United States.

As can be seen in Figure 1, the West, which in 1890 exhibited a notably higher urban/rural divergence with respect to the percentage of single women, had come considerably closer to the national norm by 1920. The initial extreme disparity between the urban and rural sectors was possibly linked to several facets of the pioneer nature of life present in much of the region. The harshness of life in many parts of the West and the isolation of many of the homesteads probably made urban life appear much more attractive for the single woman of the West in 1890 and 1900.

Figure 3, which deals with the percentage of employed NWNP women, illustrates the consistently higher urban/rural difference present in the South Central region and the consistently lower urban/rural difference in the North Atlantic states. Of all regions, the North Atlantic had the highest percentage of women employed in the rural sector. In contrast, the South Central region consistently had the lowest percentage of women employed in the rural sector. Perhaps job opportunities for women in the less urbanized and industrialized South Central region tended to be limited to larger urban units (of 25,000 people or more), whereas in the North Atlantic states the longer standing existence of industrialization and the higher degree of urbanization had allowed similar employment opportunities to penetrate even the smaller towns.

In Figure 4 the urban/rural difference with respect to the native white child/woman ratio can be seen to have been uniformly lower in the North

Figure 1. Urban/Rural Difference in Percent of Single Women vs. Percent Urbanized

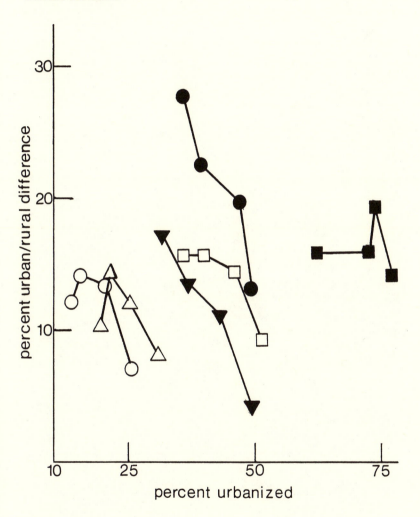

Information is for aggregate population in the total United States and by region, 1890-1920. Time moves in the same direction as percent urbanized.

KEY: Total United States □; North Atlantic ■; South Atlantic △; North Central ▼; South Central ○; West ●.

Figure 2. Rural/Urban Difference in Percent of Married Women vs. Percent Urbanized

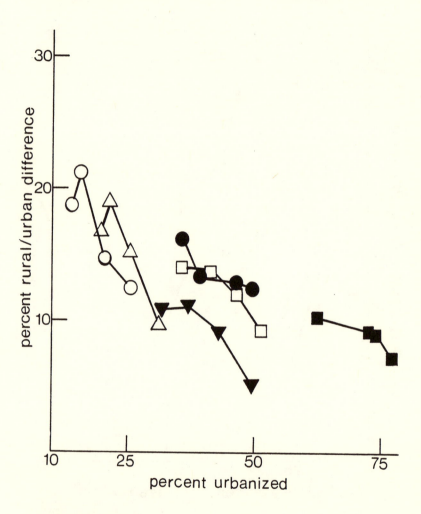

Information is for the aggregate population in the total United States and by region, 1890-1920. Time moves in the same direction as percent urbanized.

KEY: United States □; North Atlantic ■; South Atlantic △; North Central ▼; South Central ○; West ●.

Figure 3. Urban/Rural Difference in Percent of Employed Women vs. Percent Urbanized

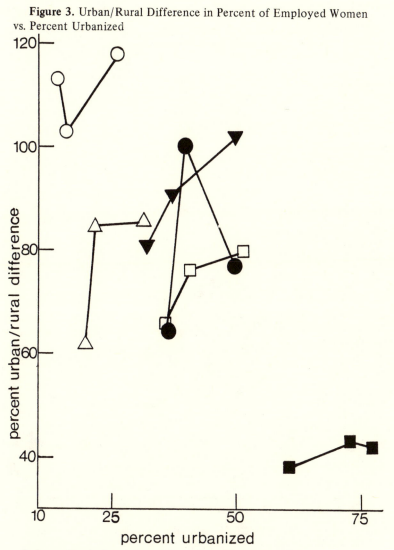

Information is for native whites of native-born parents in the total United States and by region, 1890-1920. Time moves in the same direction as percent urbanized.

KEY: Total United States ☐ North Atlantic ■; South Atlantic △; North Central ▼; South Central ○; West ●.

Figure 4. Rural/Urban Difference in Child/Woman Ratio vs. Percent Urbanized

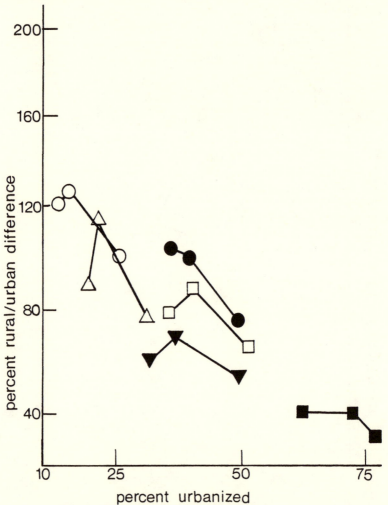

Information is for native whites in the total United States and by region, 1890-1920. Time moves in the same direction as percent urbanized.

KEY: Total United States ☐; North Atlantic ■; South Atlantic △; North Central ▼; South Central ○; West ●.

Atlantic region. The relatively lower urban/rural divergence in the North Atlantic states may have been linked to the greater percentage of rural employed women in the North Atlantic states. Employment and fertility tended to be correlated negatively in both urban and rural areas, and the lower North Atlantic urban/rural difference with respect to the native white child/woman ratio possibly reflected the relatively high employment rate in the rural sector.

Insofar as regional variation was concerned, the following conclusions can be drawn. For the four variables considered, different regional patterns were present. However, despite distinct regional patterns, the difference between the urban and rural sectors was always in the same direction: For example, if the urban rate was higher than the rural in one region, the same was true in all of the other regions. As for the degree of difference between the urban and the rural sector and the relationship between the changing differences and the extent of urbanization, the results were mixed. During the time period studied, the only indication of converging rates that could possibly be linked to the impact of increased urbanization was the diminishing difference for the native white child/woman ratio.[7] Although the urban and rural marriage rates converged during the era, the convergence could not be attributed to increased urbanization. In addition, there was a growing divergence between the percentage of employed women in urban and rural areas.

Notes

1. It should be noted that the method of analysis used in this book of studying urban and rural differences on a state-by-state basis has guarded against the pitfall of allowing the particular pattern shown by a numerically dominant region to be mistaken for a pattern applicable to the entire United States. For example, if one were to calculate the percentage of women working in urban areas in 1890 by simply dividing the total number of employed women in all urban areas, cities such as New York, Philadelphia, and Boston, and thus the North Atlantic region, would be given inordinate weight. In contrast, a state-by-state analysis, with each city in each state given equal weight, offered a much more accurate picture.

2. See, for example, "Part VI, Urban-Rural Differences," in *Urban Research Methods,* ed. Jack P. Gibbs (Princeton, N.J.: D. Van Nostrand Co., 1961), pp. 462-539, for a selection of articles. See especially pages 462-71.

3. Urbanized was calculated on the basis of communities of 2,500 or more people.

4. That the higher proportion of married women found in rural areas was not alone responsible for the rural/urban fertility differential can readily be seen from looking at child/woman ratios for only those women who were married, widowed, or divorced. In U.S., Department of Commerce, *Ratio of Children to Women,* p. 109, the child/woman ratio for married, widowed, or divorced native white women was as follows: 512 in communities of 100,000 or larger; 554 in communities of 25,000-100,000 inhabitants; 608 in those with between 10,000 and 25,000; 646 in towns between 2,500 and 10,000; and 899 in rural areas. Wilson H. Grabill, Clyde V. Kiser, and Pascal K. Whelpton, *The Fertility of American Women* (New York: John Wiley & Sons, 1958), p. 89, found similar results in 1950. They had three population categories: urban (2,500 or more people), rural-nonfarm, and rural-farm. For all women fifteen to forty-four, the child/woman ratio was 1,285 in urban areas, 1,689 in rural-nonfarm, and 2,126 in rural farm. For women fifteen to forty-four, "ever married," the corresponding numbers were 1,713, 2,128, and 2,742.

5. See the following for discussions regarding the rural/urban fertility differential. Warren Thompson and Nelle E. Jackson, "Fertility in Rural Areas in Relation to Their Distance from Cities," *Rural Sociology* 5 (June 1940): 143-62; William Ogburn and M. F. Nimkoff, *Technology and the Changing Family* (Boston: Houghton Mifflin Co., 1955); A. J. Jaffee, "Urbanization and Fertility," *American Journal of Sociology* 48 (July 1942): 48-60; Pascal Whelpton and Clyde V. Kiser, "Trends, Determinants, and Control in Human Fertility," *Annals of the American Academy of Political and Social Science* 237 (January 1945): 112-22; Bernard Okun, *Trends in Birth Rates in the United States Since 1870* (Baltimore: Johns Hopkins Press, 1958); Grabill, Kiser, and Whelpton, *Fertility of American Women;* Regine Stix and Frank W. Notestein, *Controlled Fertility: An Evaluation of Clinical Service* (Baltimore: Williams & Wilkins, 1940), pp. 144-58.

6. The aggregate child/woman ratio is a much less sensitive measure, since it includes so many different groups of women. Therefore, the discussion of this section has been confined to the native white child/woman ratio.

7. See Okun, *Trends in the Birth Rates.* Okun contends that it was not the shift in population from rural to urban areas, but rather the spread of urban values and ideas beyond urban boundaries that can explain the decline in fertility. He found lower birth rates in the most highly urbanized and industrialized states (see pp. 97 and 101).

Glossary

Child/woman ratio	The number of children under five years of age per 1,000 women twenty to forty-four years old
FW	Foreign-born whites
NWFP	Native-born whites of foreign-born parents
NWNP	Native-born whites of native-born parents
Sex ratio	The number of men per 100 women

Selected Bibliography

Books

Addams, Jane. *Twenty Years at Hull House*. New York: Macmillan Co., 1910; Signet Classic, 1960.

Alden, Isabella. *Memories of Yesterday*. Philadelphia: J. B. Lippincott Co., 1931.

Allen, Frederick Lewis. *Only Yesterday*. New York: Harper & Bros., 1931.

Ariès, Phillipe. *Centuries of Childhood*. New York: Alfred A. Knopf, 1962.

Baker, Elizabeth F. *Technology and Women's Work*. New York: Columbia University Press, 1964.

Banner, Lois W. *Women in Modern America: A Brief History*. New York: Harcourt Brace Jovanovich, Inc., 1974.

Barger, Harold. *Distribution's Place in the American Economy Since 1869*. Princeton, N.J.: Princeton University Press, 1955.

Barnes, Earl. *Woman in Modern Society*. New York: B. S. Huebsch, 1912.

Barnett, James. *Divorce and the American Novel, 1858-1937*. New York: Russell & Russell, 1939.

Beard, Ida Mae. *My Own Life, Or a Deserted Wife*. Raleigh: Edwards & Broughton, 1900.

Beard, Mary. *Women's Work in Municipalities*. New York: D. Appleton & Co., 1915.

Bennett, Arnold. *Our Women: Chapters on the Sex Discord*. New York: Cassell & Co., 1920.

Bennett, Estelline. *Old Deadwood Days*. New York: J. H. Sears & Co., 1928.

Berg, Barbara J. *The Remembered Gate: Origins of American Feminism: The Woman and the City, 1800-1860.* New York: Oxford University Press, 1978.

Bishop, Joel P. *Marriage and Divorce.* 2 vols. Boston: Little, Brown & Co., 1881.

Blake, Nelson. *The Road to Reno.* New York: Macmillan Co., 1962.

Blanc, Marie Thérèse (de Solms). *The Condition of Women in the United States.* Translated by Abby Langdon Alger. Boston: Roberts Bros., 1895; reprint ed., New York: Arno Press, 1972.

Bliven, Bruce, Jr. *The Wonderful Writing Machine.* New York: Random House, 1954.

Boone, Gladys. *The Women's Trade Union League.* New York: Columbia University Press, 1942.

Bowen, William, and Finegan, T. Aldrich. *Economics of Labor Force Participation.* Princeton, N.J.: Princeton University Press, 1969.

Bowlan, Marian. *City Types.* Chicago: T. S. Denison & Co., 1916.

Breckinridge, Sophonisba P. *Women in the Twentieth Century.* New York: McGraw-Hill Book Co., 1933.

Brooke, Mary C. *Memories of Eighty Years.* New York: Knickerbocker Press, 1916.

Brunner, Edmund S., and Hallenbeck, William C. *American Society: Urban and Rural Patterns.* New York: Harper & Bros., 1955.

Burner, David. *The Politics of Provincialism.* New York: Alfred A. Knopf, 1970.

Burrell, Caroline Frances [Caroline French Benton]. *The Complete Club Book for Women.* Boston: Page Co., 1915.

Busbey, Katherine. *Home Life in America.* New York: Macmillan Co., 1910.

Cahen, Alfred. *Statistical Analysis of American Divorce.* New York: Columbia University Press, 1932.

Calhoun, Arthur. *A Social History of the American Family from Colonial Times to the Present.* 3 vols. in one. Cleveland: A. H. Clark, 1917-19; reprint ed., New York: Arno Press, 1973.

Campaigne, Edna Foote. *I'm Fifty . . . So What?* Montclair, N.J.: n.p., 1938.

Campbell, Helen. *Women Wage Earners.* Boston: Roberts Bros., 1893.

Carlier, Auguste. *Marriage in the United States.* Translated by B. Joy Jeffries. Boston: De Vries, Ibarra & Co., 1867; reprint ed., New York: Arno Press, 1972.

Chamberlin, Marie Louise Barrett. *Looking Back from Eighty-five.* Chicago: Federal Printing Co., 1926.

Chudacoff, Howard. *The Evolution of American Urban Society*. Englewood Cliffs, N.J.: Prentice-Hall, Inc., 1975.

Clary, Anna. *Reminiscences*. Los Angeles: Printed by B. McCallister at the Adcraft Press, 1937.

Cohn, David M. *The Good Old Days*. New York: Simon & Schuster, 1940.

Crowe, Martha F. *The American Country Girl*. New York: Frederick A. Stokes Co., 1915.

Current, Richard N. *The Typewriter and the Men Who Made It*. Champaign: University of Illinois Press, 1951.

Davenport, Charles. *Heredity in Relation to Eugenics*. New York: Henry Holt & Co., 1911.

Davis, Allen F. *Spearheads for Reform: The Social Settlements and the Progressive Movement, 1890-1914*. New York: Oxford University Press, 1967.

Dennett, Mary Ware. *Birth Control Laws*. New York: Frederick H. Hitchcock, 1926.

Diaz, Mrs. A. M. *A Domestic Problem*. Boston: James Osgood & Co., 1875.

Dilnot, Frank. *The New Americans*. New York: Macmillan Co., 1919.

Ditzion, Sidney. *Marriage, Morals and Sex in America*. New York: Bookman Associates, 1953.

Dodge, Grace H., et al. *What Women Can Earn: Occupations of Women and Their Compensation*. Boston: Frederick A. Stokes Co., 1898.

Dorr, Rheta Childe. *What Eight Million Women Want*. Boston: Small, Maynard & Co., 1910.

Doyle, Helen M. *A Child Went Forth*. New York: Gotham House, 1934.

Dumond, Annie. *The Life of a Book Agent*. Cincinnati: By the Author, 1868.

Duncan, Otis E., and Reiss, Albert J., Jr. *Social Characteristics of Urban and Rural Communities, 1950*. New York: John Wiley & Sons, 1956.

Durand, John S. *The Labor Force in the United States, 1890-1960*. New York: Social Science Research Council, 1948.

Ellington, George. *Women of New York: Underworld of the Great City*. New York: New York Book Co., 1869.

Ericksen, Ephraim Gordon. *Urban Behavior*. New York: Macmillan Co., 1973.

Exner, M. J. *The Rational Sex Life for Men*. New York: Associated Press, 1914.

Finch, Bernard Ephraim, and Green, Hugh. *Contraception Through the Ages*. Springfield, Ill.: Charles C Thomas, 1963.

Finlayson, Archibald. *A Trip to America.* Glasgow: David Wilson, 1879.

Flexner, Eleanor. *Century of Struggle: The Woman's Rights Movement in the United States.* Cambridge, Mass.: Harvard University Press, 1959; reprint ed., New York: Atheneum, 1971.

Foote, Edward Bliss. *New Plain Home Talk.* New York: Murray Hill Publishing Co., 1904.

Four Years in the Underbrush. New York: Charles Scribner's Sons, 1921.

Furstenberg, Frank. "Industrialization and the American Family: A Look Backward." In *The Family and Change,* pp. 326-27. Edited by John N. Edward. New York: Alfred A. Knopf, 1969.

Gibbs, Jack P., ed. *Urban Research Methods.* Princeton, N.J.: D. Van Nostrand Co., 1967.

Gilman, Charlotte Perkins. *The Living of Charlotte Perkins Gilman: An Autobiography.* New York: D. Appleton-Century Co., 1935.

Gist, Noel P., and Fava, Sylvia F. *Urban Society.* 5th ed. New York: Thomas Y. Crowell Co., 1964.

Glaab, Charles N., and Brown, Theodore. *A History of Urban America.* New York: Macmillan Co., 1967.

Good, Harry S., and Teller, James D. *A History of American Education.* New York: Macmillan Co., 1973.

Goode, William. *World Revolutions and Family Patterns.* New York: Free Press of Glencoe, 1963.

Goodell, William. *Lessons in Gynecology.* Philadelphia: D. G. Brinton, 1879.

Goodsell, Willystine. *The Education of Women: Its Social Background and Its Problems.* New York: Macmillan Co., 1924.

_____. *A History of Marriage and the Family.* New York: Macmillan Co., 1939.

Gordon, Linda. *Woman's Body, Woman's Right: A Social History of Birth Control in America.* New York: Grossman Publishers, 1976.

Grabill, Wilson H.; Kiser, Clyde V.; and Whelpton, Pascal K. *The Fertility of American Women.* New York: John Wiley & Sons, 1958.

_____. "A Long View." In *The American Family in Social-Historical Perspective,* pp. 374-96. Edited by Michael Gordon. New York: St. Martin's Press, 1973.

Greenfield, Sidney. "Industrialization and the Family in Social Theory." In *The Family and Change,* pp. 33-49. Edited by John N. Edward. New York: Alfred A. Knopf, 1969.

Gregory, Addie. *A Greatgrandmother Remembers.* Chicago: A. Kroch & Sons, 1940.

Guenther, William. *Concepts of Statistical Inference.* New York: McGraw-Hill Book Co., 1965.

Hale, Nathan G., Jr. *Freud and the Americans: The Beginning of Psycho-analysis in the United States, 1876-1917.* 2 vols. New York: Oxford University Press, 1971.

Hart, Gordon. *Woman and the Race.* Westwood, Mass.: Ariel Press, 1907.

Hart, Hornell. "Change in Social Attitudes and Interests." In *Recent Social Trends in the United States: Report of the President's Research Committee on Social Trends,* 2 vols., 1: 382-442. New York: McGraw-Hill Book Co., 1933.

Hasmi, Sultan H. "Factors in Urban Fertility Differences in the United States." In *Contributions to Urban Sociology,* pp. 42-58. Edited by Ernest Burgess and Donald J. Bogue. Chicago: University of Chicago Press, 1964.

Hatton, Joseph. *Today in America.* London: Chapman & Hall, 1881.

Hayslett, H. T. *Statistics Made Simple.* Garden City, N.Y.: Doubleday & Co., 1968.

Herkimer County Historical Society. *The Study of the Typewriter, 1873-1923.* Herkimer, N.Y.: Herkimer County Historical Society, 1923.

Himes, Norman. *Medical History of Contraception.* Baltimore: Williams & Wilkins Co., 1936; reprint ed., New York: Schocken, 1970.

Hoerle, Helen, and Saltzberg, Florence B. *The Girl and the Job.* New York: Henry Holt & Co., 1919.

Hofstadter, Richard. *The Age of Reform.* New York: Vintage Books, 1955.

Holcombe, Lee. *Victorian Ladies at Work.* Hamden, Conn.: Anchor Books, 1973.

Hostetler, Ella M. Dogget. *Sketches Here and There Along the Way from the Year 1856.* Lincoln, Neb.: Woodruff Printing Co., 1916.

Howard, George Elliot. *A History of Matrimonial Institutions.* Chicago: University of Chicago Press, 1904.

Irwin, Inez Haynes. *Angels and Amazons.* New York: Doubleday, Doran & Co., 1933.

Jelliffee, Belinda. *For Dear Life.* New York: Charles Scribner's Sons, 1936.

Josephson, Hannah G. *The Golden Threads.* New York: Duell, Sloan & Pearce, 1949.

Kahl, Joseph A. *The American Class Structure.* New York: Rinehart & Co., 1957.

Kennedy, David. *Birth Control in America.* New Haven, Conn.: Yale University Press, 1970.

Kirkland, Edward C. *A History of Economic Life.* New York: F. S. Crofts & Co., 1947.

Kiser, Clyde V., ed. *Research in Family Planning*. Princeton, N.J.: Princeton University Press, 1962.

Knapp, Emma Benedict. *Hic Habitat Felicitas*. Boston: William B. Clarke Co., 1910.

Laselle, Mary A., and Wiley, Katherine E. *Vocations for Girls*. Boston: Houghton Mifflin Co., 1913.

Latimer, Caroline. *Girl and Woman*. New York: D. Appleton & Co., 1916.

Leslie, Gerald. *The Family in Social Context*. New York: Oxford University Press, 1967.

Lewis, Dio. *The New Gymnastics for Men, Women and Children*. Boston: Ticknor & Fields, 1862.

Lichtenberger, James P. *Divorce: A Social Interpretation*. New York: Whittlesey House, 1931.

_____. *Divorce: A Study in Social Causation*. New York: Columbia University Press, 1909.

Lipset, Seymour, and Bendix, Reinhard. *Social Mobility in Industrial America*. Berkeley: University of California Press, 1963.

Loomis, Charles P., and Beegle, U. Allan. *Rural Social Systems*. New York: Prentice-Hall, 1950.

Low, Alfred. *America at Home*. London: George Newnes, 1908.

Lowry, Edith Belle. *Herself: Talks with Women Concerning Themselves*. Chicago: Forbes & Co., 1914.

_____. *Himself: Talks with Men Concerning Themselves*. Chicago: Forbes & Co., 1914.

Lyman, Henry M.; Feneger, Christian; Jones, H. Webster; and Belfield, W. T. *The Practical Home Doctor: 20th Century Household Medical Guide*. Revised ed. Chicago: America Publishing Co., 1907.

Lynd, Robert S., and Lynd, Helen M. *Middletown: A Study in Contemporary American Culture*. New York: Harcourt Brace, 1929.

McLaughlin, Virginia Yans. "Patterns of Work and Family Organization: Buffalo's Italians." In *The Family in History*, pp. 111-26. Edited by Theodore K. Rabb and Robert Rotberg. New York: Harper & Row, 1973.

MacLean, Annie M. *Women Workers and Society*. Chicago: A. C. McClurg & Co., 1916.

McRae, David. *America Revisited*. Glasgow: John Smith & Son, 1908.

Marcus, Steven. *The Other Victorians*. New York: Basic Books, 1964.

Martin, Eleanor, and Post, Margaret. *Vocations for the Trained Woman*. New York: Longmans, Green & Co., 1914.

Martineau, Harriet. *Society in America*. 3 vols. London: Saunders & Otley, 1837.

Massachusetts State Federation of Woman's Clubs. *Progress and Achievement: A History of the Massachusetts State Federation of Woman's Clubs, 1893-1931.* Boston: 1932.

Melder, Keith. *Beginnings of Sisterhood: The American Woman's Rights Movement, 1800-1850.* New York: Schocken Books, 1977.

Millar, Mara. *Hail to Yesterday.* New York: Farrar & Rinehart, 1941.

Mohr, James C. *Abortion in America: The Origins and Evolution of National Policy, 1800-1900.* New York: Oxford University Press, 1978.

Monahan, Thomas P. *The Pattern of Age at Marriage in the United States.* 2 vols. Philadelphia: Stephenson-Bros., 1951.

Moore, Sallie Alexander. *Memories of a Long Life in Virginia.* Staunton, Va.: McClure Co., 1920.

Morantz, Regina. "The Lady and Her Physician." In *Clio's Consciousness Raised: New Perspectives on the History of Women,* pp. 38-53. Edited by Mary S. Hartman and Lois Banner. New York: Harper & Row, 1974.

Morgan, Edmund S. *The Puritan Family.* Revised ed. New York: Harper & Row, 1966.

Moroney, M. J. *Facts from Figures.* Baltimore: Penguin Books, 1951.

Nearing, Scott. *Wages in the United States, 1908-1910.* New York: Macmillan Co., 1914.

Neff, Wanda. *Victorian Working Women.* London: Frank Cass & Co., 1929.

Neville, Amelia. *The Fantastic City.* Boston: Houghton Mifflin Co., 1932.

Ogburn, William, and Nimkoff, M. F. *Technology and the Changing Family.* Boston: Houghton Mifflin Co., 1955.

Ogburn, William, and Tibbits, Clark. "The Family and Its Functions." In *Recent Social Trends in the United States: Report of the President's Research Committee in Social Trends.* 2 vols., 1: 661-708. New York: McGraw-Hill Book Co., 1933.

Okun, Bernard. *Trends in Birth Rates in the United States Since 1870.* Baltimore: Johns Hopkins Press, 1958.

O'Neill, William. *Divorce in the Progressive Era.* New Haven, Conn.: Yale University Press, 1967.

Owens-Adair, Bethenia. *Some of Her Life Experiences.* Portland, Ore.: Mann & Beach, 1906.

Parkes, Henry Bamford. *The United States of America.* New York: Alfred A. Knopf, 1968.

Penny, Virginia. *Think and Act: A Series of Articles Pertaining to Men and Women, Work and Wages.* Philadelphia: Claxton, Remsen & Haffelfinger, 1868; reprint ed., New York: Arno Press, 1971.

Pierce, Paul. *Social Survey of Three Rural Townships in Iowa.* University of Iowa Monograph Series, vol. 5, no. 2. Iowa City: University of Iowa Press, 1917.

Place, Francis. *Illustrations and Proof of the Principles of Population.* n.p.: Longman, Rees, Hurst & Orme; reprint ed., Augustus, Me.: Kelley, 1967.

Pruette, Lorine. *Women and Leisure: A Study of Social Waste.* New York: E. P. Dutton & Co., 1924.

Rayne, Martha L. *What Can a Woman Do: Or, Her Position in the Business and Literary World.* Detroit: F. B. Dickerson & Co., 1883; reprint ed., Petersburg, N.Y.: Eagle Publishing Co., 1893.

Reed, James. *From Private Vice to Public Virtue: The Birth Control Movement and American Society Since 1830.* New York: Basic Books, Inc., 1978.

Rhodes, Harrison. *On Vacation in America.* New York: Harper & Bros., 1915.

Richardson, Dorothy. "The Long Day." In *Women at Work,* pp. 1-303. Edited by William O'Neill. New York: Quadrangle Books, 1972.

Riegel, Robert E. *American Women: A Story of Social Change.* Rutherford, N.J.: Fairleigh Dickinson University Press, 1970.

Riis, Jacob. *How the Other Half Lives: Studies Among the Tenements of New York.* New York: Charles Scribner's Sons, 1890; reprint ed., New York: Hill & Wang, 1957.

Robie, W. F. *Rational Sex Ethics.* Boston: Gorham Press, 1916, 1918.

Robinson, Elsie. *I Wanted Out.* New York: Farrar & Rinehart, 1934.

Robinson, William J. *Eugenics, Marriage and Birth Control.* New York: The Critic & Guide Co., 1917.

Ruitenbeck, Hendrik. *Freud and America.* New York: Macmillan Co., 1966.

Salmon, Lucy. *Domestic Service.* New York: Macmillan Co., 1901.

Sanger, Margaret. *My Fight for Birth Control.* New York: Farrar & Rinehart, 1931.

_____. *The New Motherhood.* London: Jonathan Cape, 1922; reprint ed., Elmsford, N.Y.: Maxwell Reprint Co., 1970.

Schlesinger, Arthur M., Sr. *Rise of the City, 1878-1898.* New York: Macmillan Co., 1933.

Schmiedeler, Edgar. *The Industrial Revolution and the Home.* n.p.: By the Author, 1927.

Scott, Anne Firor. *The Southern Lady: From Pedestal to Politics, 1830-1930.* Chicago: University of Chicago Press, 1970.

Sennett, Richard. *Families Against the City.* Cambridge, Mass.: Harvard University Press, 1970.

Sherif, Muzaffer, and Sherif, Carolyn. *An Outline of Social Psychology.* New York: Harper & Row, 1948.

Sinclair, Andrew. *The Better Half: The Emancipation of the American Woman.* London: Jonathan Cape, 1966.

Sjoberg, Gideon. "The Rural-Urban Dimension in Pre-industrial, Transitional and Industrialized Societies." In *Handbook of Modern Sociology,* pp. 127-59. Edited by Robert E. Faris. Chicago: Rand McNally Co., 1964.

Smith, Daniel Scott. "The Dating of the American Sexual Revolution: Evidence and Interpretation." In *The American Family in Social-Historical Perspective,* pp. 321-35. Edited by Michael Gordon. New York: St. Martin's Press, 1973.

Smith, Thomas Lynn. *The Sociology of Rural Life.* 3rd ed. New York: Harper & Bros., 1953.

Smuts, Robert. *Women and Work in America.* New York: Columbia University Press, 1959.

Spearman, Eugenie Longerman. *Memories.* Los Angeles: Private printing by Modern Printers, 1941.

Sprague, William Forrest. *Women and the West.* Boston: Christopher Publishing House, 1940.

Stigler, George. *Trends in Employment in Service Industries.* Princeton, N.J.: Princeton University Press, 1956.

Stix, Regine K., and Notestein, Frank W. *Controlled Fertility: An Evaluation of Clinic Service.* Baltimore: Williams & Wilkins, 1940.

Stockham, Alice. *Tokology.* Boston: George Smith & Co., 1886.

Sullenger, Thomas Earl. *Sociology of Urbanization: A Study in Rurban Society.* Ann Arbor: Braun-Brumfield, 1956.

Sutro, Florentine Scholle. *My First Seventy Years.* New York: Roerich Museum Press, 1935.

Tarkington, Booth. *Alice Adams.* New York: Doubleday, Page & Co., 1926.

Thelen, David P. *The New Citizenship: Origins of Progressivism in Wisconsin, 1885-1900.* Columbia: University of Missouri Press, 1972.

Thompson, Warren, and Whelpton, Pascal K. *Population Trends in the United States.* New York: McGraw-Hill Book Co., 1933; reprint ed., New York: Kraus Reprint Co., 1969.

Towle, George. *American Society.* London: Chapman & Hall, 1870.

Tunnard, Christopher, and Reed, Henry Hope. *American Skyline.* New York: Mentor Books, 1956.

Tuttle, Florence. *The Awakening of Women: Suggestions from the Psychic Side of Feminism.* New York: Abingdon Press, 1915.

Ueland, Brenda. *Me.* New York: G. P. Putnam's Sons, 1939.

Veblen, Thorstein. *The Theory of the Leisure Class.* New York: Macmillan Co., 1899; reprint ed., New York: Mentor Books, 1953.

Warner, William Lloyd; Meeker, Marchia; and Eells, Kenneth, eds. *Social Class in America.* Chicago: Science Research Associates, 1949.

Weber, Adna. *The Growth of Cities in the Nineteenth Century.* New York: Macmillan Co., 1899.

Wiebe, Robert H. *The Search for Order, 1877-1920.* New York: Hill & Wang, 1967.

Willcox, Walter F. *The Divorce Problem: A Study in Statistics.* New York: Columbia University Press, 1891-1892.

Wilson, Grace H. *The Religious and Educational Philosophy of the Young Women's Christian Association.* New York: Columbia University Press, 1933.

Wood, Ann Douglas. " 'The Fashionable Diseases': Women's Complaints and Their Treatment in Nineteenth Century America." In *Clio's Consciousness Raised: New Perspectives on the History of Women,* pp. 1-22. Edited by Mary S. Hartman and Lois Banner. New York: Harper & Row, 1974.

Woods, Caroline H. [Belle Otis]. *The Diary of a Milliner.* New York: Hurd & Houghton, 1867.

Woodward, George. *Diary of a "Peculiar" Girl.* Buffalo: Peter Paul Book Co., 1896.

Woody, Thomas. *History of Women's Education in the United States.* 2 vols. New York: Science Press, 1929; reprint ed., New York: Octagon Books, 1966.

Zenner, Phillip. *Education in Sexual Physiology and Hygiene.* Cincinnati: Robert Clarke Co., 1910.

Journal and Magazine Articles

Abbott, Lyman. "Effect of Modern Industry upon Women." *Outlook,* May 22, 1909, pp. 137-38.

Addams, Jane. "Women's Work for Chicago." *Municipal Affairs* 2 (September 1898): 502-8.

"Advertising Means for Prevention of Conception." *Medical and Surgical Reporter* 63 (September 20, 1890): 347.

"Advice to the New Woman." *Review of Reviews,* June 1895, pp. 84-85.

"The Age of Birth Control." *New Republic,* September 25, 1915, pp. 195-97.

"Alleged Decline in Marriage." *Living Age,* June 15, 1899, pp. 198-200.

Allen, Nathan. "Divorces in New England." *North American Review,* June 1880, pp. 547-64.

American City, vols. 1-5 and 8-32, 1909-25.

"The American Ideal Woman." *Putnam's,* November 1853, pp. 527-31.

"As to Woman's Clubs." *Atlantic,* January 1909, pp. 135-36.

Atchley, Robert. "A Size-Function Typology of Cities." *Demography* 4, no. 2 (1967): 721-33.

Bachelor Maid [pseud]. "Work for Women." *Independent,* June 25, 1912, pt. 1, pp. 182-86.

Bantock, George Granville. "On the Use and Abuse of Pessaries." *Lancet* 1 (February 2, 1878): 162-64.

"The Battle over Birth Control." *Current Opinion,* November 1915, pp. 339-41.

"The Best Thing Our Club Ever Did." *Harper's Bazaar,* June 1909, pp. 614-15.

Billings, John S. "The Diminishing Birth Rate in the United States." *Forum,* June 1893, pp. 467-77.

Bixby, J. "Why Is Single Life Becoming More General." *Nation,* March 5, 1868, pp. 190-91.

Blackwood, W. R. D. "The Prevention of Conception." *Medical and Surgical Reporter* 59 (September 29, 1888): 394-96.

_____. "The Prevention of Conception." *Medical and Surgical Reporter* 59 (December 1, 1888): 698.

Blalock, H. M., Jr. "Correlated Independent Variables: The Problem of Multicollinearity." *Social Forces* 42 (December 1963): 233-36.

Blood, Robert O., Jr., and Hamblin, Robert L. "The Effects of the Wife's Employment on the Family Power Structure." *Social Forces* 36 (May 1958): 347-52.

Boyce, Mary. "The Club as an Ally to Higher Education." *Arena,* August 1892, pp. 377-83.

Bray, Frank Chapin. "The National Consumer League." *Chautauquan,* June 1910, pp. 106-15.

Bridges, William. "Family Patterns and Social Values in America, 1827-1875." *American Quarterly* 27 (September 1965): 3-11.

Brooks, Caroline. "Early History of the Anti-contraceptive Laws in Massachusetts and Connecticut." *American Quarterly* 18 (Spring 1966): 3-23.

Brownell, Jane Louise. "Significance of a Decreasing Birth Rate." *Annals of the American Academy of Political and Social Science* 5 (July 1894): 48-89.

Brunkhurst, Harriet. "The Married Woman in Business." *Collier's,* February 26, 1910, p. 20.

Burnham, John C. "The Progressive Revolution in American Attitudes Toward Sex." *Journal of American History* 59 (March 1973): 885-908.

Campbell, Helen. "Working Women of Today." *Arena,* August 1891, pp. 329-39.

Cartland, Ethel Wadsworth. "Childless Americans." *Outlook,* November 15, 1913, pp. 585-88.

Cave-North, T. "Woman's Place and Power." *Westminster Review,* September 1908, pp. 264-67.

Cirillo, Vincent J. "Edward Foote's *Medical Common Sense:* An Early American Comment on Birth Control." *Journal of the History of Medicine* 25 (July 1970): 341-45.

"City Life in America by a Non-resident American." *Contemporary,* November 1881, pp. 710-25.

Clark, Colin. "The Economic Function of a City." *Econometrica* 13 (April 1945): 97-113.

Collins, James H. "She Drifted to the City." *Saturday Evening Post,* January 1, 1921, p. 11.

Collver, Andrew. "Woman's Work Participation and Fertility in Metropolitan Areas." *Demography* 5, no. 1 (1968): 55-60.

Cooley, Winifred Harper. "The Eternal Feminine: The Future of the Woman's Club." *Arena,* April 1902, p. 380.

Corey, Lewis. "Problems of the Peace: IV. The Middle Class." *Antioch Review* 5 (Spring 1945): 68-87.

Cowan, Ruth Schwartz. "The 'Industrial Revolution' in the Home: Household Technology and Social Change in the 20th Century." *Technology and Culture* 17 (January 1976): 1-23.

_____. "Two Washes in the Morning and a Bridge Party at Night: The American Housewife Between the Wars." *Women's Studies* 3 (1976): 147-72.

Danbar, Olivia H. "The City's Housekeepers." *Harper's Bazaar,* June 1909, pp. 594-96.

Davies, Margery. "Woman's Place Is at the Typewriter: The Feminization of the Clerical Labor Force." *Radical America* 8 (July-August 1974): 1-28.

Davis, Estelle. "The New Woman: Changing Views of Women in the 1920s." *Journal of American History* 61 (September 1974): 372-93.

Davis, Ritt. "Country Girls in Town." *Independent,* July 17, 1902, pp. 1691-93.

Decker, Sarah S. Platt. "The Meaning of the Woman's Club Movement." *Annals of the American Academy of Political and Social Science* 28 (September 1906): 199-204.

Degler, Carl. "Revolution Without Ideology: The Changing Place of Women in America." *Daedalus* 93 (Spring 1964): 653-70.

_____. "What Ought to Be and What Was: Woman's Sexuality in the Nineteenth Century." *American Historical Review* 79 (December 1974): 1467-90.

Deland, Margaret. "The Change in the Feminine Ideal." *Atlantic Monthly,* March 1910, pp. 291-302.

Demos, John. "The American Family in Past Time." *American Scholar* 43 (Summer 1974): 422-46.

_____. "Families in Colonial Bristol Rhode Island: An Exercise in Historical Demography." *William and Mary Quarterly* 25 (January 1968): 40-57.

Dike, Samuel W. "The Problem of the Family in the United States." *Contemporary Review,* November 1913, pp. 724-36.

Draper, F. W. "Some of the Obstetric and Legal Relations of Infanticide." *Boston Medical and Surgical Journal* 117 (January 5, 1888): 7-11.

_____. "Some of the Obstetric and Legal Relations of Infanticide." *Boston Medical and Surgical Journal* 117 (January 12, 1888): 36-38.

Edson, Cyrus. "Evils of Early Marriage." *North American Review,* February 1894, pp. 230-34.

Eliot, Charles W. "The Normal American Woman." *Ladies' Home Journal,* January 1908, p. 15.

Fawcett, Edgar. "The Woes of the New York Working Girl." *Arena,* December 1, 1891, pp. 26-35.

Ferrero, Guglielmo. "The New Woman and the Old." *Hearst Magazine,* July 1912, pp. 70-77.

"Finding Homes for the Homeless." *Review of Reviews,* August 1899, pp. 224-25.

Forrey, Carolyn. "The New Woman Revisited." *Women's Studies* 2 (1974): 37-56.

Free, James E. "Prevention of Conception." *Medical and Surgical Reporter* 59 (December 8, 1888): 726.

Furer, Howard. "The City as a Catalyst for the Women's Rights Movement." *Wisconsin Magazine of History* 52 (Summer 1969): 285-305.

Fyffee, C. A. "The Punishment of Infanticide." *Nineteenth Century,* June 1877, pp. 583-95.

Garrison, Dee. "The Tender Technicians: The Feminization of Librarianship, 1876-1905." *Journal of Social History* 6 (Winter 1973-74): 131-59.

Gibbons, Cardinal. "Pure Womanhood." *Cosmopolitan,* September 1905, pp. 559-61.

"The Girl Who Comes to the City." *Harper's Bazaar,* January 1908, pp. 54-55; November 1908, pp. 1139-1142; and January 1909, pp. 54-57.

Glazer, Norman. "A History of Mechanical Contraception." *Medical Times* 93 (August 1965): 865-69.

Goodsell, Willystine. "The American Family in the Nineteenth Century." *Annals of the American Academy of Political and Social Science* 160 (March 1932): 13-22.

Gordon, Ann D.; Buhle, Mari Jo; and Schrom, Nancy. "Women in American Society." *Radical America* 5 (July-August 1971): 3-66.

Granger, A. D. "The Effect of Club Work in the South." *Annals of the American Academy of Political and Social Science* 28 (September 1906): 248-60.

Greven, Philip J., Jr. "Family Structure in Seventeenth Century Andover, Massachusetts." *William and Mary Quarterly* 23 (April 1966): 234-56.

Haber, Sheldon. "Trends in Work Rates of White Females, 1890-1920." *Industrial Labor Relations Review* 26 (July 1973): 1122-34.

"Half a Century of Child Saving." *Charities* 9 (December 6, 1902): 550-52.

Hareven, Tamara, and Vinovskis, Maris A. "Marital Fertility, Ethnicity, and Occupation in Urban Females: An Analysis of South Boston and the South End in 1880." *Journal of Social History* 8 (Spring 1973): 69-93.

Harland, Marion. "The Passing of the Home Daughter." *Independent,* July 13, 1911, pp. 88-90.

Hays, Samuel P. "The Changing Political Structure of the City in Industrial America." *Journal of Urban History* 1 (November 1974): 6-38.

Heberle, Rudolf. "Social Consequences of the Industrialization of Southern Cities." *Social Forces* 27 (October 1948): 29-37.

Heer, David M. "Dominance and the Working Wife." *Social Forces* 36 (May 1958): 341-47.

Helm, Ernest C. "The Prevention of Conception." *Medical and Surgical Reporter* 59 (November 24, 1888): 643-46.

"Helping My Husband Earn a Living." *Illustrated World,* April 1916, p. 251.

Henderson, Charles. "Are Modern Industry and City Life Unfavorable to the Family?" *American Journal of Sociology* 14 (March 1909): 668-80.

Henry, Josephine K. "The New Woman of the South." *Arena,* February 1895, pp. 353-62.

Hewitt, Emma C. "The 'New Woman' in Her Relation to the 'New Man.' " *Westminster Review,* March 1897, pp. 335-37.

Hogeland, Ronald W. "The Female Appendage: Feminine Styles in America, 1820-1860." *Civil War History* 17 (June 1971): 101-14.

Howard, George Elliot. "Changed Ideals and Status of the Family and the Public Activity of Women." *Annals of the American Academy of Political and Social Science* 56 (November 1914): 27-37.

Howe, Marcie. "Self Help for the Country Woman." *Harper's Bazaar,* March 1909, pp. 269-72.

Huber, L. "The Prevention of Conception." *Medical and Surgical Reporter* 59 (November 10, 1888): 580-81.

Humphreys, Mary. "Women Bachelors in New York." *Scribner's,* November 1896, pp. 626-35.

"Infant Mortality: Its Causes and Prevention." *Medical and Surgical Reporter* 59 (April 9, 1881): 409-11.

"Infanticide." *Journal of the American Medical Association* 5 (October 17, 1885): 440.

"Infants' Rights." *Living Age,* January 8, 1916, pp. 115-17.

Jaffee, Abe J. "Urbanization and Fertility." *American Journal of Sociology* 48 (July 1942): 48-60.

Kemp, Louise. "A Note on the Use of the Fertility Ratio in the Study of Rural-Urban Differences in Fertility." *Rural Sociology* 10 (September 1945): 312-13.

Kenneally, James A. "Women and Trade Unions, 1870-1920: The Quandary of the Reformer." *Labor History* 14 (Winter 1973): 42-55.

Key, William. "Rural-Urban Difference and the Family." *Sociological Quarterly* 2 (January 1961): 49-56.

Kiser, Clyde V. "Trends in the Fertility of Social Classes from 1900-1910." *Human Biology* 5 (May 1933): 256-73.

Klaczynska, Barbara. "Why Women Work: A Comparison of Various Groups—Philadelphia, 1910-1930." *Journal of Labor History* 17 (Winter 1976): 74-87.

Kleinberg, Susan. "Technology and Women's Work: The Lives of Working Class Women in Pittsburgh, 1870-1900." *Journal of Labor History* 17 (Winter 1976): 58-72.

Lasch, Christopher. "Divorce American Style." *New York Review of Books,* February 17, 1966, pp. 3-4.

_____. "Divorce and the Family in America." *Atlantic,* November 1966, pp. 57-61.

Laslett, Barbara. "The Family as a Public and Private Institution: An

Historical Perspective." *Journal of Marriage and the Family* 35 (August 1973): 480-92.

Laughlin, Clara E. "Her Sister in the Country Who Wants to Come to the City and Make Her Way." *Ladies' Home Journal,* August 1911, p. 16.

Lerner, Gerda. "The Lady and the Mill Girl: Changes in the Status of Women in the Age of Jackson." *American Studies* 10 (Spring 1969): 5-15.

_____. "Women's Rights and American Feminism." *American Scholar* 40 (Spring 1971): 235-48.

"The Limitation of Births." *Medical and Surgical Reporter* 44 (April 2, 1881): 382-85.

Linton, Eliza Lynn. "Revolt Against Matrimony." *Forum,* January 1891, pp. 585-95.

Lowell, Josephine Shaw. "Woman's Municipal League of New York City." *Municipal Affairs* 2 (September 1898): 465-66.

McCluny, Hester M. "Women's Work in Indianapolis." *Municipal Affairs* 2 (September 1898): 523-26.

McGovern, James. "The American Woman's Pre-World War I Freedom in Manners and Morals." *Journal of American History* 55 (Spring 1968): 315-33.

McMahon, A. Michael. "An American Courtship: Psychologists and Advertising Theory in the Progressive Era." *American Studies* 13 (Fall 1972): 5-18.

Malet, Lucas. "Threatened Re-subjection of Women." *Living Age,* June 17, 1905, pp. 705-15.

Martin, John. "The Married Woman in Industry." *Survey,* March 11, 1916, p. 697.

Matteson, David E. "Professional Cowardice." *Medical and Surgical Reporter* 59 (November 3, 1888): 568.

_____. "Prevention of Conception." *Medical and Surgical Reporter* 59 (December 15, 1888): 759-60.

Medico-Legal Society of Chicago. "Medico-Legal Aspect of Criminal Abortion." *Journal of the American Medical Association* 9 (December 10, 1887): 762-64.

Medusa [pseud]. "Crime That May Be Prevented." *Westminster Review,* September 1911, pp. 270-77.

Melder, Keith. "Ladies Bountiful: Organized Women's Benevolence in Early Nineteenth Century America." *New York History* 48 (July 1967): 231-54.

Modell, John, and Hareven, Tamara. "Urbanization and the Malleable Household: An Examination of Boarding and Lodging in American

Families." *Journal of Marriage and the Family* 35 (August 1973): 467-79.

Morrison, Denton E., and Henkel, Ramon E. "Significance Tests Reconsidered." *American Sociologist* 4 (May 1969): 131-39.

Morrow, Prince A. "The Relation of Social Disease to the Family." *American Journal of Sociology* 14 (March 1909): 622-35.

Morse, Nancy, and Weiss, Robert. "The Function and Meaning of Work and the Job." *American Sociological Review* 20 (April 1955): 191-98.

Murphey, Rhoads. "The City as a Center of Change: Western Europe and China." *Annals of the Association of American Geographers* 44 (December 1954): 349-62.

Murphy, Lady Blanche. "American Boardinghouse Sketches." *Catholic World,* July 1885, pp. 455-64.

Murray, Margaret Polson. "Women's Clubs in America." *Living Age,* June 1900, p. 561.

"The New Woman." *Cornhill Magazine,* October 1894, pp. 365-68.

Notestein, Frank. "The Decrease in Size of Families from 1890 to 1910." *Milbank Memorial Fund Quarterly* 9 (October 1931): 180-88.

_____. "Differential Age at Marriage According to Social Class." *American Journal of Sociology* 37 (June 1931): 22-48.

"Obstacles to Fecundation." *Medical and Surgical Reporter* 56 (January 1887): 48-50.

Ouida [pseud]. "The New Woman." *North American Review,* May 1894, pp. 610-19.

Paine, Albert Bigelow. "The Flat-Dwellers of a Great City." *The World's Work,* April 1903, pp. 3281-94.

Pelton, E. M. "New Aids to Housework." *Illustrated World,* April 1916, pp. 215-19.

Phelps, E. J. "Divorce in the United States." *Forum,* December 1889, pp. 349-64.

Pierce, Issac. "The Prevention of Conception." *Medical and Surgical Reporter* 59 (November 17, 1888): 614-16.

Pierson, Mary M. "What a Few Women in New London, Iowa, Have Accomplished." *American City* 8 (May 1913): 512-13.

Pinnelli, Antonella. "Female Labour and Fertility in Relationship to Contrasting Social and Economic Conditions." *Human Relations* 24 (December 1971): 603-10.

Poole, Hester M. "Club Life in New York." *Arena,* August 1892, p. 369.

Pope, Thomas A. "Prevention of Conception." *Medical and Surgical Reporter* 59 (October 27, 1888): 522-25.

"Prevention of Conception." *Medical and Surgical Reporter* 59 (September 15, 1888): 343-44.

"Refusal to Multiply." *Living Age,* November 29, 1913, pp. 566-69.

"Reports of Medical Societies." *Boston Medical and Surgical Journal* 6 (December 1, 1870): 359-60.

Repplier, Agnes. "Repeal of Reticence." *Atlantic,* March 1914, pp. 297-304.

Rhine, Alice Hyneman. "The Work of Women's Clubs." *Forum,* December 1891, pp. 519-28.

Rhodes, Albert. "Women's Occupations." *Galaxy,* January 1876, pp. 45-55.

Richardson, A. S. "Lure of a Double Salary." *Woman's Home Companion,* May 1920, p. 12.

Richardson, James. "The New Homes of New York." *Scribner's Monthly,* May 1874, pp. 63-76.

Ridley, Jeanne Clare. "Demographic Change and the Roles and Status of Women." *Annals of the American Academy of Political and Social Science* 375 (January 1968): 15-25.

Riley, Glenda Gates. "The Subtle Subversion: Changes in the Traditionalist Image of the American Woman." *Historian* 32 (February 1970): 210-27.

Rogers, Alma A. "The Woman's Club Movement: Its Origins, Significance, and Present Results." *Arena,* October 1905, p. 347.

Ross, Edward Alsworth. "The Significance of the Increasing Divorce Rate." *Century Magazine,* May 1909, p. 150.

Rubinow, I. M. "Discussion: Women and Economic Dependence." *American Journal of Sociology* 14 (March 1909): 614-19.

Runnalls, H. B. "The Prevention of Conception." *Medical and Surgical Reporter* 59 (December 8, 1888): 710.

Sallume, Xarifa, and Notestein, Frank. "Trends in the Size of Families Completed Prior to 1910 in Various Social Classes." *American Journal of Sociology* 38 (November 1932): 398-408.

Sangster, Margaret E. "Shall Wives Earn Money?" *Woman's Home Companion,* April 1905, p. 32.

Sauer, R. "Attitudes to Abortion in America, 1800-1973." *Population Studies* 28 (March 1974): 53-67.

Scott, Miriam Finn. "Factory Girl's Danger." *Outlook,* April 15, 1911, pp. 817-21.

Sewall, May Wright. "The General Federation of Women's Clubs." *Arena,* August 1892, pp. 362-67.

"Sex O'Clock in America." *Current Opinion,* August 1913, pp. 113-14.

Sherman, Mrs. John Dickinson. "The Woman's Club in the Midwest

States." *Annals of the American Academy of Political and Social Science* 28 (September 1906): 227-47.

Shipman, Carolyn. "The Anomalous Position of the Unmarried Woman." *North American Review,* September 1909, pp. 338-46.

Shorter, Edward. "Female Emancipation, Birth Control and Fertility in European History." *American Historical Review* 78 (June 1973): 605-40.

Sjoberg, Gideon. "Familial Organization in the Pre-industrial City." *Marriage and Family Living* 18 (February 1956): 30-36.

Smith, Daniel Scott. "Family Limitation, Sexual Control and Domestic Feminism in Victorian America." *Feminist Studies* 1 (Winter-Spring 1973): 40-57.

Smith, Julia Holms. "The Woman's Club as an Agent of Philanthropy." *Arena,* August 1892, pp. 382-84.

Smith, Mary Roberts. "Statistics of College and Non-college Women." *American Statistical Association* 8 (March 1900): 1-26.

Smith-Rosenberg, Carroll. "The Hysterical Woman: Sex Roles and Role Conflict in Nineteenth Century America." *Social Research* 39 (Winter 1972): 652-70.

Smith-Rosenberg, Carroll, and Rosenberg, Charles. "The Female Animal: Medical and Biological Views of Woman and Her Role in Nineteenth Century America." *Journal of American History* 60 (September 1973): 332-56.

Smuts, Robert. "The Female Labor Force: A Case Study in the Interpretation of Historical Statistics." *Journal of the American Statistical Association* 55 (March 1960): 71-79.

"The Spreading Movement for Birth Control." *Survey,* October 21, 1916, pp. 60-61.

Srole, Leo. "Urbanization and Mental Health: Some Reformulations." *American Scientist* 60 (September-October 1972): 576-83.

Sullivan, J. L. "Treatment of Abortion with Cases." *Boston Medical and Surgical Journal* 123 (September 3, 1885): 222-24.

Tarver, James. "Gradients of Urban Influences on the Educational, Employment and Fertility Patterns of Women." *Rural Sociology* 34 (September 1969): 356-67.

Taylor, W. H. "A Case of Infanticide." *Boston Medical and Surgical Journal* 123 (November 12, 1885): 459-60.

Thomas, W. F. "The Old and New Ideals of Marriage." *American Magazine,* April 1909, pp. 548-52.

Thompson, Warren, and Jackson, Nelle E. "Fertility in Rural Areas in Relation to Their Distance from Cities, 1930." *Rural Sociology* 5 (June 1940): 143-62.

Tisdale, Hope. "Process of Urbanization." *Social Forces* 20 (March 1942): 311-16.

Trautman, Mary E. "Woman's Health Protective Association." *Municipal Affairs* 2 (September 1898): 439-46.

"Trials of Birth Control Advocates." *Survey,* February 10, 1917, p. 555.

Turner, O. C., "Criminal Abortion." *Boston Medical and Surgical Journal* 5 (April 21, 1870): 299-300.

Ward, May Alden. "The Influence of Women's Clubs in New England and in the Middle-Eastern States." *Annals of the American Academy of Political and Social Science* 28 (September 1906): 205-26.

Warner, Anne. "The New Woman and the Old." *Century,* November 1909, pp. 85-92.

Watson, Hannah Robinson. "The Attitude of the Typical Southern Woman to Clubs." *Arena,* August 1892, pp. 363-88.

Weiss, Thomas. "The Industrial Development of the Urban and Rural Work Forces: Estimates for the United States, 1870-1910." *Journal of Economic History* 32 (December 1972): 919-37.

Wells, Kate Gannett. "The Transitional American Woman." *Atlantic,* December 1880, p. 824.

Welter, Barbara. "The Cult of True Womanhood: 1820-1860." *American Quarterly* 28 (Summer 1966): 151-74.

Wetherill, Edith. "The Civic Club of Boston." *Municipal Affairs* 2 (September 1898): 480.

Whelpton, P. K., and Kiser, Clyde V. "Trends, Determinants and Controls in Human Fertility." *Annals of the American Academy of Political and Social Science* 237 (January 1945): 112-22.

White, Martha E. D. "The Case of the Woman's Club." *Outlook,* June 25, 1898, pp. 479-81.

_____. "The Work of the Woman's Club." *Atlantic,* May 1904, p. 614.

Wilcox, Suzanne. "The Unrest of Modern Woman." *Independent,* June 8, 1909, pp. 62-66.

Willcox, Walter F. "Changes Since 1900 in the Fertility of Native White Wives." *Milbank Memorial Fund Quarterly* 10 (July 1932): 191-202.

Winchester, Boyd. "The New Woman." *Arena,* April 1902, p. 367.

Wirth, Louis. "Urbanism as a Way of Life." *American Journal of Sociology* 44 (July 1938): 1-24.

"A Woman's Reason." *Independent,* March 28, 1907, pp. 780-84.

"Woman's Work for Better Cities." *Literary Digest,* July 13, 1912, pp. 49-50.

"Women in Industry: A Racial Evil." *Literary Digest,* April 12, 1913, p. 826.

Wood, Helen M. "The Unquiet Sex." *Scribner's*, October 1897, p. 487.

Wood, Mary I. "The Woman's Club Movement." *Chautauquan*, June 1910, pp. 36-39.

Woodward, Margaret. "Why Our Boys and Girls Leave Their Homes in the Country." *Countryside Magazine and Suburban Life*, August 1915, p. 81.

X.Y.Z. [pseud]. "The Prevention of Conception." *Medical and Surgical Reporter* 59 (November 10, 1888): 600.

Yarros, Rachelle S. "Some Practical Aspects of Birth Control." *Surgery, Gynecology and Obstetrics* 23 (August 1916): 188-190.

Public Documents

Massachusetts. Bureau of Statistics of Labor. *Fifteenth Annual Report of the Massachusetts Bureau of Statistics of Labor: The Working Girls of Boston*, by Carroll Wright (1884); reprint ed., New York: Arno Press, 1967.

U.S. Department of Commerce. Bureau of the Census. *Fourteenth Census of the United States, 1920*. Vol. 1, *Population: Number and Distribution*.

U.S. Department of Commerce. Bureau of the Census. *Fourteenth Census of the United States, 1920*. Vol. 2, *General Report and Analysis Tables*.

U.S. Department of Commerce. Bureau of the Census. *Fourteenth Census of the United States, 1920*. Vol. 3, *Population: Composition and Characteristics of Population by States*.

U.S. Department of Commerce. Bureau of the Census. *Fourteenth Census of the United States, 1920*. Vol. 4, *Population: Occupations*.

U.S. Department of Commerce. Bureau of the Census. *Fourteenth Census of the United States, 1920*. Vol. 8, *Manufactures: General Report*.

U.S. Department of Commerce. Bureau of the Census. *Fourteenth Census of the United States, 1920*. Vol. 9, *Manufactures: Report by States*.

U.S. Department of Commerce. Bureau of the Census. *Fourteenth Census of the United States, 1920*. Vol. 10, *Manufactures: Report for Selected Industries*.

U.S. Department of Commerce. Bureau of the Census. *Fourteenth Census of the United States, 1920: Abstract*.

U.S. Department of Commerce. Bureau of the Census. *Women in Gainful Occupations, 1870-1920*, by Joseph A. Hill. Census Monograph No. 9. Washington, D.C.: Government Printing Office, 1929.

U.S. Department of Commerce. Bureau of the Census. *Fifteenth Census of the United States, 1930.* Vol. 5, *General Report on Occupations.*

U.S. Department of Commerce. Bureau of the Census. *Ratio of Children to Women,* by Warren Thompson. Census Monograph No. 11. Washington, D.C.: Government Printing Office, 1931.

U.S. Department of Commerce. Bureau of the Census. *Sixteenth Census of the United States, 1940: Comparative Occupational Statistics for the United States, 1870-1940.*

U.S. Department of Commerce. Bureau of the Census. *Seventeenth Census of the United States, 1950.* Vol. 2, *Characteristics of the Population,* pt. 1, U.S. Summary.

U.S. Department of Commerce. Bureau of the Census. *Statistical Abstract: Supplements. Historical Statistics of the United States from Colonial Times to 1957* (1960).

U.S. Department of Commerce. Bureau of Foreign and Domestic Commerce. *Statistical Abstract of the United States* (1923).

U.S. Department of Commerce and Labor. Bureau of the Census. Special Reports. *Streets and Electric Railways* (1903).

U.S. Department of Commerce and Labor. Bureau of the Census. *Abstract of the Annual Report of Statistics of Cities* (1907).

U.S. Department of Commerce and Labor. Bureau of the Census. *Statistics of Women at Work: Based on Unpublished Information Derived from the Schedules of the Twelfth Census: 1900* (1907).

U.S. Department of Commerce and Labor. Bureau of the Census. Special Reports. *Marriage and Divorce: 1867-1906.* 2 vols. (1909).

U.S. Department of Commerce and Labor. Bureau of the Census. Special Reports. *Telephones: 1907* (1910).

U.S. Department of Commerce and Labor. Bureau of the Census. *Thirteenth Census of the United States, 1910.* Vol. 1, *Population.*

U.S. Department of Commerce and Labor. Bureau of the Census. *Thirteenth Census of the United States, 1910.* Vol. 2, *Population: Reports by States and Counties.*

U.S. Department of Commerce and Labor. Bureau of the Census. *Thirteenth Census of the United States, 1910.* Vol. 3, *Population: Reports by States and Counties.*

U.S. Department of Commerce and Labor. Bureau of the Census. *Thirteenth Census of the United States, 1910.* Vol. 4, *Occupation Statistics.*

U.S. Department of Commerce and Labor. Bureau of the Census. *Thirteenth Census of the United States, 1910.* Vol. 8, *Manufactures: General Report.*

U.S. Department of Commerce and Labor. Bureau of the Census. *Thirteenth Census of the United States, 1910.* Vol. 9, *Manufactures: By States.*

U.S. Department of Commerce and Labor. Bureau of the Census. *Thirteenth Census of the United States, 1910.* Vol. 10, *Manufactures: Reports for Principal Industries.*

U.S. Department of Commerce and Labor. Bureau of the Census. *Thirteenth Census of the United States, 1910: Abstract.*

U.S. Department of the Interior. Office of the Census. *Eighth Census of the United States, 1860: Mortality and Miscellaneous Statistics.*

U.S. Department of the Interior. Office of the Census. *Ninth Census of the United States, 1870.* Vol. 1, *Population and Social Statistics.*

U.S. Department of the Interior. Office of the Census. *Ninth Census of the United States, 1870.* Vol. 2, *Vital Statistics.*

U.S. Department of the Interior. Office of the Census. *Ninth Census of the United States, 1870: Compendium.*

U.S. Department of the Interior. Office of the Census. *Tenth Census of the United States, 1880.* Vol. 1, *Population.*

U.S. Department of the Interior. Office of the Census. *Tenth Census of the United States, 1880.* Vol. 2, *Mortality and Vital Statistics,* pt. 1.

U.S. Department of the Interior. Office of the Census. *Tenth Census of the United States, 1880.* Vol. 21, *Report on the Defective, Dependent and Delinquent Classes.*

U.S. Department of the Interior. Office of the Census. *Tenth Census of the United States, 1880: Compendium.*

U.S. Department of the Interior. Office of the Census. *Eleventh Census of the United States, 1890: Population,* pt. 1, Total Population, Sex, Nativity, Dwellings, and Marital Status.

U.S. Department of the Interior. Office of the Census. *Eleventh Census of the United States, 1890: Population,* pt. 2, Ages and Occupations.

U.S. Department of the Interior. Office of the Census. *Eleventh Census of the United States, 1890: Vital and Social Statistics,* pt. 1, Analysis and Rate Tables.

U.S. Department of the Interior. Office of the Census. *Eleventh Census of the United States, 1890: Vital and Social Statistics,* pt. 2, Cities of 100,000 Population.

U.S. Department of the Interior. Office of the Census. *Eleventh Census of the United States, 1890: Crime, Pauperism and Benevolence,* pt. 2.

U.S. Department of the Interior. Office of the Census. *Eleventh Census of the United States, 1890: Vital and Social Statistics,* pt. 3, Statistics of Death.

U.S. Department of the Interior. Office of the Census. *Eleventh Census of the United States, 1890: Abstract.*

U.S. Department of the Interior. Office of the Census. *Eleventh Census of the United States, 1890: Compendium.*

U.S. Department of the Interior. Office of the Census. *Twelfth Census of the United States, 1900.* Vol. 1, *Population: By States.*

U.S. Department of the Interior. Office of the Census. *Twelfth Census of the United States, 1900.* Vol. 2, *Population: Ages, Marital Status, Occupations.*

U.S. Department of the Interior. Office of the Census. *Twelfth Census of the United States, 1900.* Vol. 3, *Vital Statistics,* pt. 1, Analysis and Ratio Tables.

U.S. Department of the Interior. Office of the Census. *Twelfth Census of the United States, 1900.* Vol. 4, *Vital Statistics,* pt. 2, Statistics of Death.

U.S. Department of the Interior. Office of the Census. *Twelfth Census of the United States, 1900: Abstract.*

U.S. Department of the Interior. Office of the Census. *Work and Wages of Men, Women and Children.* Eleventh Annual Report of the Commissioner of Labor (1897).

U.S. Department of State. "Marriage Statistics in the United States," by Joseph A. Hill. In *Fifteenth International Congress on Hygiene and Demography* 6:202-9 (1912).

Newspapers

Boston Weekly Transcript, April 4, 1890; April 25, 1902; and March 6, 1903.

Chicago Daily Journal, November 2, 1905.

Chicago Times, July 19, 1885, and August 7, 1893.

Cincinnati Daily Gazette, March 18, 1862.

Daily Oklahoman (Oklahoma City), May 5, 1894; May 8, 1894; May 12, 1894; January 4, 1904; September 4, 1904; October 14, 1904; July 11, 1914; November 2, 1914; and November 12, 1914.

Detroit Free Press, October 12, 1884, and November 22, 1885.

Kansas City (Missouri) *Star,* October 12, 1884; January 9, 1901; and May 24, 1914.

Los Angeles Times, February 2, 1913.

Morning Oregonian (Portland), February 20, 1872, and May 1, 1900.

New Orleans Times Picayune, October 9, 1880, and January 1, 1897.

New York Times, February 19, 1875, and August 25, 1875.

Other Sources

August, Rebecca. Interview, April 14, 1970, Los Angeles, California.

Davidson, Ruth. Interview, April 14, 1970, Pasadena, California.

Harbert Collection. Huntington Library. San Marino, California.

Kleinberg, Susan. "Technology's Stepdaughters." Ph.D. dissertation, University of Pittsburgh, 1973.

Oppenheimer, Valerie Kincade. "The Female Labor Force in the United States: Factors Governing Its Growth and Changing Composition." Ph.D. dissertation, University of California, Berkeley, 1966.

Peal, Edith. "The Atrophied Rib: Urban Middle Class Women in Jacksonian America." Ph.D. dissertation, University of Pittsburgh, 1970.

Pownall Papers. Huntington Library. San Marino, California.

Riley, Glenda Gates. "From Chattel to Challenger: The Changing Image of the American Woman, 1828-1848." Ph.D. dissertation, Ohio State University, 1967.

Ryan, Mary P. "American Society and the Cult of Domesticity: 1830-1860." Ph.D. dissertation, University of California, Santa Barbara, 1971.

Index

ABOUT THE AUTHOR

Margaret Gibbons Wilson is Director of Research, Center for Labor
Research and Studies, and Assistant Professor, School of Technology,
at Florida International University, Miami, Florida.